THE BASKING SHARK IN SCOTLAND

Frontispiece. A basking shark feeding just under the sea surface. Inside the widely distended jaws the pale branchial arches can be seen with the dark areas in between indicating the rows of gill-rakers. These filter out the small planktonic animals such as *Calanus* copepods which are the food of the basking shark. (Courtesy J. Stafford-Deitsch)

The Basking Shark in Scotland

Natural History, Fishery and Conservation

Denis Fairfax

TUCKWELL PRESS

First published in Great Britain in 1998 by
Tuckwell Press
The Mill House
Phantassie
East Linton
East Lothian EH40 3DG
Scotland

ISBN 1 86232 094 2

The publishers gratefully acknowledge subsidy from the Scotland
Inheritance Fund towards publication of this volume

British Library Cataloguing in Publication Data
A catalogue record for this book is available
on request from the British Library

Typeset by Hewer Text Ltd, Edinburgh
Printed and bound by Biddles Ltd, Guildford and King's Lynn

For Beverly

Contents

Illustrations

A basking shark feeding just under the sea surface. *Frontispiece*

Maps

Acknowledgements

My research could not have been carried out without the help of a very large number of people and I thank them all most sincerely for their willing assistance in this project. I owe much to the early encouragement of Dr Colin Martin of the Scottish Institute of Maritime Studies, University of St Andrews, and for information on the biology and conservation of the basking shark I am indebted to Dr Chris Todd, University of St Andrews; Professor I.G. 'Monty' Priede, University of Aberdeen; Dr Mark O'Connell and Dr Tim Thom of the University of Durham; David Wilson, Scottish Wildlife Trust; Ann Hunt and Samantha Pollard, Marine Conservation Society; and Sarah Fowler, Nature Conservation Bureau. Geoff Swinney of the Royal Museum, Edinburgh, guided me through the scientific literature and provided a willing ear on many occasions. Oliver Crimmen, Natural History Museum, London, and Dr Margaret Reilly, University of Glasgow, helped greatly by enabling me to examine preserved specimens. I enjoyed a fruitful correspondence with the veteran basking shark investigator, Dr F.C. Stott, Cookham Dean. My thanks also to Dr J.R. Turner, University College of North Wales; Dr Clare Eno, Joint Nature Conservation Committee; Dr Bob Earll, Dr Martin Lucas and Jill Strawbridge for their advice on various points and I record my appreciation of the camaraderie shown by the volunteer observers of 'Basking Shark 97' on the Isle of Arran.

Angus Martin of Campbeltown generously provided me with the results of his own research into the history of Scottish fishing and, with his wife Judy, was most hospitable during my fieldwork in Kintyre in 1995. In Carradale I benefited greatly from the recollections of Archibald 'Archie' Paterson and his wife Crystal, Duncan Ritchie, and Angus Paterson. I am particularly indebted to Archie and Crystal for their continuing hospitality, for facilitating other contacts, and for retrieving old photographs. The events of the 'Carradale Incident' of 1937 were related to me by the living survivor, Donald MacDonald, Paisley; and by Colin Oman, Carradale, an eyewitness. Margaret Scott recalled for me her memories of conversations with her cousin, the late Jessica Clayton (née Brown), the other survivor.

On the Isle of Soay, the late Tex Geddes was most hospitable, giving me access to the site of the shark factory and recollecting many details of the heyday of the modern fishery. My understanding of the Soay venture was greatly enhanced by the kindness of His Grace the Duke of Hamilton in allowing me to examine the records of the Island of Soay Shark Fisheries Ltd in the archives of the Hamilton and Kinneil Estates, Lennoxlove, Haddington, East Lothian. Robert Cholawo kindly made a videotape of the Soay factory site.

Tom and Ina Ralston of Lundin Links assisted my work in the West of Scotland by providing vital introductions. In Mallaig, the late William Manson patiently submitted on a number of occasions to questioning about the family involvement in the 1950s basking shark fishery. I also thank David and Rosie McMinn of Mallaig for the opportunity to examine and photograph the Kongsberg harpoon gun which was used by Mrs McMinn's father, the late William Sutherland. Ross Campbell of the Mallaig Marine World and Malcolm Poole of the Mallaig Heritage Centre both helped by letting me examine guns and harpoons in their displays. In Millport, Great Cumbrae, Howard McCrindle was very forthcoming about his Clyde shark-fishing experiences during several meetings and provided the data on his basking shark catches.

The late Dr John Lorne Campbell of Canna corresponded with information on the basking shark in the Western Isles, while Robert Smart, Keeper of Muniments, University of St Andrews, assisted by referring me to early historical sources. Virginia Wills, Bridge of Allan, made me aware of the Forfeited Estates Papers and clarified several details in those records. For other information I express my gratitude to William Anderson, Edinburgh; Douglas Botting, London; Paul Carre, Fisheries Officer, Guernsey; Gordon Christie, Tighnabruaich; David Dryhurst, Barnt Green; Fiona Gorman, Isle of Arran Museum Trust; David Henderson, McManus Gallery, Dundee; Ian Tait, Shetland Museum, Lerwick; Monica Ory, Warwick; Rudiger Bahr and Steve Liscoe, St Andrews; Trudi Overman, the Tynwald Library, Isle of Man; Derek Pieroni, Ayr; Ken Watterson, Isle of Man; M.L. Rosenthal, Robeco Inc., New York; and Matthew Callahan, Florida Museum of Natural History, Gainesville. I am grateful to M.A. Newland and the Birmingham Museum of Science and Technology for the opportunity to examine a Greener light harpoon gun.

Dr Ole Lindquist, of Reykjavik, Iceland, sent me material on the basking shark fisheries in Iceland and Norway. For further material on the Norwegian fishery I have to thank Arnold Farstad, Havforskningsinstituttet, Bergen; Odd Sævik of Leinoy; Jan Ringstad, Commander Chr. Christensen's Whaling Museum, Sandefjord; I. J. G. Rokke, Universitetsbiblioteket i Trondheim; Astri Botnen, *Naturen* magazine, Bergen; Norvald Vik, Norges Fiskerimuseum,

Bergen; Anne Ulset, Royal Norwegian Embassy, London; Laurie Skjelten, Trondheim; and Dr Colin Bain, Edinburgh.

My appreciation goes to Dr Ian Morrison of Edinburgh for transcribing several pages of Kristjansson's *Islenzskir Sjavarhættir* and to Magnus Sigurdsson and Ragnheidur Valdimarsdottir, formerly of St Andrews, for translations from Icelandic, Norwegian and Danish. For additional translations from Norwegian my thanks go to Jorgen Lovbakke, St Andrews and Dr Paul Kerswill, University of Reading; and for translations from Italian, to Elizabeth Hallum, Reading. For various etymological clarifications I thank Professor Derick Thomson, Glasgow and Dr Mark Humphries, University of Manchester.

J.S. Love, Maritime Institute of Ireland, assisted by providing material on the Irish fishery, and I am grateful to those who sent me information on the basking shark in New Zealand: Janet Ledingham, Dunedin; my daughter Katherine, Wellington; and especially Larry Paul, National Institute of Water & Atmospheric Research, Wellington. Barry and Lauren Harcourt, Lower Hutt, were especially helpful in the final stages of the work.

At the Scottish Fisheries Museum, Anstruther, Jim Lindsay, Kate Newland and John Doig were most helpful. I also owe much to the assistance given by staff of the following institutions: the Scottish Record Office, Edinburgh; the Warwickshire County Record Office; the Record Office, Isle of Anglesey; the Library of the University of St Andrews; the Special Collections at the University of Edinburgh; the Scottish Room, Central Library, Edinburgh; the Glasgow and History Room, the Mitchell Library, Glasgow; the Main Library and the Rural History Centre, University of Reading; the Reading Central Library; the Science Museum and Imperial College Library, London; the General and Zoological Library of the Natural History Museum, London; the Royal Society of Medicine, London; the Linnaean Society, London; the Map Library of the Royal Geographical Society, London; the Main Library, University of Wales, Bangor; the National Library of Wales, Aberystwyth; the Centre for Environment, Fisheries & Aquaculture, Lowestoft; and in Wellington, the Parliamentary Library and the Press & Public Affairs section of the British High Commission.

I particularly thank Dr Robert Prescott, Director of the Scottish Institute of Maritime Studies, University of St Andrews, for allowing me to use the facilities of the Institute and for his unstinting help in a number of unobtrusive but nevertheless very significant ways. A grant from the Russell Trust of Fife (founded to commemorate Major D. F. O. Russell CBE, MC) allowed me some months of full-time research and writing and I thank the trustees for their generosity.

Various chapters were read by Geoff Swinney, Mark O'Connell, Monty Priede, Sarah Fowler, and Samantha Pollard. I thank them all for their patience and for their clarifications but note that any errors remain my own.

I am grateful to the Duke of Hamilton; the Scottish Record Office; and the Warwickshire Country Record Office for permission to quote from archival sources.

For permission to quote from theses I thank Dr Ole Lindquist, Jill Strawbridge and Scott Farmery. Unsuccessful attempts were made to contact the authors of other theses consulted.

I wish to thank the following for providing illustrations and/or giving permission to use them:

Dr Simon Berrow, Cambridge (fig 55), Douglas Botting, London (fig 31), Alexander Cooke, Kew (fig 60), *The Daily Record*, Glasgow (fig 21), the Duke of Hamilton, Lennoxlove, Haddington (fig 44), Dr Bob Earll (fig 7), The Food & Agriculture Organisation of the United Nations (fig 1 & map 1), HarperCollins (fig 61), Messrs Heinemann (fig 22, 26, 43, 45, 46), Hulton Getty Picture Collection, London (figs 32, 38, 47, 48, 49, 50, 51), David Henderson, Dundee (fig 11B), Dr K. Izawa, Japan (fig 15), Howard McCrindle, Millport (fig 40), Dr Colin Martin, St Andrews (fig 3), the Trustees of the Estate of Gavin Maxwell (fig 4), the National Museums of Scotland, Edinburgh (fig 9), Crystal Paterson, Carradale (fig 9), Professor I.G. Priede, Aberdeen (figs 56, 57, 58 & 59A&B), The Royal College of Surgeons of England, London (fig 16C), The Royal Society of London (fig 14), *The Scotsman*, Edinburgh (fig 29), Secker & Warburg (fig 27), The Shetland Museum, Lerwick (fig 28), Jeremy Stafford-Deitsch, London (frontispiece & dustjacket), *The Straits Times*, Singapore (fig 53), Universitetsbiblioteket i Trondheim (fig 16A), Isabel White, Castle Douglas (fig 25), David Wilson, Lanark (fig 11A & 54).
Unacknowledged photographs and diagrams are my own.

Thanks also to Messrs Chatto & Windus for permission to quote Norman MacCaig's 'Basking Shark'.

Finally, to my wife Beverly, I owe the greatest debt of all. She has sustained me through the whole time of writing this book and with her keen eye for detail has made many improvements to the text. This book is worthily dedicated to her.

Abbreviations

DR	*Daily Record & Mail*
EU	University of Edinburgh
GH	*Glasgow Herald*
HC	House of Commons
HKIS	Island of Soay Shark Fishing Ltd papers in the archives of the Hamilton and Kinneil Estates
MWNH	*Memoirs of the Wernerian Natural History Society*
NSA	*New Statistical Account*
OED	*Oxford English Dictionary*
OSA	*Old Statistical Account* (see Sinclair, J., 1799)
S of G	States of Guernsey
SRO	Scottish Record Office
T	*The Times*
WCRO	Warwickshire County Record Office

Chapter One
Natural History

INTRODUCTION

THE AWESOME SIGHT on a calm sunlit morning of a massive dark fin slowly
and erratically circling close to the shore has been a feature of the summer
seascape of western Scotland for a very long of time, perhaps indeed for
thousands of years. The appearance of this fin, now more often than not a
solitary event, signals the annual visitation of the basking shark to its feeding
areas in the seas and firths of the western coast and the sounds and voes of the
Northern Isles.

The basking shark *Cetorhinus maximus*, the largest fish of northern temperate
and sub-polar oceans, is a harmless plankton-eater which has now become, like
the great whales, an icon of the conservation movement, but at two periods in
Scottish history its numbers sustained a small fishery. In comparison to the
main sea-fisheries, these basking shark fisheries were of minor economic
importance and, mainly owing to the the unpredictable habits of the shark
itself, flourished only intermittently and locally. Long before recorded history
the coastal inhabitants of western Scotland and the Northern Isles were
accustomed to stripping the blubber and flesh from stranded whales, and
no doubt in a similar way utilised a dead shark cast ashore for its liver oil. But it
seems that the first organised hunting of the fish in Scottish seas came
comparatively late, dating only from 1760 or thereabouts as the earliest accounts
of capturing the basking shark in Scotland all relate to the mid-to-late eighteenth century.

From undocumented obscurity, the shark emerges in the eighteenth century
in the correspondence of the Commissioners for the Annexed Estates listed in a
matter-of-fact way with other species; in the parish descriptions of the
compendium known as the *Old Statistical Account;* and in the accounts of
various travellers to the Western Isles who in the full flush of Romanticism were
describing the life and customs of the Scottish outliers for a wider British
audience. It is a matter for conjecture whether actively hunting the shark was a

truly indigenous Scottish activity or whether, as is more likely, the pioneers were inspired by knowledge of contemporary Irish and Norwegian practice. An Irish fishery may have been under way as early as the 1740s and the Norwegian fishery certainly predated the scientific description of the basking shark by Bishop Gunnerus of Trondheim in 1765 but possibly not by very many years. The basking shark may also have been fished in Anglesey, Wales, in the early 1760s.

This first fishery lasted until about 1830 and for a century the basking shark appears to have remained more of a curiosity of natural history than a potential prey until, in the mid-1930s, exceptionally large numbers appeared over several summers in the Firth of Clyde. An encounter between a basking shark and a sailing boat at Carradale, Kintyre, which drowned three people, brought the shark notoriety, while the very numbers of the fish stimulated the rebirth of a small fishery, based near the same village. This operation was interrupted by the Second World War but resumed in 1946. Gavin Maxwell's enterprise based on the island of Soay began at the same time and several other, smaller, shark-hunting ventures followed. The activities of this period, which were well publicised in the books written by the participants, had all ceased by the early 1950s when for a few seasons basking sharks were taken by a group of Mallaig fishermen and also in Shetland. In addition, the distinctive Norwegian shark-catching vessels were active in Scottish waters at this time.

Again there was a gap until 1982 when one Clyde fisherman began hunting the basking shark to increasing opprobrium from conservationist and animal rights groups. His fishing ceased in 1994 and this small decade-long effort may well prove to have been the last chapter in the history of the Scottish basking shark fishery. As this was being written, strenuous efforts were being made to give the basking shark the status of a legally-protected species in British waters.

While the historical theme is essentially a Scottish one, the natural history of the basking shark is plainly a topic of much wider significance. The summary given here of our present knowledge of its biology incorporates the fruits of many studies of the shark from its description by Bishop Gunnerus in the mid-eighteenth century, through to the early nineteenth-century anatomists, the research of Matthews and Parker at Soay in 1947 and the recent observations of basking shark behaviour in the English Channel, around the Isle of Man and in the Firth of Clyde. However, the course of scientific enquiry was not always an ordered or progressive one. While the first illustration of the basking shark to appear in a British zoological book (in 1776) was based upon a specimen from Scotland, it was also Scotland which provided some of the 'sea-monsters' which together with other oddities (all of which turned out to be basking sharks) distracted naturalists into unprofitable byways.

CLASSIFICATION

The basking shark was the first filter-feeding shark to be scientifically described and it is placed in its own family, the Cetorhinidae. It belongs, together with the comparatively recently-discovered megamouth *Megachasma pelagios,* also a filter-feeder, in the order Lamniformes, which contains many of the fast-swimming predatory oceanic sharks. The whale shark *Rhincodon typus* of tropical seas, in the order Orectolobiformes, although not closely related to the basking shark, is also a filter-feeder. These three large sharks, like all other sharks, skates and rays, belong to the sub-class Elasmobranchii within the great assemblage of cartilaginous fishes, the class Chondrichthyes.

The formal classification of the basking shark is:

class: Chondrichthyes
subclass: Elasmobranchii
superorder: Selachiformes
order: Lamniformes
family: Cetorhinidae
genus: *Cetorhinus*
species: *maximus*

It should be observed that while various other species of basking shark have been described in the past, it is now thought that these are, at best, regional forms of a worldwide species, and that the name *Cetorhinus maximus* covers all the variations once thought to be distinct species or geographical sub-populations.[1]

The basking shark is generally found in warm temperate and boreal waters in the North Atlantic and North Pacific oceans as well as around South America as far north as Ecuador, South Africa, and the southern coasts of Australia and New Zealand. In northern European waters the basking shark is mainly seen in the summer months but this is not necessarily the case in other parts of the world. In central California, for example, the greatest number of sightings are made in spring and late winter/early autumn.[2] Specimens caught from time to time in tropical regions, such as Florida, are thought to be well outside the normal range of the shark and their emaciated condition suggests that they have not been feeding.[3]

EXTERNAL MORPHOLOGY

In its external form the basking shark is similar in many respects to those large sharks such as the blue shark *Prionace glaucus* which are characterised by a relatively slender body with a markedly pointed snout. The body of the basking shark is fusiform in its general shape with a heterocercal tail (caudal fin) in which the notched upper lobe is larger than the lower. (Fig. 1) At the base of the tail, on either side, there is a horizontal keel, a feature shared by some other Lamniforms. The thrust of the tail propels the shark in a slightly tail-down, nose-up posture with the paired pectoral and pelvic fins acting as hydroplanes to steer the fish up or down.[4] The pectoral fins are relatively large, being about 1.5 metres long in a 7-metre fish. The pelvic fins are smaller, about 0.75 metres in length.[5]

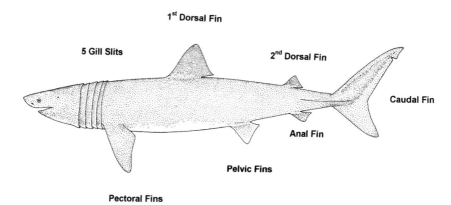

Fig. 1.   External form of the female basking shark. The dot to the rear of the head indicates the position of the spiracle. (Compagno (1984): 234. Courtesy of FAO of the UN)

There are two dorsal fins. The first can be up to (and possibly over) a metre in height in a large adult, and in an older fish the top of the fin may droop sideways when out of the water. The second dorsal fin is much shorter. Another Lamniform feature is the presence of an anal fin behind the cloaca. The two copulatory organs, the claspers, formed from the inner borders of the pelvic fins and lying along the ventral surface, distinguish the male fish but otherwise there is no external difference between the sexes, although the female may be somewhat larger than the male. (Fig. 2)

When the basking shark is swimming, but not feeding, the head of the fish in its general shape is not dissimilar to that of the blue shark. An almost conical snout (rostrum) overhangs a partially-open crescent-shaped mouth with the eyes, set well forward in the snout, being quite prominent. However, in its feeding mode the appearance of the shark is spectacularly transformed. The capacious mouth gapes open to a metre or more and the branchial region

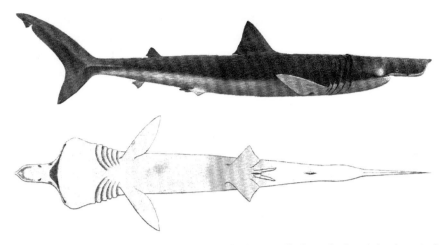

Fig. 2. A young male basking shark, distinguished externally from the female by the paired claspers. The flattened appearance of the branchial region is characteristic of preserved specimens. (Pavesi (1874): plate 1)

expands to give the forepart of the fish the distorted appearance of a giant scoop with the abdomen and tail trailing behind as the 'handle'. The five pairs of gill-slits, which almost encircle the body, open wide and from the front, the gill-arches are very obvious as creamy-white hoop-like structures forming the wall of the throat (pharynx). It is thought by some that the whiteish colour of the open mouth may serve to attract the planktonic copepods.

The jaws of the shark, pink-tinged in the living animal, bear rows of minute teeth (nine on the lower jaw and six on the upper). Immediately behind the upper jaw is a continuous flap of tissue (the buccal valve) which lies flat as water passes over it into the mouth. Matthews and Parker describe the buccal valve in detail but they do not suggest any function for it even though it is quite a conspicuous feature of the palate. An earlier researcher labelled this flap a 'maxillary breathing valve' and considered it prevented water from flowing forwards out of the mouth by engaging with the basihyoid cartilage (the 'tongue').[6] Possibly it helps to retain copepods when the fish closes its mouth to 'swallow'.

The colour of the basking shark has been described by zoologists as 'dirty blue or light slate colour' and 'dark-grey, almost black'.[7] However, under water the colours appear brighter and there is considerable variation caused by lighter patches on the darker ground colour of the fissured, highly-textured skin. Again, these variations appear more distinct when the shark is viewed under-water and the lighter areas often take the form of long streaks. (Fig. 3) Taken together with slight differences in the shape of the first dorsal fin, this variability

in colour can be used to distinguish individual fish – an important consideration if they are to be identified for research purposes. Individual sharks may
have patches of worn skin at the base of the claspers or (in the case of a female)
around the cloaca, suggesting wear caused by mating activity.

Innumerable small denticles (placoid scales) cover the skin, making it rough

Fig. 3.   A female basking shark feeding at the surface off the Outer Skerries, eastern side of
Shetland, circa 1976. (Photograph, Richard Price. Courtesy Dr Colin Martin)

to the touch, and a layer of mucus lies just below the denticles. It seems that this
mucus is a sort of 'anti-fouling' slime exuded to repel parasites, especially the
copepods which fasten onto the skin, and its corrosive nature meant that any
herring drift nets in which a shark became entangled had to be destroyed as the
mucus rotted natural fibres.[8] Some fishermen claimed to be able to smell the
mucus (malodorous to the human nose) from a distance and so detect a shoal of
sharks under the surface.[9] The lamprey *Petromyzon marinus* also utilises the skin
of the shark even though it does not seem that lampreys can actually bite into
the flesh as the skin is too tough. Perhaps the lamprey just uses the shark as a
means of transport, and in that case it is not strictly a parasite. Other external
parasites include a number of copepod species in the gills.[10]

Size

We do not know with absolute certainty the maximum size attainable by the basking shark, but it is very likely that estimates of size made by observing the shark in the water have resulted in considerable exaggeration. (Fig. 4) By carefully measuring nine dead sharks at Soay the zoologists Matthews and

Fig. 4. Diagram of the surface appearance of a basking shark with tip of the snout, 1st dorsal fin and top of the caudal fin visible. (Courtesy Trustees of Estate of Gavin Maxwell)

Parker found the average length to be 7 metres and they proposed a maximum length of 8.8 metres, at which size the fish was estimated to weigh 'about 10,000 lbs' (= 4.46 tons = 4541 kilograms), later revised to between 6 to 7 tons.[11] At a maximum length of 8.8 metres, the basking shark is quite a bit shorter than the whale shark (at least 12 metres), about the same size as an exceptionally large great white shark *Carcharodon carcharias* or a minke whale *Balaenoptera acutorostrata,* and substantially larger than the megamouth (about 4.5 metres). This work of Matthews and Parker appears to be the only systematic measurement of a number of basking sharks which has ever been undertaken. Nevertheless, much larger examples than their putative maximum size have been reported and it is possible that exceptional specimens could indeed be much longer than the largest of those in the actual Soay sample. Recent observation of a shark at very close quarters off Arran measured against a 4.5 metre inflatable boat suggests that it was just over 9 metres.[12] In the early nineteenth century two specimens discussed by the anatomist Everard Home were, even if a bit shorter than the reputed measured lengths of 30 to 31 feet (9.1 to 9.4 metres), certainly at the top end of the range.[13] Gavin Maxwell, hunting the basking shark in western Scotland in the late 1940s, was insistent that he sighted occasional specimens that were at least 40 feet (12.2 metres) long.[14] The local tradesmen who measured the Stronsay Monster (discussed in the next chapter) found it to be 55 feet (16.8 metres) in length. (Home thought it was more likely to have been about 30 to 36 feet – 9.1 to 10.9 metres.).[15] While there has been no other report of anything like that length for a basking shark before or since, very large basking sharks may indeed exist even if they have managed to elude the zoologist so far. Analysis of information sent to the Marine Conservation Society over a decade from 1986 onwards found that most of the 3000 sharks observed were in the range of 2 to 6 metres.[16]

SKELETON

A long straight spine, bending upwards at the base of the tail to support the upper lobe, forms the axis of the basking shark's cartilaginous skeleton. The 150 or so vertebrae are all similar in shape, consisting of an oval centrum (which partially calcifies as the fish ages) surmounted by a neural arch through which runs the spinal cord. The vertebrae are held together by strong ligaments such that each intervertebral cavity is filled with incompressible fluid and 'forms a ball round which the concave surfaces of the vertebrae are moved' – a very strong but flexible structure.[17] The skull (chondrocranium), containing the auditory and olfactory capsules, is more or less rectangular with three forward-extending rostral elements supporting the snout. The lower one of the three (the median rostral cartilage) is quite substantial and curves upwards while the upper two (dorsolaterals) are lighter struts, joined together at the front in the form of a 'y'.[18] The dorsolateral cartilages may lose their forward attachment in the adult, becoming blunt prongs.[19] Considering the size of the fish, the skull is surprisingly small (30 to 50 centimetres long in an adult). The upper and lower jaws are joined to the neurocranium with the massive cartilages of the gill-arches extending behind the lower jaw. (Fig. 5)

Gill Arches
The basking shark has five gill slits on either side, each opening being between two gill arches, so that there are twelve gill arches altogether. In each gill arch there are two main skeletal elements which are substantial curved rods with thickened ends. The uppermost (the epibranchial cartilage) is attached to the base of a vertebra while the lower (the ceratobranchial) is joined to a hypobranchial element. The epibranchial and the ceratobranchial abut, forming a hinge joint somewhat like the human elbow and it is this hinge joint

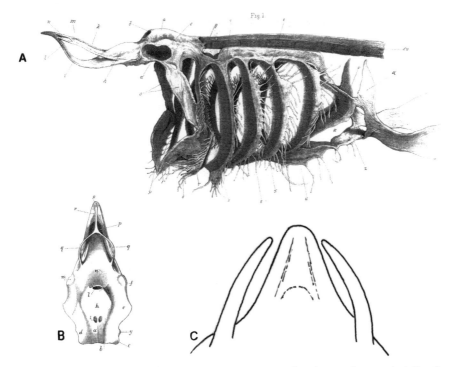

Fig. 5.   Skeleton. **A**. The skull, vertebral column, jaws, gill-arches, and pectoral girdle of a 2.95m basking shark. The bowed shape of the median rostral cartilage (i) is transitional form between the very young shark and the adult. The gill-rakers (x) are still attached to the gill-arches but the spiky branchial rays (s) are badly distorted probably because the cartilaginous skeleton typically warps as it dries out. (Pavesi 1874): plate 2) **B**. Dorsal view of the skull (40 centimetres long), possibly at a later stage when the dorsolateral rostral cartilages (q & r) have altered their shape slightly. (Pavesi (1878): 360) **C**. A later stage in an adult shark. The dorsolateral cartilages have lost their forward attachment to the median rostral cartilage to become merely two prongs. (Barnard (1937): 44)

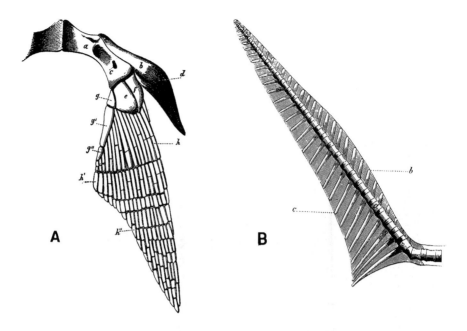

Fig. 6. Skeleton. **A**. Part of pectoral girdle and the left pectoral fin. **B**. The caudal fin (tail). b & c are rays running out from the caudal vertebrae. (Pavesi (1878): 375 & 381)

which enables the contraction and expansion of the gill-arches during feeding. Attached at intervals to these two main cartilages and radiating outwards are long flattened spurs (branchial rays) which support the gill-rakers and the tissue of the gills, and continue under the outer skin. A thin semi-circular cartilage (the extrabranchial) curves around the outer ends of the branchial rays under the outermost layer of skin. The gill-arches are held together at their bases by the complex of hypobranchial and basibranchial cartilages. The first of these, the basihyoidal cartilage, is large and wedge-shaped and lying as it does directly behind the lower jaw looks very like a tongue.

The whole structure of gill-arches overlain with connective tissue and skin is only semi-rigid, giving it flexibility so that the gill-slits can be opened widely and then closed. This lack of rigidity contributes to the distorted appearance of the dead shark cast ashore when the branchial region, lacking muscle tone and without the buoyancy provided by water, becomes a flaccid mass. In a suspended carcass the gill-arches flop downwards and forwards with the gill clefts hanging open, and the abdominal organs also slump downwards, further distorting the shape.

Fins and Claspers

The pectoral fins are attached to a substantial pectoral girdle which is joined to the vertebral column. The pelvic girdle is not attached to the spine but lies embedded in the ventral muscles. The fins are given rigidity and flexibility by multiple cartilages (the basals) which support long fin-rays (radials). (Fig. 6) The claspers also have a complex skeletal support composed of several curved elements having a rather scroll-like appearance.

Fig. 7. A feeding basking shark off the Isle of Man viewed from above. The branchial arches are fully expanded with the gill-slits wide open and a lamprey can be seen hanging from the second arch. (Photographer not known. Courtesy Dr Bob Earll)

FEEDING AND RESPIRATION

Sustained research into the environmental biology of the basking shark is still at a very early stage. Practically all the studies that have been done have been conducted in comparatively small areas or have been limited to one or two seasons. What is presented here must be regarded as a very tentative assessment of our understanding of the animal's behaviour and the inferences currently made may well be proved wrong as research continues.

The basking shark is thought to be attracted to coastal waters where there is a 'blooming' of plankton in the spring and summer, and judging by one small-scale Isle of Man study the key predictor of its likely presence is the concentration of zooplankton species. The types of phytoplankton present and other characteristics of the water mass such as thermal stratification, chorophyll concentration and acidity do not seem to be as directly relevant as zooplankton density.[20] The shark is generally not seen in British seas until the minimum sea surface temperature is circa 10 degrees C.[21] It is commonly found with schools of herring and mackerel which are feeding on the same plankton and it is possible that its olfactory sense guides it to the dense plankton swarms. It has often been seen feeding quite close to the shore and may be particularly attracted to 'tide line' areas around headlands. In these, long streaks of foam and floating debris mark the confluence of different water masses where plankton may be concentrated. That the basking shark also feeds well below the surface can be inferred from the reports of sharks being caught in gill nets 60 to 600 metres deep in Newfoundland. They have been taken by deep water trawlers off the west coast of New Zealand, and have also been found off Japan feeding at night deeper than 100 metres.[22]

The basking shark feeds by cruising slowly through the plankton 'soup' with its mouth agape and the gill-arches fully expanded to open the gill-slits to their maximum extent. (Fig. 7) Water streams into the cavernous mouth and pharynx and exits via the gill slits so that feeding and respiration go on simultaneously. Some denizens of the plankton such as the many types of very small crustacean are the food species which provide the most energy, while jelly-fish and comb-jellies are nutritionally poorer, being composed almost entirely of water. In British waters the reddish copepod *Calanus finmarchicus*, about 5 millimetres in length, has been found to be one of the main items in the shark's stomach, together with fish eggs and various larvae.[23] (Fig. 8)

Another study of feeding basking sharks off the Isle of Man showed that other copepod species (*Paracalanus parvus*, *Temora longicornis* and *Acartia clausi*) formed a high proportion of the planktonic crustacea. However, the most abundant species are not necessarily the preferred food and *Calanus finmarchicus* was the only one to be positively correlated with the presence of the basking shark.[24] In other words the shark may be capable of selectively seeking out *Calanus* swarms, and in this it has the herring *Clupea harengus* as one competitor, for *Calanus* is the preferred food of the adult fish. The most recent research in the Channel confirms selective foraging for dense *Calanus* patches.[25] In New Zealand, *Calanus tonsus* together with the rather larger krill (euphausiid species) and *Munida gregaria* were recorded as the stomach contents of sharks harpooned in 1964 during a period of marked *Calanus* [now *Neocalanus*] swarming.[26] By the very way in which it feeds, it would seem unlikely that the basking shark could

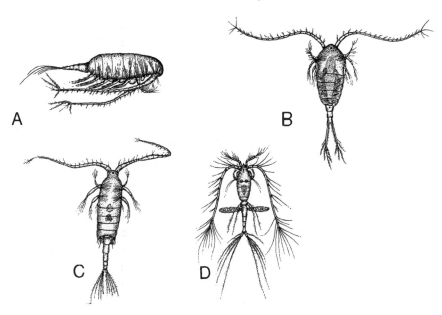

Fig. 8. Some planktonic copepods, important food species for the basking shark. **A**. A female *Calanus finmarchicus*. *Calanus* may be the preferred food species. The adult is 4–5 mm long and reddish in colour. **B**. *Temora longicornis*. **C**. *Caudacia armata*. **D**. *Oithonia spinirostra*. (Graham (1956): plates 6 & 7)

discriminate in its food intake but the fish has been observed to turn aside from the larger jelly-fish without closing its mouth.[27]

Feeding Mechanism

Each gill arch is the skeleton which supports crescent-shaped surfaces containing gill-rakers and gill tissue. Eight of these surfaces on each side are back-to-back and may be considered to form 'free-standing' branchial septa as the gill slits which bound them front and rear almost encircle the fish. In the relaxed state a branchial septum has the shape of a 'u' on its side, but when the shark is feeding, it expands to a shape which is more like a flattened 'v'. (Figs. 9 & 10)

The inner side (front and rear) of each septum carries 1000 to 1300 erectile gill-rakers in a single series facing inwards towards the pharynx. The gill-rakers are composed of keratin, the same substance that forms human hair and nails and the baleen of whales, and in a large shark the longest examples in the centre row are about 11.5 centimetres. Fossil gill-rakers have been found and may indicate a forerunner of the present species.[28] While the baleen plates of a whale and the gill-rakers of the shark are chemically the same and have the similar function of straining out small food organisms, there are marked differences in their physical character.

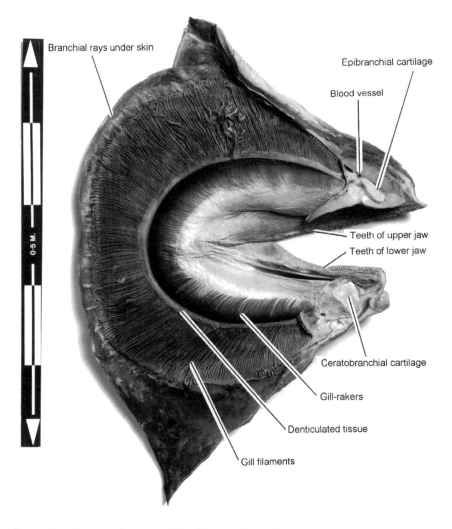

Fig. 9. Interior view of the 1st left-hand branchial arch from the angle of the jaws to the 1st gill cleft. Compare the transverse section of the septum in Fig. 10 which has gill-rakers and gill filaments on both sides. The specimen here is c. 60 x 45cm and is taken from a head sent to the Royal Scottish Museum about 1980. Length of the complete shark understood to have been 6 metres. (Courtesy G. Swinney, & National Museums of Scotland)

Baleen plates, fused into long leathery sheets, are worn down by the whale's tongue and end in fringes of fine, frayed material rather like coarse hair to the touch. In contrast, with their lustrous dark-brown surface, the gill-rakers of the shark look anything but frayed and are very flexible with a pronounced springiness evident even in specimens that have been preserved in alcohol for

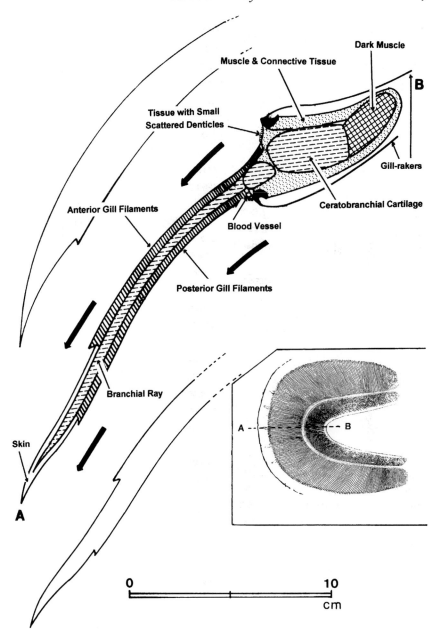

Fig. 10. Transverse section of a left-side branchial septum; probably the 2nd arch. The arrows indicate the direction of water flow from the pharynx outwards. Drawn from a specimen taken from a 4.95 metre female shark from St Ives, Cornwall, in the Natural History Museum, London (BM(NH) 1988. 3.1.1)

Fig. 11. A 'sea-monster' in the making. **A**. A fairly recently dead female basking shark on the south coast of Arran in November 1997. The flexibility of the branchial region which has collapsed inwards, opening the gill-slits and exposing the branchial septa, is clearly evident. **B**. A long-dead basking shark washed ashore at East Haven, north of Dundee, in early 1978. The jaws and branchial cartilages have come away from the vertebrae leaving the skull attached to the spine which gives the appearance of a long neck. The larger cartilages visible are elements of the jaws. (**A**. Courtesy David Wilson, Lanark. **B**. Courtesy David Henderson, Dundee)

many years. Although the rakers are numerous and densely-packed (about 13 per centimetre), each is a distinct bristle with an embedded curved base. On its inner (pharyngeal) side the base is held by connective tissue with elastic fibres; on its outer side it is gripped by a layer of muscle fibres.

In their relaxed position, when the gill-slits are open for respiration but are not wide open for feeding, the rakers lie tightly against the surface of the branchial septum. (They may be actively held down in the living animal, but even in a spirit specimen they flick back onto the connective tissue surface after being lifted, implying that they have this flexibility in life). In this state they are under considerable tension so a commensurate muscular effort is needed to bring them erect as the whole gill-arch structure expands and the gill slits open fully. The erect rakers standing against the out-flowing current now form a stiff fringe. This fringe appears to intersect with a similar fringe on the adjacent septum to form a sieve which strains out the planktonic animals. The mesh of gill-rakers is probably covered with mucus exuded from the glands around the bases of the rakers. About every minute or so, the mouth closes as the head drops down; the fish 'gulps' and the gill-arches contract, collapsing the rakers. The mass of plankton mixed with mucus passes down through the oesophagus (lined with branched papillae which form a valve) into the stomach. The head is then raised, the mouth opens wide and feeding continues.[29]

Matthews and Parker calculated that in a shark 7 metres long with an area of open mouth of 0.5 square metres and swimming at a speed of 2 knots, 1484 cubic metres of seawater were filtered every hour.[30] Although this rate of 2 knots while feeding has been widely quoted, more recent research suggests a greater range of swimming speeds. Sharks have been studied in the Firth of Clyde that were moving while feeding at estimated speeds of less than 1 knot and at from 2 to 4 knots, possibly indicating that feeding swimming speed varies with the density of the zooplankton. Perhaps, when not feeding, basking sharks are capable of sustained swimming speeds in excess of 5 knots.[31]

Filter feeding

The basking shark, whale shark and the megamouth all possess minute teeth but the filtration structure in the gills and the feeding behaviour of the whale shark and the megamouth differ from that of the basking shark. The whale shark has a huge flattened head with an unshark-like almost terminal mouth. While it is very large as befits the colossal size of the animal, the mouth has the shape of an enormous slot rather than the extended scoop of the basking shark. The flow of water through the mouth and out through the gill-clefts brings planktonic food which is strained out by a thin layer of sieve-like tissue formed from modified denticles and supported by cartilaginous struts extending from the gill-arch.[32] As well as filtering plankton, the whale shark also apparently ingests larger fish and squid, possibly by sucking them into its mouth.

The megamouth shark, unknown until 1976, is a deepwater Indo-Pacific species with an extensible gaping mouth that gleams with a silvery luminescence to attract the small shrimp-like crustaceans on which it feeds. It seems that the straining out of the food animals is done by rows of papillae covered with flattened denticles lining the inside surfaces of the gill slits and that the large 'tongue' formed by the basihyoidal cartilage and its tissues forces the filtered water out.[33]

The Gills

A narrow band of denticulated tissue which has the feel of fine sandpaper separates the gill-rakers from the next outer crescent of the branchial septum (about 20 centimetres wide) containing the complex vascular surface of the gill proper.

Each gill consists of some 250 radial filaments, each of which (in a fairly large shark) is a narrow free-standing strip 2 centimetres high and about 18 centimetres long richly supplied with blood vessels. A distinct dark-coloured rim forms the free outer edge of the filament. Running at right angles to this rim are very thin plates (lamellae) each about 2.5 millimetres wide and in these the blood is separated from the flow of water only by a membrane a few cells thick. This system of filaments with its myriads of lamellae gives an extremely large surface for the absorption of oxygen from the water and the release of carbon dioxide. Matthews and Parker estimated that the total respiratory area of a shark 7 metres long was some 270 square metres.[34]

Most sharks obtain their oxygen requirements in two rather different ways. When the fish is swimming, a current of water is being forced across the gills. This is 'ram ventilation'. However, if the fish is resting, it has to move the branchial region to keep a water flow through the gills – 'pump ventilation'.The proportion of oxygen obtained by each method of ventilation varies between species, but since the basking shark possibly hibernates, pump ventilation is presumably used in that resting state. A basking shark caught in a net and unable to move will, in time, drown, and the most probable explanation for this is that its struggles have caused a high oxygen debt for which the water flow produced by pump ventilation cannot compensate.

THE STOMACH AND LIVER

The stomach is a 'J'-shaped organ about two metres long in a large fish, containing (in the words of Matthews and Parker): '. . . over half a ton . . . of a bright red semi-liquid mass of disintegrating planktonic crustacea mixed with a great quantity of mucus'.[35] A specialised portion of the pyloric section – the *bursa entiana* – is full of a clear red oil derived from the stomach contents which is in the process of being transferred to the liver. (Fig. 12) Sharks have a comparatively small intestine, most of it taking the form of a compact and internally-complex spiral valve, and the basking shark is no exception. This organ in the adult is about a metre in length with 50 turns in it. Inside the spiral valve enzymes act on the contents and nutrients are absorbed. After the spiral valve a short colon follows ending at the the rectum which has a large salt-excreting rectal gland associated with it.

The lobed liver is a truly enormous organ even in such a large fish and may contribute as much as 25 per cent of the shark's total weight. There is a small median lobe but this is dwarfed by the two main lobes, huge dull-red slabs of oil-rich tissue extending along the sides and bottom of the abdominal cavity for its full length and almost completely enclosing the other viscera. The outer surface of each lobe (that seen first when the fish is cut open) is rounded in shape with the pattern of the blood vessels of the abdominal wall impressed in it, whereas the inner surface is moulded to the shapes of the organs it lies against.

The very size of the liver is a clue to one of its principal functions. The oil it holds is itself a nutritional reserve. Basking sharks that have been examined, known to be either not feeding or caught in an area of low plankton density, have been found to be thin with a reduced liver volume. From this it is presumed that the liver is a source of energy in the winter during hibernation (if this does occur). The basking shark, like the other elasmobranchs, does not have the gas-filled swim bladder typically found in the bony fishes, so that the liver also acts as a 'hydrostatic float' keeping the fish at almost neutral buoyancy. This buoyancy is given by the complex hydrocarbon squalene, the main constituent of the liver oil, which has a low specific gravity.[36] Laboratory analysis of oil samples from the 1940s Scottish fishery found that squalene comprised 38 percent of the oil.[37]

The elongated strap-shaped kidneys stretch nearly the whole length of the abdomen lying alongside the reproductive organs. Some of the urea, a metabolic product of the liver, is filtered from the blood but some remains in the tissue fluids for osmotic balance and this gives the flesh of the shark, as it ages, its characteristic smell of ammonia.

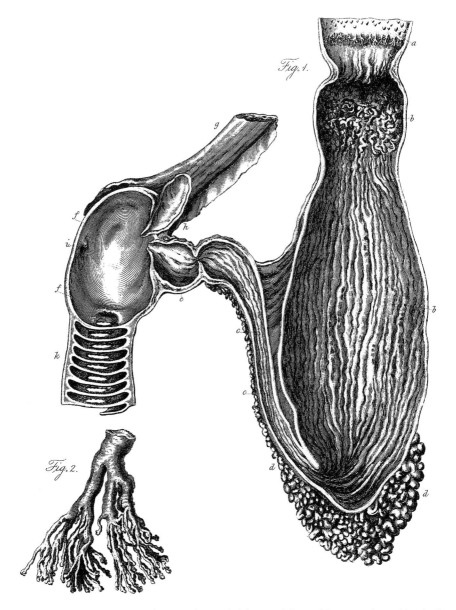

Fig. 12. Digestive organs. The oesophagus (1a) has cauliflower-like appendages (2) which may act as a valve for the stomach (b-b). The spleen = d-d. The bursa entiana (e) is a sac containing clear red oil, derived from the digestion of planktonic crustacea, which passes to the liver. Nutrients are finally absorbed in the spiral valve (k). Length of stomach circa 2.4 m. Appendage in (2) = 6 cm. (Home (1813): plate 17)

SENSES

The senses of the basking shark may differ from those reported for sharks generally, given that it is not a predatory feeder, but little research has been done in this area specifically on the basking shark.[38] The brain is small, surprisingly so at about 10 centimetres long. (Fig. 13) Its puny size is accentuated by its singular position, suspended in the centre of a much larger cerebral cavity by a network of fine filaments – 'rather like cotton wool' – and surrounded by fluid. It has been suggested that this arrangement could protect the brain from damage should the skull be deformed under pressure 'when the shark descends to great depths to lie in the canyons of the slopes of the Continental Shelf during its winter disappearance . . .' (if indeed it does do this – there is as yet no direct evidence).[39]

The olfactory lobes of the forebrain are well-developed with olfactory nerves connecting with paired olfactory sacs immediately behind the nasal flaps which partially protrude from the underside of the snout just forward of the level of the eyes. A current of water is diverted through the nostrils and this brings scents to the olfactory sacs. Pit organs, present along the body in all sharks, but very imperfectly understood, may also have an olfactory function (or may sense vibration). Sharks are extremely sensitive to certain scents in the water, even in very dilute amounts. (The effect of even a small amount of blood in attracting the larger man-eating sharks from a considerable distance is well known.) It is thus possible but not yet demonstrated, that a basking shark can seek out dense concentrations of plankton by 'smelling' them. Evidence for a keen olfactory sense in the basking shark comes from the Clyde ring-net fishermen who poured diesel oil around their nets to discourage the shark from blundering through them. When basking sharks were about, the Manson brothers of Mallaig used to puncture a small drum to allow a dribble of diesel and lower it over the side of a boat when herring fishing. They also noticed that oil oozing from the tar on their ring-nets deterred the shark. In Shetland a copper vessel 'washed' in the sea had the same effect.[40]

Research on the sight of sharks suggests that in many species the eyes are well adapted to discerning 'the brief flickering movements of prospective prey' in the dim greenish underwater world but are probably not good at focusing on near objects.[41] A slow-swimming species such as the basking shark, whose minute 'prey' is passively engulfed, probably has little need of acute sight. Nevertheless, it is noticeable that when approached by divers they stop feeding and veer away for a short distance, resuming feeding when they have overtaken the swimmers. They no doubt see the divers but also would sense their presence through their lateral line system which monitors water flow. A canal under the skin,

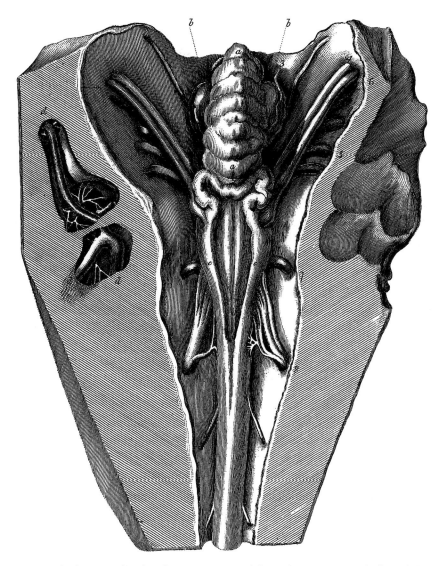

Fig. 13. The brain in the chondrocranium viewed from above. a-a = cerebellum. b-b = tubercula quadrigemina. c = oval band giving rise to peripheral nerves. d = semi-circular canals of the ear. Numbers indicate the cranial nerves. (Home (1813): plate 20)

perforated at intervals and containing sensory cells, runs the full length of each side, branching into a complex pattern on the head and jaws. The inputs from the lateral line system go to the inner ear, which with its three semicircular canals and associated sacs is an organ highly sensitive to motion, changes in direction and sound. As, however, there is no eardrum it is thought that sharks cannot distinguish specific sounds, unless they are pulsed and of low frequency.

Whatever the senses employed – hearing, vibration perception or a combination of these, it is known that the basking shark is alarmed by loud outboard motors and anecdotal evidence from the 1950s would suggest that the sharks learnt to be wary of their hunters. As recollected by one Mallaig man, the sharks were so 'tame' early in the summer that the fishing boat could get so close 'you could throw an anchor in their mouths'. But later in the season, as the harpoon gun did its deadly work, the sharks became 'timid' and would move away from the approaching boat.[42] More recent observations by biologists studying the sharks off the Isle of Man showed that they behaved in two different ways when approached by a motorboat. Some of the fish, apparently perceiving the boat as a threat, swam rapidly away in 'erratic zig-zagging movements' and often went deeper, while others, not appearing to feel threatened, would merely change course to avoid it.[43]

There are other sense organs. Scattered around the body of the shark and along the lateral line (but with a concentration on the top of the snout) are a large number of tubules known as the Ampullae of Lorenzini which are probably sensitive to electrical fields. Many sharks can locate prey by sensing small electrical fields. It is not improbable that the basking shark can locate its prey by this means as a moving mass of tiny animals or the counterflow of bodies of water may produce detectable electrical fields. There is the further possibility that sharks can sense changes in the earth's magnetic field through these ampullae and can use this input to navigate long distances. Such a capability would certainly be of great importance to a migratory species like the basking shark.

REPRODUCTION

In the male basking shark, the testes lie well forward in the abdomen on either side of the stomach and from each testis a long duct, the ampulla ductus deferens, runs to the urogenital sinus which opens into the cloaca. Each duct is intensively folded internally, holding a large volume of spermatophores and, in each spermatophore, about 3 centimetres in diameter, sperm is enclosed within a layer of clear jelly.[44]

The external sexual organs of the male – the claspers – are misnamed as they are not used to 'clasp' the female but in a similar manner to the action of the mammalian penis, one of the pair is inserted into the female to deliver the spermatophores. Each clasper, arising from the inner border of the pelvic fin, is composed of compact fibrous tissue over cartilaginous elements and is strongly muscled on the ventral (outer) side. (Fig. 14) The claspers, about 1 metre long in an adult fish, normally lie close to the belly facing to the rear, but in preparation for copulation the strong muscles of a clasper contract, curving the organ forwards and its clawed cartilage is extended to engage with a fibrous pad on the inner wall of the vagina of the female. Many litres of spermatophores then pass down the clasper through the groove formed by folds of tissue.

There is no published account of the act of copulation in a basking shark but behaviour has been observed which may have been mating activity. Two sharks seen in the Clyde in the late 1960s lying side by side facing each other and thrashing about were possibly copulating as were a pair observed close to the shore at Corrie, Arran, in the 1980s. Similar behaviour has been observed in the great white shark with the male and female slowly rotating.[45] Skin wear around the cloaca has already been described and this feature may be a pointer to this type of amatory behaviour in these large sharks.

The gonads of the female basking shark likewise lie almost the full length of the abdominal cavity. Only the right-side ovary of the pair is functional, producing an estimated 6 million ova. As the number of young produced by a female shark is small it is probable that only a very few of the ova which enter the oviduct are fertilised by the sperm released from the spermatophores which liquify once they are deposited in the female. A section of the oviduct is a nidamentary gland secreting a membrane over the fertilised egg. In the oviparous shark species, this membrane takes the form of a horny case with twisted tendrils containing an embryo which is left to develop quite independently after the eggcase has been laid. From the little evidence we have it seems that the basking shark is probably ovoviviparous, with the new-born pup breaking out of the egg while still inside the mother. In this case the membrane secreted by the nidamentary gland would be merely a filmy covering which would break open as the embryo develops, leaving the newly hatched pup free to subsist on its yolk-sac.

The Young Basking Shark

In many species of shark, newly hatched young are known to be cannibalistic while still inside the mother, the first one or two to hatch eating the later arrivals. While such behaviour seems unlikely in the case of basking shark pups, equipped only with insignificant teeth, it not impossible that the 'toothless' pups could feed on eggs. (The fertilisation of some eggs may suppress the development of others which then become a food source.) In the account of the basking shark given in his 1769 *British Zoology* (discussed in Chapter 2) the naturalist, Thomas Pennant, describes an embryo: 'They were viviparous, a young one about a foot in length being found in the belly of a fish of this kind'.[46]

The only eye-witness description so far of new-born young is the little-

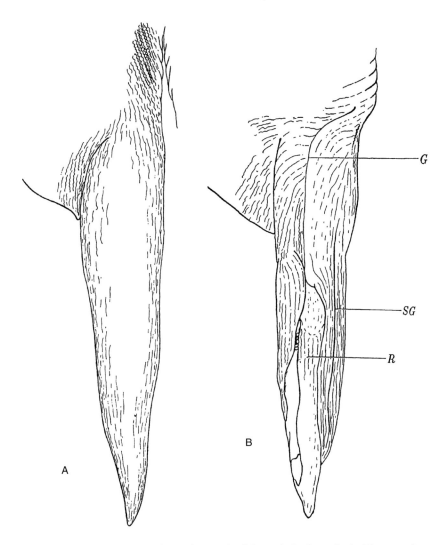

Fig. 14.   The claspers (external sexual organs) of the male basking shark. They are about a metre long in a large shark. **A** is the right side, ventral surface. **B** is the left side, dorsal surface. G = clasper groove. SG = second subsidiary groove. R = rhipidion (a long narrow lobe). (Matthews (1950): 258. Courtesy the Royal Society)

known Norwegian account of two fishermen, Hans Goksoyr and Jonas Sordal, who were hunting basking sharks off the mid-western coast of Norway in the boat *Holmefjord* near the end of August 1936. The second shark they caught was being towed into port when:

. . . it threw a live young shark roughly as large as a common habrand [porbeagle shark, *Lamna nasus*].The young shark was alive and immediately started swimming at the surface. Then another young shark and so on to five young sharks, and a sixth which was dead.

The parent fish appeared to be 'plump' but became leaner bit by bit as the young were disgorged. Sordal retrieved one of the pups and noted that it had neither a 'blommesekk' [yolk-sac] nor a 'navlestreng' [umbilical cord]. He added that its 'snout [was] narrow in front with a little bend downwards' and that it came swimming with its mouth open in the usual way when feeding. He considered the pup to be about 1.5 metres long and confirmed that the pups observed generally could have been about 2 metres long like the 'ordinary porbeagle'.[47] The adult porbeagle grows to 3 metres so presumably Sordal was referring to the size of the sub-adult specimens that he usually caught. His assessed length of the new-born shark agrees well with the theoretical figure (1.5 metres) arrived at by Parker and Stott who constructed a hypothetical growth curve for the basking shark based on their analysis of the rate of calcification in the centrum of the vertebra. The male shark was thought to become sexually mature at six to eight years of age. The age of sexual maturity of the female shark was not determined (although it was probably in the same bracket) and the gestation period was estimated to be three and a half years.These figures would now be considered to be too low by some shark biologists. Sexual maturity at a size of 5 to 7 metres (= 12 to 16 years) for the male and at 8.1 to 9.8 metres (= about 20 years) for the female, has been proposed.[48] As pregnant females were almost unknown Parker and Stott suggested that they remained hidden offshore for the gestation period. Their general conclusion was that the basking shark had 'an extremely slow reproductive rate'.[49]

The shape of the snout as observed by Sordal seems to distinguish the young fish for some years, possibly until it is about 3 metres long. While Matthews and Parker who critically examined the evidence from earlier authors for a 'proboscis-like snout' in the juvenile were not fully convinced, speculating that shrinkage in the snout of partially dessicated specimens had produced this effect, young sharks observed at sea do seem to have snouts which are pointed and even twisted slightly downwards.[50] However, the form of the 'hook-shaped' snout in a 2.6 metre shark estimated to be six months old taken off Japan in 1977 fully vindicates Sordal's account. (Fig. 15) The snout has a pronounced ventral groove which could be an adaptation to an egg-eating habit in the embryo and improve feeding efficiency in the very young fish by increasing the water current into the mouth.[51] The snout appears to develop to the mature rounded form through a stage in which, even though of a full shape and losing the ventral groove, it still retains a short hooked end. This transitional stage, in which the median rostral cartilage assumes the shape of a bow, may characterise fish in the 3 to 5 metre range.[52] P.F. O'Connor, fishing in the Minch, found that the 2-metre young sharks he observed in May

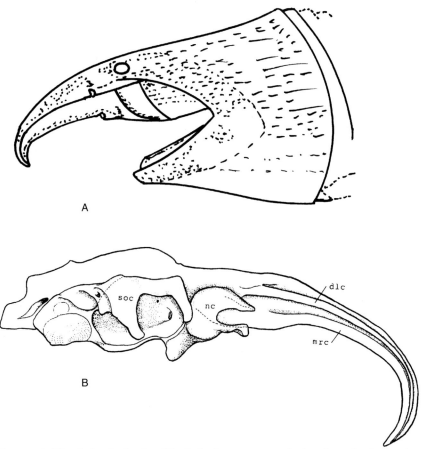

Fig. 15. **A.** The distinctive head and **B**, skull of a 2.6 m metre shark estimated to be less than six months old. There is a pronounced ventral groove in the curved snout. The median rostral cartilage (mrc) becomes bow-shaped in older fish to assume the shape shown in Fig. 5A. dlc = dorsolateral cartilages. (Izawa & Shibata 1993: 238 & 242)

were more active at the surface than older fish in the same shoal.[53] Research on basking sharks off the coast of southern England indicates that the larger sharks appear early in the season, in May, in conditions of high zooplankton density but that sharks less than 3 metres presumed to be the 'young-of -the-year' tend to appear somewhat later, in mid-June, as zooplankton density lessens, suggesting 'parturition occurring offshore around May and June'.[54]

The life expectancy of the basking shark is not known, but a twenty-year lifespan is not improbable. The adult would seem to have few natural enemies. Great white sharks have been seen to scavenge the carcasses of dead basking sharks but there is no report of their attacking the living adult fish although it is possible that juveniles may be taken.[55] In 1956 a 2.5 metre basking shark with a very obvious drooping snout was taken from the stomach of a sperm whale *Physeter catodon* captured at the Azores. From the photograph it appears to be fresh and intact which suggests that it had been stunned with a sonic blast like the large deepwater squids which are the whale's main food.[56] The mortality rate of young basking sharks is as yet quite unknown, but even if the adults are relatively safe from natural enemies, it may be that the young fish are preyed upon by large carnivores such as the great white shark and the killer whale *Orcinus orca* as well as by the sperm whale. In spite of this predation, if it is indeed significant, the overall mortality rate of juvenile sharks is more likely to be determined by the availability of their planktonic food.

HABITS

To the casual observer on the shore the characteristic sign of the basking shark is the appearance of its massive first dorsal fin tracking slowly and apparently aimlessly through the water. As has been noted, to gain its considerable energy requirements from tiny planktonic life, the basking shark needs to seek out the densest concentrations of the plankton. This probably accounts for a feeding pattern at the surface which seems erratic to the observer but is in reality the sign of a specific foraging strategy. A shark seems to find a rich patch of plankton and swim through it in a zigzag fashion, possibly exhausting the food potential of one plankton mass before moving on to the next. It may be that this zigzag feeding pattern indicates that the shark is in low density zooplankton, with a circular pattern or a series of loose 'u'-turns signifying that the shark is feeding in a denser patch.[57]

The daily movements of the plankton swarms account for the shark usually being seen feeding in the early morning or in the evening. The swimming zooplankton species such as *Calanus,* which are near the surface at dawn, descend many metres as the light intensity increases during the day and do not begin to rise again until the late afternoon.[58] This general pattern is, however, not immutable as the existence of a rich phytoplankton bloom may encourage a copepod swarm to remain near the surface apparently indifferent to the increasing light intensity. Strong upwelling currents around islands and headlands may also slow the rate of descent of the plankton masses. In recent observations off the island of Arran, most of the sightings of the basking shark were between 1500 hrs and 1900 hrs indicating a late afternoon surface feeding pattern there.[59]

Calanus copepods often congregate right at the surface on calm sunny days, even bumping against the surface film and causing small circular ripples which give the sea a speckled look perceptible to the experienced herring fisherman.[60] In these conditions the basking shark, with the tip of its snout, the first dorsal fin and the upper tail lobe all conspicuously out of the water, is possibly feeding at maximum efficiency. It may be postulated that more time and thus more energy has to be expended by a shark which is feeding on plankton masses dispersed by rough seas and it is thought that strong winds deter the shark from feeding in the surface layer.[61] However, other observers have found sharks feeding in rough windy conditions so the true situation has yet to be fully elucidated.[62]

Shoals and Mating Activity

In recent years in Scottish waters basking sharks have been generally sighted singly or sometimes in small groups. Further south, off the Isle of Man, shoals of between 50 to 200 fish have been seen occasionally but most of the sharks studied there were solitary fish or in a small group of two or three only.[63] The situation in Scotland was quite different in the late 1930s and during the fishery of the late 1940s when very large numbers of the shark were evident. One Carradale man recalls counting 177 sharks in one evening in June or July 1943 – undoubtedly a large shoal like the one encountered by Gavin Maxwell in the summer of 1947 'halfway between Barra and Canna':

> It was a gigantic shoal . . . at one moment we counted fifty-four dorsal
> fins in sight at the same time . . . we could see the fish down below us
> in the green water as a practically continuous mass, crossing and
> recrossing, ponderous and mighty; only the topmost layer, and not all of
> them, were breaking the surface.[64]

And that shoal was merely one of several he came across.

When basking sharks occur in groups, are these merely the incidental result of a number of animals exploiting the same food source or are the sharks gathering for some sort of social behaviour? As there is some evidence that the basking shark feeds at depths well below the surface it is postulated that the surface-swimming habit may have another purpose as well as feeding.[65] Surface feeding brings sharks to the upper boundary of their habitat and comparatively shallow waters as well as local oceanographic features would further define a space conducive to shoal formation to bring the sexes together for reproductive activity in a season when energy levels were high.[66] Again, Maxwell gives some confirmation of this possible reason for shoaling. In the shoal he described above, he found:

> There was one group that was more often visible than other parts of the shoal, a group of five fish that followed each other almost nose to tail . . . we shot the hindmost fish and . . . the next as well. This was a male fish, and . . . during a tremendous struggle . . . he emitted a great quantity of what we afterwards found to be sperm.[67]

Thus it seems that the circling behaviour is very likely a preliminary to copulation, as is the behaviour of sharks swimming in pairs or threes in a 'wedge-shaped formation' or 'swimming in a nose to tail manner'.[68] William Manson of Mallaig recalled that in the early 1950s when they came across a pair at the surface they would try to pass by the male in the rear to take the female (which in their opinion had a much richer liver). This manoeuvre had to be done with some care as the male, if alarmed, could somehow warn the female which would submerge. They also noticed that often when the female shark was being gutted the male would circle the boat and sometimes follow it for a distance.[69]

From the catches of the Scottish fishery of the 1940s and 1950s we know that in the summer female fish far outnumber males, but the fish that have been examined in the winter, when the shark is uncommon, are predominantly male. Females caught in the summer were all impregnated or showed other evidence of recent copulation and this seems to indicate that breeding takes place in spring, possibly 'prior to the main feeding period'.[70]

Breaching

Another aspect of basking shark behaviour which probably has a social purpose is 'breaching' when the shark jumps totally or partially out of the water – to the observer a spectacular, indeed unnerving, sight as a six-ton fish unexpectedly erupts from the sea and then crashes back with a thunderous splash. Breaching, which is a well-known phenomenon in whales, was, for the basking shark, long doubted by scientists even though described by Pennant as far back as 1769.[71] Matthews and Parker in the paper summarising the results of their 1949 Soay investigations considered it 'very improbable' that breaching occurred. Several years later they recanted after receiving a detailed account of a breaching observed off the Shiant Isles.[72] Breaching was commonly observed in the Clyde in the 1930s and has been seen often by those studying the shark off the Isle of Man in the last decade, and it may be a fairly common item of basking shark behaviour.[73] Possibly, breaching is more prevalent late in the summer.[74] A breaching basking shark seen at some distance could be confused with a small whale such as a minke but the absence of spouting before or after the event strongly suggests that the animal in question is a basking shark.

The reason for breaching can only be speculated upon at this stage of basking shark research. Of the two theories in vogue the older suggestion that breaching is a means of ridding the shark of lampreys seems the least likely. Even though circular bite marks have been observed around the vent there is so far no proof that the lampreys actually chew into the shark and the shark may not even be aware of their presence. The sharks do, however, occasionally rub against a boat, a jetty or the seabed in shallow water and this behaviour is likely to be related to the removal of parasites.[75] Alternatively, and given more credence by researchers, breaching could be a form of social behaviour possibly with the noise made communicating a shark's presence to others, or part of mating activity, or, if the breaching sharks are male, a form of agonistic or warning display associated with territory and mating. Some breachings are solitary sharks, others breach from a group.[76]

Eyewitnesses describe the shark as leaping out of the water often but not always with the tail right out, landing on its belly or coming out at an angle. Double breachings are known and are taken to be two fish, although one fast shark could breach twice and in the flurry of spray it would be very difficult to distinguish whether there was only one fish present. In two breachings (one a double) observed close to shore off Arran in two consecutive days conditions were fine and calm. However, even though breaching may be a phenomenon associated with this type of weather, the exact time of day does not seem to be significant as one occurred at 1220 hrs, a presumed non-feeding time and the other at 1930 hrs when feeding was likely.[77]

MIGRATION

Basking sharks appear every year on the western coats of Britain and Ireland from the Channel to the Northern Isles in a presumed migratory surge from late spring to late summer (occurrences on the east coast of Britain are sporadic and probably represent stragglers). The sharks are usually first seen in the western Channel in May, then on the south and west Irish coasts and around the Isle of Man by June, and in July in the Firth of Clyde, the Sea of the Hebrides and the Minch, with smaller numbers around Orkney and Shetland. The fish have generally disappeared from British seas by late September but occasionally an individual is reported in midwinter.[78] This sequence of seasonal arrivals and departures in British and Irish seas conforms with the overall pattern observed for the northeastern Atlantic: Portugal to the Channel Islands and Brittany; and further north, Iceland and the coast of Norway, even into the Barents Sea.

There can be little doubt that the primary purpose of this movement of sharks is to bring the fish to their feeding grounds in temperate seas 'where production shows a strongly seasonal cycle'. A complementary reason for the 'migration circuit' followed by the basking shark is bringing together dispersed groups to provide an opportunity for mating.[79]

While it is generally accepted that there is an exodus of the sharks from a deepwater winter retreat to the plankton-rich coastal waters in spring, many questions relating to the migration remain unanswered. We do not yet know whether there is one sizeable North Atlantic stock which radiates across the western European continental shelf or whether there are smaller distinct stocks, regional or local, which do not transit over great distances, have definite geographic boundaries and in winter move into pockets of deep water within the general range of their feeding areas. It does seem, from the recognition of individual sharks off the Isle of Man in consecutive years, that whatever their area of origin, adult sharks may continue to return to the same coastal region.[80]

If there is indeed one North Atlantic stock on the move, is there a well-defined movement from south to north, or is the broad trend west to east, but with a northerly bias? A south-to-north migratory trend would tend to favour the concept of the members of a single population going north from a hibernation area somewhere well to the west of North Africa. By contrast a west-to-east trend could support either a theoretical single stock spreading on a broad front across the North Atlantic or (an equally theoretical concept) dispersed local populations which hibernate on the closest edge of the continental shelf.

Theories of Migration
The earliest attempt to provide a comprehensive explanation of basking shark migration – the 'South-North' theory – proposed that one discrete population spent the winter off the Atlantic coast of Morocco and then streamed north, progressively appearing along the the western European coasts from Portugal to northern Norway. In the absence of evidence of a return autumn migration, this theory was found to be unconvincing and was abandoned in favour of the 'Inshore-Offshore' theory. As originally formulated by Parker and Stott in the 1960s to explain the decline in basking shark catches in the Irish fishery at Achill Island, the 'Inshore-Offshore' theory postulated a distinct local population migrating shorewards from the edge of the continental shelf in the spring to feed and mate and then returning to deep water in the autumn.[81] The theory was then refined to account for the observed movement of sharks northwards along the west coasts of Ireland and Scotland and the shoals of sharks off

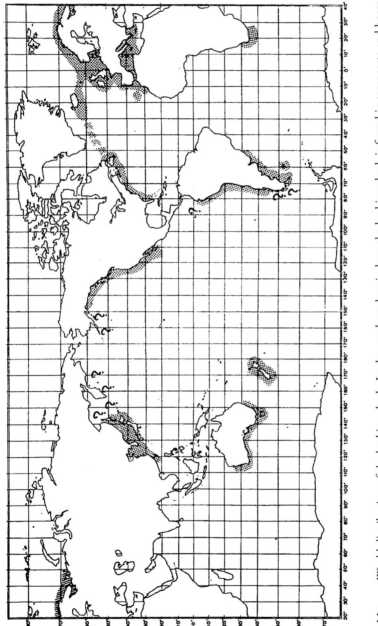

Map 1. World distribution of the basking shark. In the northern hemisphere the basking shark is found in temperate and boreal seas. In the southern hemisphere it ranges from warm temperate regions to sub-Antarctic waters. (Compagno (1984): 235. Courtesy FAO of the UN)

northern Norway.[82] This theory had the merit of apparently explaining the connection between the fishery and the numbers of the shark. An intense fishing effort (even though the numbers of sharks caught were not high in an absolute sense) would deplete a slow-breeding local stock by overfishing without necessarily affecting other populations. Implicit in this theory was the assumption that a local population would be inflexibly dependent upon a single bountiful but restricted feeding area.

Acknowledging that 'the whereabouts of the basking sharks in the winter months, whilst they are assumed to be in an offshore habitat, is unknown . . .', Stagg in 1990 proposed a modified Inshore-Offshore theory which accepted the fundamental proposition that the sharks migrate from deep water but on a broad westerly front rather than a south-to-north course. The sharks arriving off the coasts of the British Isles in the Western Approaches are thought to move regionally, that is within several hundred kilometres, searching out the most prolific areas of zooplankton. This regional movement inevitably, as the summer goes on, takes the sharks northwards, following the advancing seasonal blooms. However, given the coastal topography of Britain and Ireland, their progress is impeded by peninsulas, headlands and islands such that they are 'entrained' and spend time feeding in a local area before moving on. In Scottish terms, this would see sharks from the vicinity of the Isle of Man entering the Firth of Clyde, feeding for some weeks in the Firth, especially around Arran and Ailsa Craig, and then leaving for the Sea of the Hebrides where again they would circulate for some time before moving further north.

This modified theory has the merit of explaining why basking sharks appear off southern Britain and Norway at much the same time and it accounts for the monthly 'timetable' by which the sharks progress northwards around Britain and Ireland. Though not fully expounded in this theory, there still seems room for the concept of one 'British Isles' population which arrives first off the Western Approaches, rather than coming in from the Atlantic to the north of Ireland, because the plankton bloom is earlier in the southern Celtic Sea. There must of course on all coasts be a return migration; but since few sharks are noticed in the autumn, whether they are swimming southwards or westwards, it is presumed that the sharks leaving on the return migration are neither feeding at the surface nor mating and thus a horde of sharks streams back to the ocean depths unseen by any human observer.[83]

Hibernation

The exact winter quarters of the basking shark in any ocean of the world are quite unknown but it has long been presumed that the sharks hibernate in deep locations – 'perhaps in the heads of the canyons at the edge of the continental shelf.[84] The evidence for this is indirect. High quantities of squalene in the liver oil are characteristic of shark species which are known only from deepwater habitats, and the intermediate level of squalene in the basking shark liver points to a life history where some period is spent at a considerable depth.[85] From time to time, torpid sharks are caught during the winter in trawls in the Firth of Clyde, and they were not uncommon in the 1950s especially in deep water to the north of Arran.[86] Also during January and February the occasional shark is seen swimming in the Clyde. Do these represent sharks that, lagging behind the main group in autumn, lose the migratory impulse and are forced to over-winter in the Clyde or does a small local stock regularly stay there in deep water in a non-active state? The answer to this would have considerable implications for the migration theories discussed above. Another puzzle is presented by the finding of sharks with non-functional gill-rakers which, flabby and incomple-tely formed, lie underneath a thin layer of epidermis. These sharks, and there have been very few of them, have all been found in autumn, leading to the conclusion that there is a resting, non-feeding and thus non-growing period in autumn and winter. The picture presented here, however, is not definitive as in the same seasons about half of the few sharks that were caught and examined still had gill-rakers, so presumably were still feeding.[87] Also, although the existence of a quiescent state in which gill-rakers worn down by a season of feeding (or damaged by parasites) are renewed is an entirely logical theory, the fact that the rakerless sharks have all been found in the comparatively shallow North Sea or the Channel gives no indication of where the great mass of North Atlantic sharks might spend the winter.

Notes

1. Compagno (1984): 236.
2. Squire (1990): 11.
3. Springer & Gilbert (1976): 47.
4. Thomson & Simanek (1977): 343 & 353.
5. The description of anatomy and biology in this chapter is based on Matthews & Parker (1950) & Daniel (1922). The measurements given here and in the rest of the chapter relate to a 7-metre fish. (See Matthews & Parker (1950): 537-538.)
6. Matthews & Parker (1950): 544 & Gudger (1935): 95–98.
7. Home (1809b): 206 & Matthews & Parker (1950): 537.
8. Martin (1981): 171.
9. Watkins (1958): 149.
10. Matthews & Parker (1950): 568.
11. Matthews & Parker (1950): 537 & Matthews & Parker (1952): 256.
12. The shark was estimated to be twice as long as the 15-ft rubber dinghy alongside it. M. O'Connell & T. Thom, *pers. comm.* 1997.

13. Home (1809b): 206 & 213.
14. Maxwell (1952): 266-267.
15. Heuvelmans (1968): 118 & Home (1809b): 216.
16. Pollard (1997): 4.
17. Home (1809a): 179.
18. Pavesi (1878): 360 & Senna (1925): plate 9.
19. Barnard (1937): 44.
20. Strong (1991): 59.
21. Earll & Turner (1992): 30.
22. Lien & Fawcett (1986): 247; Tennyson (1992): 41; & Mutoh & Omori (1978) *in* Stagg (1990): 135.
23. Matthews & Parker (1950): 566.
24. Farmery (1992): 32, 35.
25. Lucas (1956): 124; & Sims & Quayle (1998): 460.
26. Grieve (1966).
27. J. Strawbridge *pers. comm.* 1997.
28. Turner (1879): 282.
29. Hallacher (1977). Movement of head – M O'Connell & T. Thom *pers. comm.* 1997.
30. Matthews (1962): 757.
31. Priede (1984): 211 & M. O'Connell & T. Thom *pers. comm.* 1997.
32. White (1937): 61.
33. Taylor, Compagno & Struhsaker (1983): 108-109.
34. Matthews & Parker (1950): 565
35. Matthews & Parker (1950): 548
36. Pelster (1997): 216–217.
37. Kunzlik (1988): 5.
38. This section on 'Senses' is based on 'Sensory organs' in Steel (1992): 63-73.
39. Stott (1980): 667.
40. Ralston (1995): 15; W. Manson *pers. comm.* 1995; & (Shetland) Sandison (1968): 61.
41. Steel (1992): 65.
42. W. Manson *pers. comm.* 1995.
43. Strawbridge (1992): 78.
44. This section 'Reproduction' is based on Matthews (1950).
45. H. McCrindle (Clyde) *pers. comm.* 1995 & M. O'Connell (Corrie, Arran) *pers. comm.* 1997. For the great white shark see Francis (1996): 171-172.
46. Pennant (1769): 80.
47. Sund (1943). The title 'Et brugdebarsel' translates as 'A basking shark giving birth'; 'habrand' is an older form of 'habrann'.
48. Fowler (1996): 4.
49. Parker & Stott (1965): 316.
50. Matthews & Parker (1950): 541-542; & Earll & Turner (1992): 34.
51. Izawa & Shibata (1993): 237, 238 & Yano (1978) in Izawa & Shibata (1993): 244.
52. Izawa & Shibata (1993): 242-244.
53. O'Connor (1953): 145 & 235.
54. Sims, Fox & Merrett (1997): 440.
55. Long & Jones (1996): 296.
56. Clarke (1950): 261 & plate 2, fig 4.

57. Earll & Turner (1992): 41 & 44.
58. Stagg (1990): 49.
59. M. O'Connell *pers. comm.* 1997.
60. Marshall & Orr (1955): 127.
61. McLachan (1991): 121.
62. Farmery (1992): 12.
63. Earll & Turner (1992): 33 & 37.
64. Angus Paterson *pers. comm.* 1995 (Carradale) & Maxwell (1952): 194.
65. Matthews (1950): 303.
66. Stagg (1990): 133.
67. Maxwell (1952): 194.
68. Stagg (1990): 99.
69. W. Manson *pers. comm.* 1995.
70. McLachlan (1991): 121.
71. Pennant (1769): 79.
72. Matthews & Parker (1950): 567; & Matthews & Parker (1951).
73. Earll & Turner (1992): 45.
74. H. McCrindle *pers. comm.* 1997.
75. Darling (1947): 171 for rubbing against a jetty.
76. Earll & Turner (1992): 45-46.
77. 1930 hrs, 8 July 1997 – M. Lucas *pers. comm.* 1997. 1220 hrs, 9 July 1997 (double breaching) – H. Reid & M. Auns *pers. comm.* 1997.
78. C. Oman *pers. comm.* 1997.
79. Stagg (1990): 28-29.
80. S. Fowler *pers. comm.* 1995.
81. Parker & Stott (1965): 307.
82. Stott (1974).
83. Stagg (1990): 129 & 135–140.
84. Matthews (1962): 758.
85. Kunzlik (1988): 9.
86. H. McCrindle *pers. comm.* 1995; 1950s – A. Paterson *pers. comm.* 1995.
87. van Diense & Adriani (1953); & Parker & Boeseman (1954): 189.

Chapter Two

Early Scientists

THERE CAN BE LITTLE DOUBT that the sight of the basking shark off the
western coasts of Britain and Scandinavia was a familiar occurrence long before
the fish came to the attention of naturalists who were both curious about its
form and habits and competent to describe it in a scientific fashion. In 1662 the
English scholar, Sir Thomas Browne, writing on the fishes of Norfolk, noted a
nine foot shark, a 'scrape', which had become entangled in herring nets. The
'vastnesse of the optick nerves & 3 conicall hard pillars wch supported the
extraordinarie elevated nose ' led a later English ichthyologist to conclude that
the scrape was a young basking shark.[1] The exact identification of the fish is not
made easy by Browne comparing it to the *canis carcharias alter* [*alius*] one of the
grotesque fanged forms in a 1649 illustrated work on fishes and whales by the
Silesian physician, Joannes Jonstonus.[2] The '3 conicall hard pillars' are the real
clue to its identity as the words are a very accurate description of the rostral
cartilages of a porbeagle *Lamna nasus* and this combined with the Jonstonus
illustration of a fiercely toothed shark forces agreement with Browne's editor
that the Norfolk shark was indeed most likely a porbeagle rather than a basking
shark.[3]

As far as can be ascertained the first written account of the basking shark,
separating it out as a distinctive kind of fish (but before the concept of a
scientifically described species had been clearly defined) appears to be the entry
for 'bein-hakall' in Jon Olafsson's *Icthyographica Islandica*, an early eighteenth-
century treatise on the fish fauna of Iceland which gives a short description of
each kind. Olafsson noted that the skeleton of the 'bein-hakall' was a
cartilaginous one, and even that some parts that were cartilaginous in other
sharks 'were bone in him' – a probable reference to the partially calcified
vertebrae of the basking shark. The oil and typical shark skin were also
mentioned.[4] A decade or so later, in Norway (which was at that time, together
with Iceland, part of the Danish-Norwegian realm) the bishop of Bergen, Erik
Pontoppidan, published his remarkable volumes on the natural history of
Norway. This comprehensive work, still of great interest for its extensive

treatment of the kraken or 'great sea serpent', was soon translated into the main European languages. An English edition appeared in 1755 and British naturalists became quite familiar with it.[5]

Pontoppidan was well aware of the distinction between the bony fishes and the 'haae, the shark' types with cartilaginous skeletons and although he described a number of sharks accurately including the Greenland shark (haae-kiaeringen), which was caught with carrion-baited hooks, he becomes confused in dealing with the basking shark. His 'brigde, the fin-fish . . . a large fish, 40 feet or more in length . . .' which provided oil from its liver is included with the bony fishes and he notes that others thought it could even be a cetacean. A little later he describes the 'haae-maeren', noting again that some considered it to be 'of the whale kind but it is truly and properly a shark . . . cartilaginous fish'. Both the 'brigde' and the 'haae -maeren' became entangled in nets and the livers of both provided oil. Undoubtedly both were the basking shark.[6]

As described by Olafsson and Pontoppidan, the basking shark, tentatively recognised as a distinct type of shark, and indeed as a fish rather than a whale, was making a rather hesitant debut in the literature of natural history. Given its size and its plankton-eating habit, the belief that it may have been more akin to a right whale than the sharks commonly encountered by seafarers was not entirely illogical and it needed more discerning investigators to establish its true place in the animal kingdom.

The two naturalists who gave the first comprehensive accounts of the basking shark which unequivocally established its anomalous position as a filter-feeding shark were mid-eighteenth century contemporaries and correspondents. Both also corresponded with the distinguished Swedish naturalist and systematist, Carl von Linne (Linnaeus). Johan Ernst Gunnerus was the vigorous bishop of Trondheim who amid his episcopal visitations over a large diocese found the time to make notable contributions to the botany and zoology of Norway. He first scientifically named, described and illustrated the basking shark in 1765. (Fig. 16A) The Welshman, Thomas Pennant, two years younger and with antiquarian interests as well as an enthusiasm for natural history, had four years earlier begun writing his *British Zoology*, an exhaustive treatise on the British fauna. This work came out in stages and in several editions between 1766 and 1812 with the basking shark first appearing in Volume 3 'Reptiles and Fishes' in 1769. (Fig. 16B)

SCIENTIFIC DESCRIPTION BY J.E. GUNNERUS

In 1765, in an article in *Det Trondhiemske Selskabs Skrifter* (Transactions of the Trondheim Society), Gunnerus described at some length the 'brugde' (basking

A

B

Fig. 16. Early naturalists. **A.** J. E. Gunnerus, bishop of Trondheim, who first scientifically described and illustrated the basking shark in 1765; **B.** Thomas Pennant, naturalist and antiquarian, author of *British Zoology* (1769), the first British treatise to include the basking shark – the name invented by Pennant. **C.** Sir Everard Home, English anatomist and surgeon, who debunked the 'Stronsay Monster', identifying it as a large basking shark. (Gunnerus portrait by J. F. Schweier, courtesy Universitetsbiblioteket i Trondheim; Pennant – frontispiece of Pennant (1793); Home by kind permission of President and Fellows, Royal College of Surgeons of England)

C

shark) and its natural history.[7] By his own account, Gunnerus became interested in the basking shark at a time when its fishery was expanding in Norway, and in the circumstances considered it his 'duty' to make a description of the fish more generally known. While travelling through the district of Nordland, north of Trondheim, in the spring of 1762, he met a landowner in Naero parish whose men were about to go fishing for the shark and Gunnerus asked that the foreman send him a careful description of the creature. When he returned to Naero in the autumn he was given an oral account of the fish, a drawing, a piece of its skin and, remarkably, a wooden model of it a half metre or so in length.

In the summer of 1763 'a well-stuffed basking shark skin' nearly 5 fathoms (9 metres) long was sent to Gunnerus from Smolen, an island west of Trondheim, and he based his scientific description on this specimen, reviewing earlier writers and remarking on Pontoppidan's confusion. The five gill-slits convinced him that the brugde was a shark. He measured the fins, noted the skin denticles, described the planktonic food as 'insects' and differentiated between the gills of the shark with rakers 'like a feather on a pen but somewhat looser' and the baleen of a whale.[8] Even though he appears to have overlooked the minute teeth, Gunnerus clearly saw the connection between the lack of biting teeth, the type of food and the narrow gullet. Concluding that the brugde, significantly different from the toothed sharks, was neither the female of the Greenland shark *Somniosus microcephalus* nor an old toothless example of the same species, Gunnerus stated that he had 'sought this fish with Linnaeus [and other authors] to no avail, therefore it must be considered a new, and so far to the learned, unknown species of shark'.[9] (Fig. 17A) As an interesting footnote we may observe that, soon after describing the basking shark, Gunnerus also first described and illustrated one of its principal food species, the planktonic copepod *Calanus finmarchicus*. He examined living specimens of these 'wingless insects', which he put in the genus *Monoculus*, that had been collected in the sea off Rensholmen, near Hammerfest, West Finmark, in 1767.[10]

Using the recently-devised binomial system of Linnaeus, Gunnerus named his new shark *Squalus maximus*. This name was incorporated by Linnaeus in the 12th edition of his *Systema Naturae* (1776), which for the purposes of zoological nomenclature definitively established the name as well as the claim of Gunnerus to be acknowledged as the first person to describe it scientifically.[11] In calling the brugde *Squalus maximus* (literally 'the largest shark') Gunnerus was of course unaware of the existence of the bigger whale shark which was not described scientifically until 1829. *Squalus* was the term used by the Roman naturalist Pliny for cartilaginous fish generally and is now just a genus of dog-fish, but as applied by Linnaeus it was a large catch-all genus which included all

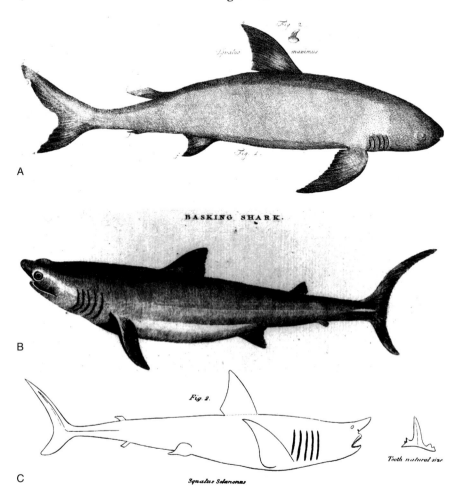

A

B

C

Fig. 17. **A.** Basking shark *Squalus maximus* as depicted by Gunnerus (1765). 'Fig. 2' is a skin denticle. **B.** Basking shark from volume 3 of the 1776 edition of Pennant's *British Zoology*. Probably based on a specimen from Lochranza, Isle of Arran, examined by Pennant in June 1772. **C.** W. E. Leach's *Squalus selanosius*, a young basking shark from Loch Fyne. (Leach 1818)

known sharks. Eventually *Squalus* had to be split up and in 1816, M.H. de Blainville of the Paris Natural History Museum erected a new sub-genus *Cetorhinus* for the basking shark. The following year Georges Baron Cuvier, another French zoologist, put the basking shark in the sub-genus *Selache* (Aristotle's name for sharks and rays as a group).[12] Even though other generic names have from time to time been proposed, the basking shark remains in the genus *Cetorhinus* with Gunnerus' name by convention bracketed after it to show that a change of genus has occurred – *Cetorhinus maximus* (Gunnerus 1765). The meaning of *Cetorhinus* is obscure as De Blainville proposed the name without explanation. 'Ceto' probably stands for *cetos*, an unusual form of the Latin *cetus* (from Greek κῆτος) for a whale, or a sea monster or even a shark, for classical authors used the term rather indiscriminately. 'Rhinus' poses a problem. Aristotle's name for the angel shark, ῥίνη, the term for a carpenter's rasp, has the secondary meaning of 'rough-skinned'. 'Shark with a rough skin' seems a little too obvious and doesn't distinguish the basking shark from most other sharks. Perhaps more likely, de Blainville derived 'rhinus' from ῥινός, the genitive form of ῥίς a nose or snout.[13] We have seen that the snout of the basking shark is quite pronounced, so 'shark with a [prominent] snout' seems a fair translation of *Cetorhinus*.

THOMAS PENNANT'S *BRITISH ZOOLOGY*

Writing on the basking shark in the third edition of his *British Zoology* (1769), Pennant claimed to have been the first (presumably the first in Britain, that is) to distinguish it from a whale – by its 'branchial orifices . . . and the perpendicular site of its tail'.[14] He mentioned a former fishery in Anglesey, Wales, and, most notably invented the popular name 'basking shark' for it (this point is discussed under 'Basking Shark' in Chapter 3). At this stage Pennant had seen only pieces of skin and the jaws and a sample of 'what is styled whalebone' (gill-rakers) and there is no suggestion that, unlike Gunnerus, Pennant, as he wrote this four-page account, was personally familiar with the fish beyond the samples sent to him. This first British description was based on information that had been supplied to Pennant by two rectors in Anglesey and he was obviously unaware of Scottish occurrences, although he noted the Irish aspects. In a footnote Pennant admits that his basking shark closely resembled the *Squalus maximus* of Linnaeus which he considered 'differs in having a small anal fin'– a feature which had plainly been overlooked by the Anglesey rectors.

Several years later, while travelling around Scotland for the second time gathering material for an expanded version of his successful work *A Tour in Scotland*, Pennant included in his itinerary 'a voyage to the Hebrides'. On 20 June 1772 he landed at '. . . Loch Ranza, a fine bay, at the N end of The isle of Arran . . .' and being informed of a captured basking shark lying on a nearby beach, went to inspect it. Here we see Pennant as the practical naturalist: he measured the shark (27 feet 4 inches – 8.3 metres) and described its distinctive features, speculated on its food, and gave a vivid description of the method of taking it.[15] Thus, these pages of *A Tour in Scotland* 1769 and a *Voyage to the Hebrides* 1772 published in 1774 anticipate the much expanded account of the basking shark which appeared in the 1776 edition of *British Zoology*. The accompanying plate 'Loch Ranza Bay And the manner of taking the basking Shark' is the first depiction of a basking shark being harpooned in British or Irish waters.[16] (Fig. 24)

The 1776 *British Zoology* entry on the shark includes Scotland – 'They appear in the Firth of Clyde and among the Hebrides in . . . the month of June . . . till the latter end of July'. It has an engraving of the fish, a grotesque goggle-eyed creature.[17](Fig. 17B) This has significance as the first illustration of a British specimen of the basking shark, so we may justified in some speculation on its origins. It is known that Pennant took an artist, Moses Griffith, with him on his second Scottish tour. Griffith drew the Lochranza scene, so it is most likely that Pennant, intending that any future edition of *British Zoology* should have a depiction of the shark, instructed Griffith to sketch the fish.[18] There is, however, a second, intriguing possibility. The Anglesey rectors were not Pennant's only clerical correspondents. Another long-standing informant on biological and historical topics was the Reverend George Low, minister of Birsay in Orkney, and many of his letters to Pennant survive in various repositories. Low wrote on 27 May 1773 with a long narrative of a basking shark which had appeared in the local harbour and had been harpooned. In this letter, Low supplied an extremely detailed description of the shark and, showing that his Orkney manse was up-to-date with its reference books, correctly identified the animal as *Squalus maximus* using both *British Zoology* and *Systema Naturae*. Low's letter spurred Pennant to ask for a drawing and on 6 August 1773, Low wrote again:

> According to your desire I have enclosed a sketch of the Basking Shark which was caught here, the shapes as far as I could is exact – the shading you will excuse as I have only just to do it as fast as possible to hit the first post lest you should have any particular design with it.[19]

George Low's drawing has not so far been located but it is reasonable to suppose that based either on the Arran fish, or an Orkney one, the first published figure of a basking shark in Britain was derived from a Scottish specimen.

Pennant's personal annotated copy of the 1776 edition of *British Zoology* which is held in the library of the Natural History Museum in London demonstrates that he customarily remained alert for new information. In the entry for the basking shark, a pasted slip notes a 26-foot long fish caught off Anglesey in 1760 and the plate has the manuscript notation 'female' added. Of particular interest is a newspaper cutting advertising the exhibition in London of a basking shark caught off Dorset in May 1801 (see page 61). As Pennant died in 1798, this must have been inserted by another hand, very likely by his son

David who used these volumes as a working copy while he prepared the 1812 edition.[20] The annotations later appeared as footnotes in the final, 1812, edition.

SEA-MONSTERS AND ODDITIES

A curious sideline to the mainstream of scientific interest in the basking shark was the describing of what may usefully be called 'pseudo' species. (The word 'fake' if used here would imply a deliberate intention to deceive, which generally, was not the case). This phenomenon took two distinct forms. In the first, the decaying carcass of a basking shark suggested to those unfamiliar with the rather unexpected way in which the body of this fish decomposes that a species unknown to science had been cast ashore. A 'sea-monster' no less. Such 'monsters' appear not infrequently on the coasts of those countries whose seas are visited by the shark and are documented for Canada and New Zealand as well as from Scotland with its notorious Stronsay monster of 1808.[21]

The second category was rather different. Some attribute of the shark was given undue significance as a specific character, or a crude sketch of the cast-up animal on the shore was accepted at face value, leading to the publication of a new species based on very slender evidence. The various aberrant shark species described by the Cornish naturalist Jonathan Couch are cautionary examples of this category.

The Stronsay Monster

We have seen in the section on the cartilaginous skeleton of the shark that the long axial spine, composed of vertebrae which are all very similar in shape, is joined to a disproportionately small skull. A 'monster' is created when the jaws and large gill-arch cartilages which are not firmly attached to the skull, fall away during decomposition, leaving the skull at the end of a long 'neck'. The cartilages of the pectoral girdle and fins remain, suggesting 'legs', and the semblance of a third pair of 'legs' is provided by the substantial skeletal elements of the claspers.

Even if sensationalised in press reports, these 'monsters' are now treated matter-of-factly by zoologists. But such was certainly not the case early in the last century. In late September 1808 several fishermen found the putrefying carcass of a large sea creature which they took to be a whale floating near Rothiesholm, in Stronsay, an easterly island of the Orkney group.[22] A week or so later, the carcass washed ashore and the news soon spread to Edinburgh. At a meeting of the Wernerian Natural History Society on 19 November, Patrick Neill, the secretary, announced the finding of a 'singular Animal, of great size, and corresponding to the description given by Egede and Pontoppidan, of the

Great Sea Snake of the Northern Ocean'.[23] Thus was born a celebrated scientific controversy which spluttered on for many years.

In the event, the carcass lasted only a short time, a storm soon completing its disintegration. Some pieces: the skull, a number of attached vertebrae, part of a pectoral fin and two gill cartilages, were retrieved and sent to the distinguished English surgeon, Edward Home, who was a prolific writer on anatomical topics in the *Philosophical Transactions of the Royal Society of London*. (Fig. 16 C) Home also had at hand the lengthy November 1808 affidavits made in Kirkwall by the local men who had viewed the 'monster': Thomas Fotheringham, John Peace, William Folsetter and George Sheran. These depositions had been sent to Sir Joseph Banks in London who passed them on to Home as well as giving him the drawing done by a local artist 'from memory six weeks after the fish had been seen by those, who describe[d] it, during which interval it had been their principal subject of conversation'.[24] (Fig. 18 A & B)

Examining the specimens, Home determined from various anatomical features that it was 'very probable that it is a *Squalus maximus*', a species which was a particular study of his at the time.[25] Home let the witnesses who had influenced the artist down fairly lightly: 'It is deserving of remark that there is no one structure represented in this drawing, which was not actually seen'. However, he also observed caustically that the contortions of the spine as depicted by the Orkney artist were an impossibility and made it 'highly probable that the account of Pontoppidan's sea snake had been read by the spectators of this fish, in the interval of time between their seeing it and their depositions being taken'.[26]

No such scepticism had been exhibited in the northern capital. In January 1809, four months before Home's account appeared (it was read at the Royal Society in London on 11 May 1809), the Wernerian Society was treated to a discourse on the 'Great Sea Snake' by Dr John Barclay, a prominent anatomist and founder-member, who based his observations on some caudal vertebrae only.[27] At the same meeting Patrick Neill proposed a new genus for the animal – *Halsydrus* (from Greek *hals*, the sea and *hydros*, a water snake). To honour the father of the great sea serpent (and thus unwittingly justifying Home's sneer) he put forward the specific name *Pontoppidani*.[28] The Stronsay monster had now formally entered the world of science. Later, in May, a minister from the Small Isles wrote reporting a 'great Sea Snake' in the Hebrides in June 1808.[29] The Wernerian Society itself did not publish anything on the 'monster' *Halsydrus* until 1811 when John Barclay's paper appeared in its *Memoirs*, but journals as such as the *Scots Magazine and Edinburgh Miscellany* and *The Philosophical Magazine* carried reports of the society's doings to a wide audience throughout Britain. A letter of September 1808 written by Alexander Maitland of

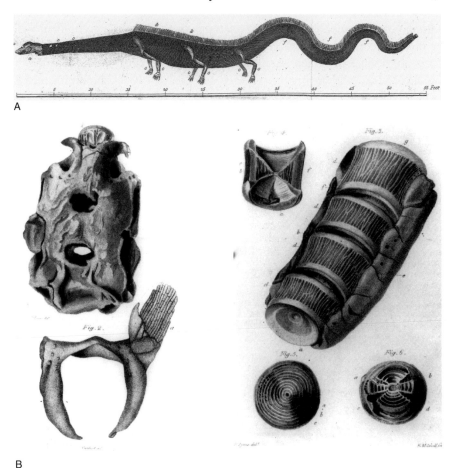

Fig. 18. The 'Stronsay monster' of 1808. Given the name *Halsydrus pontoppidani*, it was taken to be a new vertebrate species of immense size. **A.** The drawing of the monster done by a local Orkney artist and sent to Sir Joseph Banks in London, who passed it on to Sir Everard Home. The '55 feet' length, resulting from measurements taken by local men, was disbelieved by Home, who thought it was about 30 to 36 feet, i.e. appropriate to an extremely large basking shark. (Home 1809b: plate 6). **B.** The drawings from John Barclay's account of the monster showing (left) the skull with distorted cartilages curving out, the pectoral girdle and one fin and (right) a section of the vertebral column. (Barclay 1811: plates 9 & 10)

Edinburgh to his son James in Ceylon survives as evidence that the monster was indeed a popular sensation. Maitland not only describes the monster in some detail but draws it twice.[30]

The controversy rumbled on, with Scottish zoologists supporting Barclay against Home. One writing under the pseudonym 'Orcadensis' repudiated

Home's conclusions by emphasising the tough 'imperishable' 'cirri or filaments' of the 'mane' which he had personally examined (he may have got hold of a strip of gill-rakers).[31] Neill continued to assert the claims of the 'Great Sea Snake of Orkney'. With its length of 55 feet and a 'row of shining filaments along the back' it was 'inadmissable' that it could be the *Squalus maximus* of Linnaeus or their own basking shark. Neill patently doubted that the two were the same species, even forty years after Pennant's full description and illustration. However, his spirited defence of the unique zoological status of the monster was rather undermined by the title under which it appeared – 'Sea-Snake and Mermaid' (the 'mermaid' had been seen by two young ladies in Caithness). Perhaps, by giving Neill's piece this heading the editor of the *Scots Magazine* reflected the wider scepticism current a year after the discovery.[32]

After the best part of a year considering Home's conclusions, Barclay refuted them at a meeting of the Society in May 1810 and in 1811 he published a full justification of his first assessment that the monster really was a new marine animal, not a basking shark. His evidence remained weak – it is not actually clear that he examined any specimens other than four vertebrae and he put excessive reliance on the depositions of the Orcadian witnesses. We may question Barclay's competence as a comparative anatomist when he expresses surprise at the shape of the vertebrae: 'What occasions a singular appearance in these vertebrae is their want of processes'. Sharks as a group have simple rounded vertebrae without processes and in their general shape the vertebrae of a basking shark differ from those of a dogfish only by their much greater size. Barclay figured the skull but he did not discuss it and as it had been sent to Home, one may wonder if Barclay examined it, even though it was reputedly in his collection when he died.[33] Although Barclay had much to say in expounding his thesis that the 'Animal cast ashore on the Island of Stronsa' was *not* a basking shark, he is strangely diffident when it comes to stating positively what the monster actually *is*. His conclusion that 'the facts before us lead to nothing precise and determinate as to the species or genus of the animal' is vague and unsatisfying. He does not adopt *Halsydrus pontoppidani* as a scientific name and it may be conjectured that by this time Barclay himself had strong doubts that he was not prepared to admit to in a public forum.

Perusal of the later *Memoirs* reveals that, ignoring the belated minutes of the 1808 and 1809 meetings which appeared in the volume for 1818, Barclay's 1811 paper is the only account of the monster. This strongly suggests that majority scientific opinion in Edinburgh overcame national pride to grudgingly accept the Home verdict. No formal description of *Halsydrus pontoppidani* ever appeared and Barclay in the few years that remained to him turned to other interests. But not all naturalists were convinced and echoes of the affair persisted for many years. The Fife minister, John Fleming, in his *History of British Animals*, 1828, at the end of the section on cartilaginous fishes stated that the Orkney 'Sea Snake' merited some notice and could be Pontoppidan's sea snake.[34] He urged this claim again for the *Halsydrus* 'sea-snake' in the ichthyology section of David Brewster's *Edinburgh Encyclopaedia* of 1830.[35] Even as late as 1854, in the wake of another sensation, the sea serpent seen from HMS *Daedalus* in the South Atlantic in 1848, an Orkney naturalist, T.S. Traill, continued to assert that the Stronsay monster was not to 'be confounded with any known shark'.[36] All that now remains of the Stronsay monster is a sample of 'hair' and three vertebrae in a jar of alcohol in the Royal Museum, Edinburgh, the type specimens of *Halsydrus pontoppidani*.[37]

The priority of an early zoological name is important and as *Halsydrus* (1809) appeared before *Cetorhinus* (1816), *Halsydrus* continued to appear intermittently in zoological literature until the 1940s. In 1941 another Orkney 'sea monster' carcass, again a basking shark, was given the generic name *Scapasaurus*.[38] These 'sea-monsters' cast ashore from time to time will always excite comment and the mystery lingers in popular perception long after the clear light of scientific analysis has established the true nature of the creature. It would seem that we need our monsters and are reluctant to see them debunked.

The Loch Fyne Shark

Like *Halsydrus,* this species was based on a Scottish specimen in the museum of the University of Edinburgh, but it was not a monster, nor, unlike the grotesque Couch types to come, was it really too much of an oddity. W.E. Leach, who published a description and illustration of it in 1818, took the scientific name of the fish *Squalus selanosus* from a drawing in the manuscript papers of the Reverend Dr John Walker, professor of natural history in the University of Edinburgh, who had died in 1803.[39] The museum specimen was an eight-and-a-half feet long fish from Loch Fyne and Leach was well aware that it was a basking shark, most likely the one in Pennant's *British Zoology*. But, as we have seen, there was a reluctance to accept that the basking shark, as described and illustrated by Pennant, was in fact identical with the *Squalus maximus* of Linnaeus. Given that the principle of *Systema Naturae* was the cataloguing of names of species, not expansive illustrated accounts of their characteristics, Linnaeus' entry for *Squalus maximus* is very brief and some disinclination to admit that his *Squalus* and the basking shark were the same species is perhaps understandable. Did the doubters think to look at the original lengthy description and plate given by Gunnerus? There is no hint that they did. Leach was dismissive, even insulting, about Pennant's illustration of the basking shark, considering that: 'an ignorant artist, and still more stupid engraver fashioned the animal to suit their fancy, carefully rounding angles, to give elegance to their works'. He thought that Pennant and Home had described two different species under the one name so for Leach *Squalus selanosus* was intended to be the scientific name for Pennant's basking shark. Even though the type specimen was 'in a dried state', when its size is taken into account, its 'porrected [= extended] nose' suggests the typical outline of the head of an immature shark.[40]

Leach did not quote any text from Dr Walker's manuscripts and it is only from John Fleming's later entry on the species in *History of British Animals* that we find that Walker had composed a Latin description of the fish as early as 1769. The name, which seems to have been given by Walker himself even though it was left to Leach to formally publish it, comes from the rather absurd idea that an indentation in Ptolemy's second-century map of Britain – Sinus Selanosus – was Loch Fyne. Walker was adamant that his new Scottish shark was not a basking shark – 'There is not a vestige of this animal in Linnaeus, Willoughby, Artedi, or Pennant'. Fleming did not stop at that. Purely, it seems, on the basis of Dr Walker's description, and with no mention of Leach ten years before, he decided that a new genus was called for, to be placed between the great white shark and the porbeagle. And so '*Selanonius Walkeri*' made its brief appearance in zoological literature.[41]

The Loch Broom Monster

In August 1906, the papers reported a 'strange monster' observed outside Loch Broom Sutherland by a party of excise officers who had fired on it. A correspondence regarding its identity followed in the 'Notes and Queries' pages of the *Zoologist*, a serious natural history magazine akin to the *Scottish Naturalist*. The discussion of its possible identity over two issues of the journal was very sober in contrast to the earlier excitement over the Stronsay Monster ninety years before; indeed in an oblique reference to that episode one correspondent expressed his relief that the letters were 'refreshing in absence of the sea serpent and mermaid tone'. The animal seen, possessing a large dorsal fin and a tail fin, was thought to be 50 to 60 feet in length, but even if this exceptional length was perhaps accepted too uncritically, all agreed on its identification as a basking shark. [42] The Loch Broom 'sea-monster' seems to have been the last Scottish one discussed in a reputable scientific journal, the much later '*Scapasaurus*' never getting beyond the pages of the local newspaper.

The 'Rashleigh Shark' and the 'Broad-headed Gazer'

Except for his schooling and his medical training, Dr Jonathan Couch spent the whole of his long life in his home village of Polperro, a small picturesque fishing

Fig. 19. Dr Jonathan Couch's Channel oddities, both basking sharks. **A**. The Rashleigh Shark (*Polyprosopus rashleighanus*). **B**. The Broad-headed Gazer (*Polyprosopus macer*). (Couch 1862 plate 15 & pp 68–69)

port on the south coast of Cornwall. Being their physician, he was able to use his relationship with the local fishermen to great advantage in pursuing his hobby of ichthyology, recording and drawing the fresh specimens that were regularly brought to him. His researches led to various papers in learned journals and culminated in the four-volume *History of the Fishes of the British Islands* (1860-1865). Volume 1 includes not only the basking shark, (illustrated very poorly – a sort of hybrid shark and bottle-nosed whale in appearance) but two new species, the Rashleigh shark (*Polyprosopus rashleighanus*) and the broad-headed gazer (*Polyprosopus macer*).[43] (Fig. 19)

Couch had already described the Rashleigh shark in 1825 on the sole authority of a drawing sent to him by 'William Rashleigh, Esq., of Menabilly in Cornwall, himself a competent naturalist . . .' observing that 'This fish seems to resemble the Basking Shark, but differs from it in the form of the head and situation of the eye'.[44] The broad-headed gazer similarly depended on the drawing of an 1852 Plymouth specimen made by 'a gentleman of the Royal Navy'.[45] In erecting the genus *Polyprosopus* to indicate that the eyes of these sharks looked forwards, not to the sides, Couch conceded that the gill openings were the same as in the basking shark. In both cases Couch was too ready to accept the distortions of the snout caused by the dead sharks drying out as significant diagnostic characters. Couch appears to have had a reputation for naming new species on very slender evidence, a common failing of nineteenth-century scientists:

> Of the multiplication of nominal species one must admit that Couch was what the modern systematist calls a 'splitter' – the fault of working in isolation.[46]

NINETEENTH CENTURY ANATOMISTS

It is necessary to return to Everard Home to pick up the thread of mainstream scientific study of the shark. The excitement over sea monsters was only a distraction to Home. He was a surgeon and his real interest was the field of comparative anatomy and physiology, not just for its own sake but so that the fruits of his research could be applied to the treatment of human disorders. His dissection of the vertebral column of the basking shark was intended to elucidate the 'general principle upon which all intervertebral joints are formed' so that the knowledge gained could be applied to the treatment of curvatures of the spine.[47] Two papers on the general anatomy of the basking shark followed this one on the intervertebral joint. In the first, he described the anatomy of a large male shark which had been caught off Brighton in November 1808.

Unfortunately he put undue reliance on the structure of the stomach and came to the untenable conclusion that the basking shark was an intermediate form between the sharks and the whales.[48] A female shark brought to London from Brighton in 1812 provided the material for his final paper devoted to the anatomy of the brain and the mechanics of the circulation of blood through the gills.[49] In neither of these papers did he discuss the structure and function of the gill-rakers which, in hindsight, seems a strange omission.

At the same time as Home was preparing his two major papers, M.H. de Blainville was also making an extensive study of the basking shark which was published in 1811.[50] This tradition of comparative anatomy continued through to the late 1870s with a series of major studies principally in French and Italian, all of which were well-illustrated by the standards of the time.[51] After these, the thrust of what was written about the basking shark became more general, relying on the work of the earlier authors and often being little more than distribution records.

EPILOGUE: MATTHEWS AND PARKER 1947

The small factory erected on the island of Soay, the site of Gavin Maxwell's shark-fishing enterprise, was the scene of the last great comprehensive study of the anatomy and biology of the basking shark, the work of the distinguished zoologists L. Harrison Matthews and H.W.Parker which has been referred to so often in the previous chapter on Natural History. At that time Matthews was the director of the Zoological Society of London and Parker was on the staff of the British Museum (Natural History) as the Natural History Museum was then known. They had met Maxwell at a meeting of the Linnean Society in London in January 1947, when he gave a lecture on the basking shark and the Soay operation. Realising that the Soay factory gave an unequalled opportunity to minutely examine and dissect a good sample of sharks, they took up Maxwell's invitation to go up there for a few weeks and began their work in mid-May of that year. The sheer bulk of the sharks and the size and weight of their organs made dissection a difficult and awkward task with its own peculiar hazards as Harrison Matthews later told Maxwell's biographer:

> It was an enormous help to be able to use the machinery Gavin had installed for cutting up the sharks, because these creatures were not easy things to dissect – some of the organs were so big and heavy we could barely handle them, and if your scalpel slipped and you punctured the stomach you could release half-a-ton of semi-digested plankton all over your dissection.[52]

Matthews and Parker focused their studies on the internal anatomy of the basking shark; its reproductive biology; its feeding habits and the composition of its food; and the variety of parasites it is host to. Perhaps most importantly, they had a distinct advantage over previous anatomists in that they were able to examine a good sample of the sharks instead of the ones and twos that had provided the raw material for the earlier workers.[53] Their work resulted in two major papers which were bench-mark studies in the natural history of the basking shark and will remain essential for the serious student of the fish for years to come.[54] Gavin Maxwell's Soay venture was to fail spectacularly leaving the remains of the shark factory in their charming isolated setting on Soay harbour to become merely a minor detail of Scottish industrial archaeology. In the long term it is the scientific work done at Soay by Matthews and Parker which unquestionably remains the most significant outcome of that ambitious short-lived Hebridean scheme.[55]

Notes

1. Browne (1902): 36-37; Day (1884): 305.
2. Jonstonus [1649]: tab vi, no 6.
3. Browne (1902): 37.
4. Lindquist (1994): 1054.
5. Pontoppidan (1755).
6. Pontoppidan (1755): 109-110 & 116.
7. Gunnerus (1765). For the life of J.E. Gunnerus, see Nordgard (1931).
8. Gunnerus (1765): 46.
9. Gunnerus (1765): 49.
10. Gunnerus (1770); & Marshall & Orr (1955): 1-2 & fig 1.
11. Linnaeus (1776): 400.
12. de Blainville (1816): 121; & Cuvier (1817): 129. For a full synonymy, see Bigelow & Schroeder (1948): 156-160.
13. M. Humphries *pers. comm.* 1997.
14. Pennant (1769): 78. The bibliography of *British Zoology* is complicated and no attempt to unravel it is made here. For chronology see Pennant (1793). For Pennant's life and works see Wroth (1895).
15. Pennant (1793): 15; & Pennant (1774): 168-170.
16. Pennant (1774): 168, plate 13.
17. Pennant (1776a): 102-103 & plate 13.
18. For Moses Griffith, see Cust (1890).
19. WCRO CR 2017/TP 290/4 (27 May 1773 letter); & TP 290/8 (6 Aug 1773 letter). For the life and work of George Low, see Cuthbert (1995); & Seccombe (1893).
20. Pennant (1776b): plate 8. David Pennant – M. Ory *pers. comm.* 1996.
21. See Heuvelmans (1968) for a full treatment of sea-monsters. For a Canadian example of a basking shark 'monster' see Scott & Scott (1988): 18. For a New Zealand sensation see Kuban (1997).

22. This account of the Stronsay monster is based on Barclay (1811), Home (1809b), Bland & Swinney (1978) and Swinney (1983). For a discussion of the scientific names see Bland & Swinney (1978). For the principal protagonists, Barclay and Home, see Bettany (1885 & 1891).
23. *MWNH* vol 2, 1818: 638; & Anon (1808): 805.
24. Home (1809b); 216.
25. Home (1809b): 217.
26. Home (1809b): 216 & 218-219.
27. *MWNH* vol 2 1818: 638 & Barclay (1811): 418-423.
28. Anon (1809a): 5-6.
29. *MWNH* vol 2 (1818): 640 & text of letter – Barclay (1811): 442-444.
30. Swinney (1983): 16.
31. 'Orcadensis' (1809): 508.
32. N. (1809): 645.
33. Barclay (1811): 418-430; & Bland & Swinney (1978): 133. (Barclay's article, published in 1811, was probably written in late 1810.)
34. Fleming (1828): 173-174.
35. Fleming (1830): 691.
36. Traill (1854): 212.
37. Herman, McGowan & Swinney (1990): 1.
38. Bland & Swinney (1978): 134.
39. Leach (1818): 64-65. For Walker's life and work see Boulger (1909) & McKay (1980).
40. Leach (1818): 65. For Pennant's illustration see Pennant (1776a): 101 plate 13.
41. Name & description (but not original drawing) – Walker misc. papers: [105–106] (EU Dc 2.39/1); Fleming (1828): 168-169.
42. Workman (1906); quote: 396.
43. Couch (1862): 60-66 & plate 14 (basking shark); 67-68 & plate 15 (Rashleigh shark) & 68-69 & plate 15 (broad-headed gazer). For life & work of Couch, see Bettany (1887) & Tucker (1956).
44. Couch (1825): 91 & (1862): 67-68.
45. Couch (1825): 92 & (1862): 68-69.
46. Tucker (1956): 141.
47. Home (1809a): 178.
48. Home (1809b): 212.
49. Home (1813).
50. de Blainville (1811).
51. Examples are Gervais & Gervais (1876) & Pavesi (1874 & 1878).
52. Botting (1993): 97-98. For L.H. Matthews see Harrison (1987), especially 422-424: 'Bats and Basking Sharks'.
53. Matthews & Parker (1952): 255.
54. Matthews (1950); Matthews & Parker (1950). See Bibliography for other papers and articles.
55. Suggested by I.G. Priede *pers. comm.* 1995.

Chapter Three
Names, Beliefs and Attitudes

THROUGHOUT SCOTTISH HISTORY the basking shark has had a surprising variety of names reflecting the diverse origins of the nation. 'Basking shark' is itself an invention which has only recently displaced some of the older names. Beliefs and superstitions which are closely tied to underlying cultural and religious patterns are less persistent than names and consequently are harder to track down in the historical record. The literary references are the outcome of the shark engaging the imagination of the author of verse or fable and are interesting though not numerous.

POPULAR NAMES

In spite of the absence of archaeological evidence, the existence of a Gaelic name and names derived from Old Norse would appear to indicate that knowledge of the basking shark in Scotland is of some antiquity. In the west, Gaelic-speaking into modern times, *cearban* is the proper name of the fish and this gave rise to the Scots forms *cairban*, *carbin*, and *carfin*. *Cairban* and its variants apparently lapsed in the nineteenth century. Another Gaelic name is *seoldair* (sailor) used in the Loch Fyne area in the 1950's and no doubt earlier. *Muldoan*, a word of uncertain origin, given as a Scots name for Argyll and, oddly, Aberdeen, was commonly used in the west until recent years. According to Gavin Maxwell it was the 'fisherman's name for the sharks'.[1] For the north-east, *pricker* is recorded as a name used at Peterhead in the early part of the last century. *Hoe-mother*, with its variant *homer* (mother of the dogfish) is given as the Orkney name, while *brigda*, a Norse derivative, was the earlier Shetland name. *Brigda* in time became *brigdie* and this name spread to the northern mainland of Scotland.

The parish ministers who provided the various narratives which comprise the *Old Statistical Account* of the 1790s use *sail-fish* or *sun-fish* for the basking shark as often as *cearban* or *cairbin*, indicating that the vocabulary of the Scots-educated minister of a parish such as South Uist differed from that of his Gaelic-speaking flock. The term *sun-fish* probably came to Scotland from the west of Ireland, but it may be slightly more recent than *sail-fish* which, as used for the basking shark (there are other 'sail-fish'), appears to be an original Scots word, certainly used earlier than 1808, the date of the first reference given by the *Oxford English Dictionary*.[2] All these names are quite specific and it is only for Inveraray, Loch Fyne, in the 1840s that we find the careless use of 'whale' for the basking shark by fishermen when the welcome sight of the fins announced the presence of herring shoals. The English name *basking shark* with its curious implication that the fish sunbathes, seems to have begun to displace *sail-fish* very early in the last century and is now universal (although *sail-fish* lingered on in Carradale until recently). *Basker* is recent colloquial usage among those studying the shark off the Isle of Man and may be restricted to that area. (See Appendix A for a full list of popular names.)

'BASKING SHARK'

Thomas Pennant invented the name 'basking shark' in 1769 to replace the 'Irish and Welsh' term 'sun-fish' as this was already commonly in use for the very large, almost circular *Orthagoriscus mola* which occasionally drifts into British and Irish waters, carried from warmer waters by the Gulf Stream. Pennant stated that the Irish and Welsh had applied the term 'sun-fish' to the shark: '. . . from its lying as if to sun itself on the surface of the water; and for the same reason we have taken the liberty of calling it the basking shark'.[3]

Although a fool in Shakespeare's *As You Like It* had 'bask'd him in the sun' as early as 1600, it seems that 'to bask' in a sense approximating to our understanding of 'sunbathe', floridly described by the *OED* as 'to expose oneself to, or disport oneself in an ambient flood of genial warmth, as in the sunshine' dates from 1697 and 'basking' itself only from 1742.[4] The same work in its listing for 'basking shark' recognises Pennant's innovation but inexplicably uses a quotation from a later naturalist, William Bingley, to establish the name. His *Animal Biography* of 1802 (the *OED*'s source) obviously took its explanation of the shark's name directly from Pennant's text: 'The basking shark has derived its name from its propensity to lie on the surface of the water, as if to bask itself in the sun'.[5]

Much later a major ichthyological work of the 1950s suggested a sunbathing 'propensity' without offering any reason for the activity:

It spends much time sunning itself at the surface of the water, often lying with its back awash and dorsal fin high out of the water, or on its side, or even on its back; sometimes it loafs along with the snout out of the water, the mouth open, gathering its provender of plankton.[6]

In the absence of any rational explanation, it seems that the early idea of 'sunfish', perhaps meaning nothing more than that the shark was commonly seen in fine, sunny weather, became subtly altered by Pennant's invention of 'basking shark' to the belief that the fish deliberately sought the sun by coming to the surface. The ostensible origin of the name and the account of the shark supposedly 'sunning itself' in Pennant and later authors is merely unscientific anthropomorphism. The most likely explanation of the shark being at the sea surface is because the planktonic animals on which it feeds are there, or possibly for mating activity, and any warmth from the sun is quite incidental and irrelevant.

Bone-shark

One other name recorded by the *OED* should be mentioned. *Bone-shark* for the basking shark, is referred to as an 1802 usage in Massachusetts and may be considered an Americanism.[7] It does not seem to have been used in Scotland, and it is doubtful that it was ever a name in regular use in England or Ireland. 'Bone-shark' is the literal translation of the Icelandic *bein-hakarl* and most likely entered American whaling usage quite separately.

SUPERSTITIONS AND LITERARY REFERENCES

It seems very likely that until the 1937 Carradale Incident the basking shark was generally perceived as being harmless, although its very size would have amazed those who came across it at sea for the first time. Bishop Pontoppidan writing of the 'brigde' in 1755 claimed that the Norwegian fishermen were 'as much afraid of them as of the most dangerous sea-monster' when the sharks came around their boats.[8] But when they could the same fishermen lanced the sharks caught in their nets, so familiarity quickly overcame their fear and there was soon a thriving fishery off the coast of Norway. If there were similar feelings in those who engaged in the early Scottish fishery, the existing records do not hint at them. In the Scottish context traditional beliefs, superstitions or literary references to the shark are very rare and as a wealth of traditional beliefs and customs have been recorded for the nineteenth-century Scottish fishing culture, the lack of these can only imply the shark was not vital to the interests of the fisherfolk. This supports other indications that it was not fished for much of the century. Nevertheless, one strange belief if not a 'superstition' in the strict meaning of the word is recorded for Shetland about 1800:

The fisherman have a tradition, that this shark claps its belly to the bottom of a boat, and seizing it with its fins, drags it under water. They are very much alarmed when they see it, although I do not believe there is any authentic instance of it ever having injured them.[9]

A reluctance by basking shark fishers to bring a shark carcass ashore in the belief that this action would cause the sharks to leave the area is recorded for the Irish fishery of the 1840s but they often fished offshore well out of sight of land.[10] The early Scots shark fishers operated quite close to beaches which were conveniently placed for cutting out the livers of the fish and such a superstition, if taken seriously, would have hindered their work, so it is not surprising that it is not recorded for Scotland. The contemporary fisherman disavows any particular beliefs or ritual behaviour in regard to the basking shark and we may take it if any did exist they have been long forgotten.

St Kilda
The isolated St Kilda community engaged in very little fishing, let alone hunting basking sharks, but some lines from an early duet suggest that the shark was viewed very positively. These verses composed by a young couple about 1780 seem to imbue the basking shark with 'heroic' qualities:

He:
Thug mi gaol dhut 's tu 'nad leanabh,
Gaol nach claon gun tèid mi 's talamh.
Cailin dubh ciar dubh, etc.

I gave thee love when thou wast but a child,
Love that shall not wane till I go beneath the earth.
    Dark dusky maid, etc.

She:
Is tu mo chugar, is tu mo chearban,
Thug thu am buit dhomh 's thug thu an gearr-
    bhreac.
Cailin dubh ciar dubh, etc.

Thou art my hero, thou art my basking sunfish,
Thou gavest me the puffin and the black-headed
    guillemot.
Dark dusky maid, etc. [11]

It was nearly two centuries before the basking shark became the subject of a poem of its own with Norman MacCaig's 'Basking Shark' (1969) where the shark's very size and the shock of its abrupt emergence causes the poet to reflect on his remote ancestry – and to remain disquieted by the thoughts the sight of the shark provokes.

Basking Shark

To stub an oar on a rock where none should be,
To have it rise with a slounge out of the sea
Is a thing that happened once (too often) to me.

But not too often – though enough. I count as gain
That once I met, on a sea tin-tacked with rain,
That roomsized monster with a matchbox brain.

He displaced more than water. He shoggled me
Centuries back – this decadent townee
Shook on a wrong branch of his family tree.

Swish up the dirt and, when it settles, a spring
Is all the clearer. I saw me, in one fling,
Emerging from the slime of everything.

So who's the monster? The thought made me grow pale
For twenty seconds while, sail after sail,
The tall fin slid away and then the tail.[12]

ATTITUDES

Those who hunted the basking shark in the eighteenth century are unlikely to have had any fine feelings about it. It was probably regarded quite unemotionally as a desirable prey, once it had been decided that the shark was not too daunting to be tackled, and its value would have been assessed purely in terms of the number of barrels of oil obtained.

An unsentimental view of the shark probably also prevailed in the nineteenth and early twentieth centuries: naturalists in Scotland gave it only perfunctory attention; the holidaymaker in the Clyde or the Western Isles no doubt commented on its presence with some excitement; but the fishermen, drawing in the herring harvest, accepted its visitations while cursing the

The extraordinary FISH now offered for the Inspection of the Public, was taken at ABBOTSBURY, in the County of DOR-SET, on MONDAY the 4th of May, 1801, in the Fishing Seine of HARDY and Co . . . after it was entangled in the Net it received SEVENTEEN MUSKET BALLS, and many other Wounds before it expired.

Its enormous Weight for a long Time baffled all efforts to drag it to Shore, which was at length done by the united exertions of SEVEN HORSES and a number of MEN: . . . It measures 28 feet in length, and near to 20 Feet in Girth; its Tail from Point to Point is near Eight Feet, it has also Two Legs, and FOUR THOUSAND TEETH.

This fish, By Their Majesties Command, was exhibited before them in LORD CATHCART'S GARDENS, Windsor, who expressed much Admiration and Approbation thereat.

Admittance One Shilling.

N.B. FIRES CONSTANTLY KEPT IN ROOMS

OPEN FROM TEN TO FIVE, AND FROM SIX TO NINE

Fig. 20. The above London advertisement of 1801, 'A Nondescript Or, WONDER OF THE DEEP' shows that although the shark had been fished for forty years in Scotland, it could be exploited to amaze city dwellers who had probably never even heard of it. At 1 shilling, it was a very expensive treat, and with 'fires constantly kept in the rooms' the smell must have been appalling. The original is in Pennant (1776b). (Courtesy Zoology Library, Natural History Museum, London).

occasional ruined net. All this was to change in a dramatic and sombre fashion from 1936 onwards when, to the consternation of the local fishermen, thinking of their nets, and the wonder of Glasgow people on holiday, impressively large numbers of the sharks returned to the Firth of Clyde. The numbers excited comment, but until the events of late 1937, it does not seem that the sharks were feared.

THE CARRADALE INCIDENT

Carradale is an attractive township, lying in the lee of the Kintyre hills on Kilbrannan Sound looking across to the peaks of Arran. Its dispersed houses and farms are spread over a large rounded peninsula and surround three different bays. To the north with its jetty is Port Crainnach, the fishing harbour. Carradale Bay, a wide tidal stretch of sand, is on the southern side. In between the two, facing east, is Port Righ, which, sheltered on both sides by rocky ridges ending in skerries, has a curving sandy beach backed by a high brae on which there are several cottages. Carradale is not on the main road to Campbeltown and nowadays a detour must be made to visit it, but like so many places on the shores of the Clyde, it could easily be reached by steamer in a few hours from Glasgow and was a popular summer resort over many decades before the Second World War (see Map 5).

Captain Angus Brown, originally from Carradale but for many years resident in Swansea where he was the master of the Hay Line steamer, the *Duchess,* had brought his wife and two young children, Jessica (aged ten) and Neil (six) up to Carradale for a summer holiday. His brother Robert was a fisherman who, with another brother, Archibald, made some extra money by hiring out boats to visitors in the summer. Their largest boat, the *Eagle*, was a solidly constructed 15-foot planked dinghy which was usually rowed when they were out lifting lobster creels but could be sailed when required. Donald MacDonald, a local boy who was then aged 14, was employed by Robert Brown to help out during the summer.[13] (Fig. 21)

On Wednesday, 1 September 1937, the weather was overcast, possibly with sunny patches, with some wind and a noticeable swell from the south, as there had been a few days of stormy weather. For a while there had been plenty of basking sharks about and on that day, outside Port Righ in the sound, sharks were 'leaping out of the water non-stop'.[14] Angus and Robert Brown took the children out for a sail in the *Eagle* just before midday, possibly to do some dredging for natural history specimens. Angus, Jessica and Neil were sitting in the stern, with Robert Brown at the bow and Donald MacDonald amidships holding the oars. With the sail set, the *Eagle* was 'going like a clipper' out of the bay when, about one to two hundred yards off Point Balfadgen, the northern promontory, the main halliard snapped and the sail came down.[15] The two men began rowing and turned the boat back towards Port Righ.[16] In the words of Donald MacDonald 'the next thing I knew I was eight or ten feet under the water' with the others.[17] His nine-year-old friend, Colin Oman, who was lying on the grass outside his house on the brae watching the *Eagle* go out, saw a big splash and then the boat was on its side with the mast at an

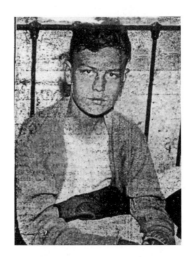

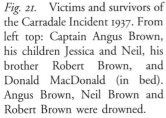

Fig. 21. Victims and survivors of the Carradale Incident 1937. From left top: Captain Angus Brown, his children Jessica and Neil, his brother Robert Brown, and Donald MacDonald (in bed). Angus Brown, Neil Brown and Robert Brown were drowned.

The survivors, Jessica Brown and Donald MacDonald, were each presented with a watch by the Royal National Lifeboat Institution for their attempts to rescue the others. Jessica is shown being presented with her watch by the Mayor of Swansea. (Brown photographs courtesy Sylvia Paterson, Carradale; D. MacDonald courtesy the *Daily Record*, Glasgow)

acute angle. The men righted the boat and put Jessica and Neil in it, but it was apparently capsized again and possibly even a third time. Jessica shouted to Neil to fling his arms out, to help him float as he could not swim. Jessica and Donald clung to the boat and dragged Angus Brown partially onto it. Angus Brown died as they were holding onto him and it may have been that his death was due to a coronary attack rather than drowning. The incident was seen from the shore and several boats went out immediately, rescuing Donald and Jessica, and bringing in the bodies of Angus and Neil Brown. The body of Robert Brown was recovered several days later. When brought ashore, the *Eagle* was found to have a broken tabernacle (the housing for the base of the mast). The newspapers suggested that there was a hole in the side but in the recollection of Donald MacDonald, while the side of the boat outside where he had been sitting was 'bruised and cracked' otherwise the hull appeared to be intact.

In the December, Donald and Jessica each received an engraved wrist-watch from the Royal National Lifeboat Institution in recognition of their efforts, and the men who went out to the rescue received £1.[18]

There can be no doubt that a basking shark caused the fatal capsize of the *Eagle;* it was thought so at the time and no credible alternative explanation has ever been advanced. Newspaper reports spoke of a shark 'attack' and in due course the incident joined those lists of attacks on swimmers by the great white shark and similar species which comprise an appendix in so many books about sharks. However, a deliberate attack on the *Eagle* by a basking shark with the intention of destroying it, although it cannot be totally ruled out, is the least probable of several explanations. Other interpretations of shark behaviour are more plausible.

Breaching sharks had been a common sight all that summer and apparently excited no alarm as visitors had engaged in swimming and boating '. . . unperturbed by the near presence of the sharks in the water'.[19] It is just possible that basking sharks, when present in sufficient numbers to stimulate breaching, may at least butt one another in some sort of territorial or mating interaction, and might in these circumstances take on a boat, but not enough is known about the group behaviour of the sharks to verify this. Against this is the evidence that the *Eagle* was not too badly damaged. One would imagine that the sheer mass of a basking shark, should it decide to ram a wooden boat, would reduce the boat to splintered timber, but this was not the case with the *Eagle.* Similarly a breaching shark landing directly on the *Eagle* would have smashed it in pieces, forcing the broken hull under the water and no doubt killing everyone in the boat in the process. Neither Donald nor Jessica appear to have seen the shark that overturned the boat, nor is there any suggestion that anything fell on them, so a deliberate attack, or the impact of a breaching shark coming down on the boat can be eliminated. This leaves the real probability of a glancing blow from a shark being responsible for overturning the *Eagle* and two possible explanations for such a blow could be considered.

Colin Oman was not the only eyewitness. A reporter interviewed a 'woman holidaymaker' who saw a shark breaching: ' the sight was such an amazing one it was only when we noticed through the haze which lay over the water that the mast of the *Eagle* had disappeared that we suspected that something was wrong and gave the alarm'.[20] The water depth off Point Balfadgen, about ten metres, increases rapidly to 26 metres and the *Eagle* was probably near the deeper part – deep enough for a shark to breach from. So the *Eagle* could have been caught a glancing blow by the rapidly ascending shark, accounting for the suddenness with which everyone was tipped out and also for the relative lack of damage to the boat's hull. Interviewed the day after the incident, Donald MacDonald recalled 'the boat seemed to stand right up on her end'.[21] This would suggest the effect of the momentum of an ascending shark, rather than a tail flick which would more likely have forced the boat downwards or sideways. An alternative possibility which would fit with Colin Oman's testimony of one big splash but disregard the holidaymakers who saw a breaching, is that when the Brown brothers were rowing they touched the tail of a shark. Touching the tail of a fish can provoke a sudden escape reflex in which a powerful thrust of the tail drives the fish rapidly out of danger.[22] A flick from a basking shark's tail against the side of the *Eagle* could easily have overturned the boat, chafing and cracking the planks of one side without necessarily breaking the hull, and the convulsive swirl as the shark swam away could account for the boat being overturned again. It may be that these theories are not exclusive and that in fact both actions took place. Colin Oman's father who went out in one of the rescue boats told him that when they got to the scene (about fifteen minutes later) the shark was still at the surface and going around the boat lashing its tail. Perhaps the *Eagle* was initially overturned by a glancing blow from a breaching shark, and then the shark, possibly injured and staying at the surface, clipped the *Eagle* once or twice with its tail at the end of its breaching sequence.

These speculations rely upon what is known about the actual behaviour of the shark and other fish. But there is some evidence for one more, disquieting, possibility, namely that there are occasional 'rogue' basking sharks which would charge at a boat. The whale shark, the largest filter-feeding shark, is usually regarded as a placid, harmless animal which divers can hold onto, but there is one account of a whale shark attacking three small boats that had hooked fish in a shoal. The shark 'raised his head out of the water and came straight for the boat'.[23] The whale shark at times ingests fish and it may have seen the boats as rivals interfering in a shoal it was feeding on.

Less than a week after the Carradale tragedy a Campbeltown fishing boat, the *Lady Charlotte*, returning home from Arran fully laden with herring was subjected to a foray by a basking shark for which, if the newspaper is to be believed, the word 'attack' is quite appropriate. A member of the crew standing at the stern:

> saw a large shark charge at the boat. The shark struck the propellor a glancing blow. The stern of the boat was lifted 3ft out of the water by the impact and came down again with a crash, fortunately on an even keel . . .[24]

A few days later, the passenger steamer *Dalriada* was entering Carradale with the sea, in the words of the master, 'alive with sharks'. All of these submerged as the vessel approached except for one very large individual which 'made straight for the *Dalriada*. It circled round and round the steamer leaping high out of the water and lashing its tail furiously'. It did not, however attack the ship. Local fishermen claimed to be able to identify the shark responsible for the *Eagle* tragedy (which they named the 'man-eater'), claiming that it was much larger and much more aggressive than the other basking sharks usually observed.[25]

The theme of dangerous sharks was taken up by a leading article in *The Times* two weeks later. Rather unfeelingly, so soon after the Carradale deaths, the tone is flippant: 'It comes as a shock to most of us to find that the waters surrounding this sceptred isle are shark-infested . . .' and a shark had 'tried conclusions' with a Clyde pleasure steamer [the *Glen Sannox*, a 664-ton LMS Railway excursion steamer], '. . . breaking the windows in the saloon and perturbing the passengers . . .' The writer debated whether the species responsible for attacks on small boats was the basking shark or the blue shark and concluded that a reputation for sharks would enliven a humdrum British holiday scene.[26] Anthony Watkins (whose exploits in the *Myrtle* are described in the next chapter) wrote to deny that basking sharks would ever deliberately attack a boat or a swimmer, but admitted that they might sometimes follow a boat out of curiosity. He found the idea that basking sharks had 'suddenly become ferocious' to be 'ludicrous' with no evidence to support it.[27] Watkins was undoubtedly right in regard to swimmers. He had just had personal experience of being a reluctant swimmer among basking sharks when he and a companion harpooned a shark from a dinghy and were left floundering as the shark pulled the craft under the water. A number of sharks near them purposefully swam up close to inspect the two – 'the sharks sniffed around us, like a pack of dogs around a tree'- and then abruptly sank out of sight.[28] But considering the attitude of sharks to boats, even if the mass of basking sharks in the Clyde that summer were timid and harmless, the episodes of the *Lady Charlotte* and the steamers show that the odd shark could behave quite aggressively. The verdict must be that the *Eagle* itself was unfortunately just above a breaching shark; but there is enough evidence to show that in certain rare circumstances, a basking shark will attack a boat, not of course like other sharks to seize prey but nevertheless to deliver an aggressive 'thump'.

CHANGING PERCEPTIONS

Four books were written by those who were active in the early phase of the modern fishery and a number of pictorial articles appeared in popular magazines. The years immediately post-World War 2 saw a proliferation of books about sharks and it may be that the public interest in shark stories was heightened by awareness of the gruesome events during the war when the survivors of torpedoed ships were attacked by schools of man-eaters. It is otherwise hard to account for a market for no less than four books from Scottish shark-hunters. As the general theme was one in which the hunters were pitted against a formidable adversary, the emphasis was on the dangers of the hunt and the human interest of those men who engaged with the shark. One may doubt that the publishers made any effort to enlighten their potential readers that the basking shark was in reality a large, slow, inoffensive, effectively toothless plankton-eater. Even the naturalist John Hillaby, a guest of Maxwell at Soay, and one who should have known better, describes the fins of the sharks arriving in the Minch in spring as 'indescribably sinister'.[29]

When it came to the actual mechanics of killing the basking shark, Watkins admitted that the sight of a shark, gutted of its liver, still struggling while an embedded harpoon was chopped out of it did harrow his feelings somewhat. He tried to kill these mutilated sharks by shooting them in the head and by bludgeoning them with a sledge-hammer, but to no avail – the sharks just kept on writhing.[30] However, it was Maxwell who in his writing most clearly expressed the growing sense of doubt about the ethics of killing the basking shark, admitting that he had a certain repugnance towards harpooning it:

All this harpooning has its unpleasant side, no matter how much it may be forgotten in the excitement of the moment. If a warm-blooded animal were concerned, and more especially if it were a warm-blooded land animal, ninety-nine people out of a hundred (of whom I should be one) would hold it to be unthinkable cruelty. Yet is one justified, because this monstrous bulk of flesh and muscle is cold-blooded and directed by a brain which could almost be enclosed in a match-box, in assuming that the experience undergone by the shark is so widely different than our own.[31]

For Maxwell, this question was answered by the principle that in any consideration of pain, or of cruelty, 'the size of the animal is completely unimportant' and thus in considering both a harpooned basking shark and a hooked salmon, our sense of revulsion should equate the two. After all, multitudes of fish were being eaten by other fish 'at every moment in the sea' and so, continuing to live uneasily with his sensitivities, Maxwell kept on harpooning sharks.[32] But attitudes do change in time and some of those who hunted the basking shark as young men in the 1950s would not do so now, having been converted to more conservationist attitudes as they aged.[33]

By the time the fishery resumed with McCrindle in the Clyde in 1983, attitudes to sharks in general and to the basking shark in particular had changed very markedly. While most people might remain ambivalent about 'real' sharks, the conservationist campaign to have the basking shark protected emphasised its harmless nature and so the general perception of it as a fish quite distinct from the dangerous sharks gained strength. The basking shark had two advantages which enabled it as it were to ride on the skirts of the 'Save the Whales' campaigns. One of these was the fact that it is a large beast, and size does matter in this area of gaining public sympathy, as Maxwell had clearly seen and a 1987 *Glasgow Herald* article referring to McCrindle well expressed:

> Big animals attract a lot of public sympathy when they are made the focus of conservation campaigns while their persecutors are bestowed with an unwanted, sometimes undeserved, infamy.[34]

The second distinct advantage in terms of public awareness is that the basking shark was being killed by the use of a harpoon. When we think of the visual images that supported anti-whaling campaigns, it is hard to imagine anything more abhorrent to the contemporary mind than the sight on colour television of a large marine creature being harpooned in a welter of bloody spray. The emotions roused are so powerful that any plea by a fisherman that the basking shark is just a fish like any other, for example a herring or a haddock, and thus a fit object for his livelihood is seen as self-justification and dismissed out of hand. Stigmatised by some of the more intemperate animal rights spokesmen as 'that hellish trade', hunting of the basking shark in Scotland can never again be compared with more mundane types of fishing, even if it could be demonstrated that the nervous system of the shark may make it virtually immune to pain.[35]

Pictorial images of the basking shark have also changed significantly since the Scottish shark-hunter books of the post-war years. The dust-jackets of three of them show large sharks and in Watkin's *The Sea My Hunting Ground* in particular the scene depicted is a very dramatic one with the dorsal fin and lashing tail of a large harpooned shark overshadowing the frail dinghy containing Watkins and his helper.[36] (Fig. 22) In the photographs in all these books the shark, except when it is shown dead, is usually seen only as a fin above the surface. Such an image is of course common to all large sharks – the circling fin of the man-eater is a cliché, and with its prominent fin as the main sign of its presence the basking shark therefore shared in the dread inspired by this image. But the advent of scuba diving and underwater photography was to change all this. Divers could swim alongside the basking shark and photograph it from the front. The imagery of fin and tail soon gave way to that of a huge gaping maw, which, obviously lacking the serrated teeth of the dangerous shark, emphasised

Fig. 22. Dustjacket illustration of A. Watkins' *The Sea My Hunting Ground*, 1958, depicting the 1937 episode when he and a *Myrtle* crewman harpooned a shark from a dinghy and were towed out into the Atlantic. This depiction by Clive Uptton emphasises the dorsal fins to give an impression of sinister menace.

the innocuous nature of the beast. The very size and disproportion of the head and gills from the front somehow give the impression of ponderous, unhurried movement in contrast to the ferocity implicit in the massive snout of a great white charging an underwater cage to seize a slab of meat. Under water, viewed from the front, the fin and tail are also less prominent, so the great bizarre open mouth, the shark's peculiar characteristic when feeding, is emphasised rather than the fins and tail which confirm its common identity with the shark tribe. Even if the underwater cameraman takes shots of the basking shark with its mouth closed, these more typically 'shark-like' images are seldom used. Fortunately for the conservationist lobby, spectacular underwater photographs of the shark feeding were exactly the visual material they needed for their campaign to transform the image of the basking shark from one of a 'sinister' animal into a 'gentle giant'.

Notes

1. Maxwell (1952): 125.
2. *OED* vol 14: 374.
3. Pennant (1769): 78.
4. *OED* vol 1: 985 & 987.
5. *OED* vol 1: 987 & Bingley (1804) 212 1st ed. not seen.
6. Bigelow & Schroeder (1953): 29.
7. *OED* vol 2: 385.
8. Pontoppidan (1755): 109.
9. Edmonston (1809): 303.
10. W. Brabazon 1848 quoted in Couch (1862): 64.
11. Carmichael (1941): 110-111. McLean (1961): 325-327 & 471-472 gives *chearban* as 'shark of the sea' and in the notes confuses the shark with the sunfish (*Orthagoriscus mola*).
12. MacCaig (1969): 38.
13. This account is compiled from interviews of D. MacDonald (survivor) & C. Oman (eyewitness); the recollections of M.Scott (for her cousin J. Clayton, née Brown) & C. Paterson, another Brown cousin; & newspaper reports.
14. Weather – D. MacDonald & C. Oman agree except for the sun. The day was generally dull, possibly overcast. Quote – C. Oman *pers. comm.* 1997.
15. D. MacDonald *pers. comm.* 1997.
16. *GH:* 3 Sept 1937: 7c.
17. D. MacDonald *pers. comm.* 1997.
18. Anon (1938) & *GH* 11 Dec 1937: 9b.
19. *GH* 2 Sept 1937: 9c.
20. *GH* 2 Sept 1937: 9c; *T* 2 Sept 1937: 12e.
21. D. MacDonald in *GH* 3 Sept 1937: 7c but not mentioned in 1997 interview.
22. M. Lucas *pers. comm.* 1997
23. Smith (1967): 237.
24. *T* 6 Sept 1937: 17d.

25. Unidentified newspaper. (From internal evidence 9 Sep 1937.)
26. Anon (1937a): 13d & letter – Hett (1937): 13e. Anon (1937b) reports the *Glenn Sannox* episode.
27. Watkins (1937).
28. Watkins (1958): 38-39.
29. Hillaby (1947): 7.
30. Watkins (1958): 152-153.
31. Maxwell (1952): 167.
32. Maxwell (1952): 167; & Botting (1993): 98.
33. A. Paterson *pers. comm.* 1995.
34. Cramb, A. (1987).
35. Quote from J. Robins of Animal Concern – *Largs & Millport Weekly News*, 9 Sept 1994: 1.
36. Watkins (1958): painting by Clive Uptton on dust jacket.

Chapter Four

The Early Fishery

UNDOUBTEDLY THE basking shark, whether it was called cearban, brigda or sunfish, had been familiar to the coastal folk of Scotland for a very long time, but the capturing of it at sea came comparatively late in Scottish history. To establish the origins of the basking shark fishery as an identifiable, distinctive activity in Scotland, a number of interrelated questions need to be resolved as far as possible, even if the evidence is scattered and inconclusive. As the basking shark up until very recent times was hunted principally for the large volume of oil which could be extracted from its liver the historical background of the use of fish oils by the people of coastal Scotland is important. A second question is whether a date, precise or approximate, for the beginning of a fishery can be determined (a 'fishery' being the organised, systematic exploitation of a species). Finally, is it possible to discern whether the hunting of the basking shark was an indigenous activity, having much in common with everyday fishing practices, or was it a novel concept, a conscious imitation of fishing methods in use outside Scotland and an introduction of technology and techniques new to the area?

FISH OIL AND ITS USES

The extraction of oil from whole fish and fish livers is so fully documented in the seventeenth and eighteenth centuries that it is reasonable to suppose the practice must have been a feature of the economy of the inhabitants of the northern and western coasts for many centuries before that. Fish oils were supplemented by the oils obtained from other marine animals. Seals were caught for their flesh, hide and blubber oil. The smaller whales such as the blackfish (= pilot or caaing whale, *Globicephala melaena*), which were slaughtered after being driven into shallow water, were valued principally for the oil from their blubber. Some oil was also obtained from otter-fat.[1] A few communities, notably that of St Kilda, were surrounded by such an abundance of sea-birds that they could utilise them for food and oil and had little need either to fish or to attempt the capture of marine mammals.[2] In the Northern Isles at least as early as the 1600s young coalfish *Gadus vivens* known as 'sillock' were caught in large numbers for their livers. These were boiled for the oil they gave and the livers of full-grown coalfish 'saithe' or 'seth' were treated in the same way. Saithe were 'abundant on all coasts' so their use as described here was no doubt a feature of all coastal communities, even if unrecorded.[3] The early traveller, Martin Martin, in the late 1690s confirms that the livers of 'seths' were boiled in Shetland, and writing about 'seths' and 'silluks' in the Northern Isles some years later, John Brand noted:

> The Oyl they get after this Manner. They put the Liver into a Pot or Pan half full of Water, which when seething, the Oyle by the face of the fire or boiling Water, is drawn from the Liver, which so being separated, and sweeming above, they take or scum it off, and puts in vessels for use.[4]

Shetland and Orkney were stable communities which had traded extensively with Norway and Scotland for centuries. It is known that the Shetlanders exported 'oyl' to Scotland in the early sixteenth century and in the same period fish oil was used as a commodity in land rentals. By contrast, the western isles had smaller, scattered populations and, at least in the inner Hebrides, were long subject to the disruption of clan feuding which was followed by the turmoil of the Jacobite risings in the early eighteenth century. So while contemporary practice in the actual processing of oil from fish-livers in the scattered communities of the western coasts of Scotland was most likely very similar to that of Orkney and Shetland, the Northern Isles, at any period, the earliest written evidence comes much later. With perhaps the exception of the larger settlements, such as Stornoway on Lewis, or particular islands such as Barra, for most of the eighteenth century fishing beyond the subsistence level was not a significant activity in the West. The generality of Highland tenant-farmers, living on islands or on the mainland shores, put their energies into cultivating their arable crops and the raising of cattle. The fishing done was a small-scale activity geared to the family's own needs for protein and fish-oil, with little if any surplus – 'neither fish nor fish-oil constituted part of the rent or casualties of land there so far as is known'.[5]

From the mid-eighteenth century onwards the Highlands and Islands were subject to various improving schemes. These, whether initiatives of the Crown, private groups or landlords, had in common the aim of creating enterprises which would bring the scattered communities of the region into the wider British trading economy. One important government-appointed group were the Commissioners of the Annexed Estates, installed in office in 1755 to administer the lands of Stuart sympathisers which had been forfeited in the aftermath of the 1745 rebellion and then 'annexed' to the Crown by an Act of 1752. The mandate of the Commissioners was a broad one. Beyond their varied administrative responsibilities they were required to promote industry and manufactures, which included fisheries, not just amongst the inhabitants of the annexed estates but in 'other parts of the Highlands and Islands'. An example of a later private initiative, after the annexed estates had been returned to their owners, is the British Fisheries Society set up in 1786 as a joint stock company for the purpose of 'Extending the Fisheries and Improving the Sea Coasts of the Kingdom'. Unlike the Commissioners, for whom fishing was only one interest among many, the directors of the Society concentrated on the possibilities of commercial fisheries and to that end sought to establish 'fishing stations' in suitable areas.[6]

The Commissioners for the Annexed Estates assiduously sent out various agents and inspectors to investigate the state of the communities they were responsible for, and one of these was the Reverend Dr John Walker whom we met in an earlier chapter as the discoverer of the Loch Fyne shark, *Squalus selanosus*. Touring the Highlands and Western Isles in 1764, he remarked of Lewis that oil from dogfish was produced 'in prodigious quantities' with 140 barrels valued at £315 exported from the island in 1763.[7] Walker apparently believed that this was peculiar to Lewis as, discussing the other Hebridean islands, he expressed his view that 'the Dog Fish is equally numerous but no where fished'.[8] This may have been true for the outer Hebrides, but in 1768, only four years later, Archibald Menzies, the Inspector General for the Commissioners, was in the western Highlands and islands assessing 'the present state of Farming, Manufactures and fisherys upon these Coasts'. He observed of Mull that dogfish were in such abundance that they could be caught by hand and that the inhabitants 'make Oyll of their Liver and eat the fish when dry'd'.[9] The directors of the British Fisheries Society, who also wanted first-hand experience of conditions in the West, sent a committee of their number to travel through the same territory in 1787. In their report, judging solely by the numbers involved, Lewis seems to have been outstanding in its utilisation of dogfish:

> About 17,000 score of dog-fish are annually caught by the inhabitants of this island; these yield near to L.800 worth of oil. The fish is dried in the stacks of corn, and sold as food for the people at 4d. per score; it is said not to be a bad fish.[10]

These dogfish would have been small sharks of various species, probably the greatest number being the spurdog *Squalus acanthias* which arrived in very large shoals and were easily caught on a line. Besides the flesh of the dogfish, eaten after drying or curing, the rough skin provided a useful rasping surface, the equivalent of modern sandpaper, for various tasks.[11]

The island of Canna was also on the itinerary of the Fisheries Society directors who found that '*scythes* or *whiting pollock*' were caught in large numbers 'and, after taking out the livers for their oil, the rest of the fish are carried to the dunghill'.[12]

Touring the Hebrides a few years later with Dr Samuel Johnson, James Boswell, with his impressive eye for detail, describes how the fish liver oil was used. Speaking of Coll he notes that:

> Every man can tan . . . and they all make oil of fish [and] boil their livers to make it. They sell some oil out of the island, and they use it much for light in their houses, in little iron (or unpainted black metal) lamps . . .[13]

These accounts all suggest that the extraction of oil from fish livers was probably widespread in the Western Isles by this time.

The importance of fish liver oil, especially that extracted from dogfish, in the coastal economy of Scotland in the late eighteenth century is confirmed by Sir John Sinclair's *Statistical Account of Scotland*, the first comprehensive systematic survey of Scottish social and economic life, compiled from the reports of parish ministers. (Usually know as the *Old Statistical Account*.) The use of dogfish, if not a definite dogfish fishery, is noted in a number of parishes on both the east and west coasts and in the Northern Isles, especially as a characteristic activity of high summer. At Nigg, Kincardineshire:

> the sea-dog . . . is taken in considerable quantities; 20 yielding, when good, one Scotch pint of oil (10d or 1s.) from the liver, and the fish being sold to country people, or dried for use.

A similar observation was made of Peterhead, a thriving fishing port. Plenty of oil was extracted from dogfish but the townspeople rejected the flesh as food and it was 'frequently . . . cast into the dunghill . . .' The country-dwellers were more thrifty: some of them 'relished' the flesh and would buy 20 dogfish for 3½d for food or for making 'an excellent manure' by mixing the fishes with soil.[14]

For Orkney and Shetland there is much mention of sillocks and dogfish for oil, and the importance of the dogfish to at least one parish is emphasised by the minister of Ophir:

> When the dog-fishing fails, which sometimes happens, the people are in the utmost difficulty for want of oil; which then rises from 6d or 8d per Scotch pint, to 1s. or even 1s.6d.[15]

The various references which point to a specific summer dogfish fishery suggest that by the mid-eighteenth century the earlier pattern of utilising this fish primarily for food, with liver oil as a by-product, was changing. The dogfish had come to be sought principally for its liver oil; its flesh was a by-product which might or might not be used or sold depending on local prejudices and the availability of alternatives. By the 1840s the dogfish, still caught in the Moray Firth in immense numbers, was 'sold by the cartload for manure to the ground'- apparently being ignored as food even by the poor.[16]

Scottish coast and island dwellers used fish oil in various ways. Its main use, along with whale and seal oil, was as an illuminant in 'cruisies', the open metal lamps used in their cottages, and of all the fish oils available to them, basking shark oil was probably preferred as being the least smoky. These marine oils were more readily available than the tallow candles used in rural communities where sheep were common. The wealthier town-dwellers sought the best quality oils for their lamps, and here basking shark oil found a ready market when seed oil, their first preference, was hard to obtain. From the early 1700s municipalities were striving to provide street lighting and this development of a civic amenity intensified the demand for great quantities of 'sperm oil and [right] whale oil, together with a shark oil from the basking shark'.[17] Basking shark oil was more like whale oil in its flammable qualities than the oils from bony fishes.

Besides its major use in lighting, fish oil featured in several other aspects of the cottager's domestic economy. Those tanning their own hides rubbed fish oil into the skins for the oxidation products of the oil to harden them, and this use of fish oils was to extend to the small industry which developed in Scotland in the late eighteenth century with hides from Ireland as the raw material.[18] Some village blacksmiths too had a use for fish oil, quenching hot steel in oil to give a tough but flexible blade, in the application of a very old tempering technique.[19] Folk medicine made use of basking shark oil, if not other fish oils, as an embrocation for joint pains and an ointment for burns, while fish oil was a common leather softening application, in a process known as 'currying' and was recommended as a leather dressing to the nineteenth century householder in Mrs Beeton's magisterial *Household Management*.[20]

In the wider industrial sphere fish oils were used in many applications where, even if they were less preferred than the higher quality imported whale oil, they remained in demand as a cheaper, more consistently available product. From early times these oils had been used extensively in the preparation of textiles. Washed wool was prepared for carding by being sprinkled with oil and some idea of the volume of oil required can be gained by reflecting on the fact that textiles were Britain's prime export in the eighteenth century.[21] In rope-making, an important process in any sizeable naval dockyard, oil was poured onto bundles of hemp in the first stage to soften the fibres for combing (hatchelling).[22] It is not unlikely that basking shark oil, when available, was used in at least some of these applications.

The demand for whale and fish oils accelerated during the latter half of the eighteenth century owing to the ever-expanding requirements of the Industrial Revolution. Whale oil, at first mainly from the right whale *Balaena glacialis* and the bowhead *Balaena mysticetus* was preferred in industry and when available could be supplied in much greater quantities than other oils. The fish oils rivalled whale oil only when the latter was in short supply. Against a background of ever-increasing demand, the story of the fluctuating supply of whale oil from the mid-eighteenth century to the end of the Napoleonic wars in 1815 is a complex one where the varying fortunes of the various whale fisheries are intertwined with the destructive effects of continous international rivalry. As whale oil, whether from the declining right whales and the bowheads, or from the burgeoning sperm whale fishery, was the main commodity in demand, it suffices here to say that the requirement for other oils, including fish oils, depended upon the availability of whale oil at any given time. Shortages of whale oil not only pushed its price up but by doing so made the production of other oils more economically attractive. It is within this context that the appearance of a basking shark fishery in Scotland in the early 1760s and its survival until early in the next century must be examined.

THE WESTERN ISLES AND THE FIRTH OF CLYDE

Every so often a dead basking shark washes ashore on a Scottish beach and there is no reason to believe that this has not always been the case. Coastal people who were accustomed to stripping the blubber from beached whales would be unlikely to leave a shark carcass unexamined for some potential use of its organs, cartilage or skin, and there are apparent records in Icelandic history of liver oil being extracted from basking sharks that had drifted ashore.[23] Fishermen who were in the habit of extracting the livers from dogfish would have recognised the liver lobes, of similar shape to those of a dogfish but vastly larger, in the slashed-open belly of a stranded shark. Once the liver of a basking shark had been cut up and boiled its enormous potential as a source of oil would have quickly become evident. Unfortunately, unlike bone, cartilage usually decays quite quickly in the ground so it cannot be expected to survive in archaeological sites save in very exceptional circumstances. Surviving bone tells us that the early inhabitants of Scotland did make use of whales but unless skin denticles of the basking shark are found by fine sifting in coastal archaeological sites, the utilisation of these sharks by coastal-dwelling folk must remain a speculation.[24] Whatever the uses made of a stranded basking shark over a long span of time it seems fairly certain that it was only comparatively recently that a practical method of catching such a large fish at sea presented itself.

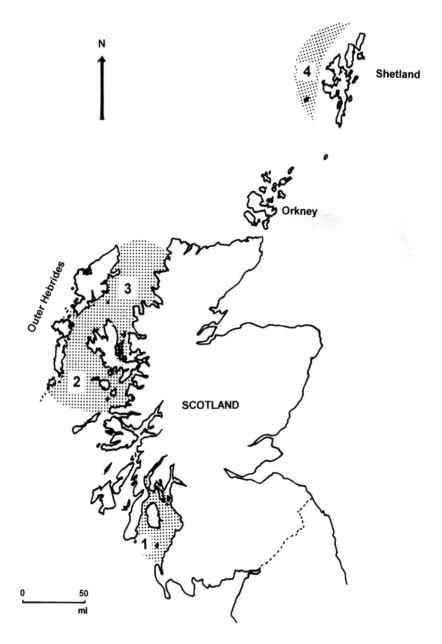

Map 2. The Scottish Basking Shark Fishery. The principal areas where fishing for the basking shark was carried out. 1 = Firth of Clyde, 2 = Sea of the Hebrides, 3 = the Minch, 4 = West of Shetland

Map 3.   The Firth of Clyde. X marks the area of deep water north of Arran (greatest depth 160m).

In early 1766 Donald MacLeod, tacksman of the island of Canna, petitioned the Commissioners for the Annexed Estates for a grant to purchase a boat and gear for hunting the *cairban*. In this 'memorial' he claimed to be:

> . . . the first that ever discovered the cairban and proved successful in killing them; and that he has instructed several people on the west coast in the method of catching them.[25]

Donald MacLeod was a young man – too young to afford the expense of a boat and gear for shark hunting – and the Commissioners needed some persuasion, as MacLeod complains that having had to go to Edinburgh to put his case 'during the two last seasons of the cairban fishery' had been an expensive and time-wasting exercise.[26] Their grant of £250 shows that they eventually accepted the recommendation of the Reverend Dr Walker, familiar with the Western Isles from his 1764 tour, and entrusted MacLeod with a valuable boat and equipment although too late for effective use in the summer season of 1766.[27] This grant neatly illustrates the wide brief of the Commissioners as Canna was not an 'annexed estate' and we may also conclude, from his journey to Edinburgh to lobby the Commissioners in person, that Donald McLeod was a particularly energetic tacksman for the times as well as an innovative one. Two hundred and fifty pounds was a considerable sum of money for the stated purpose. Unless there was a precipitate decline in the value of money a 'small wherry' – a two-masted sailing boat – could be bought a decade later for about £20. The wages of three men and a boy for a summer season were only just over £7.[28] The boat MacLeod purchased must have been a very substantial one indeed because as we see he soon sold it and bought two smaller ones. In October 1768 MacLeod wrote to the Commissioners from Oban reporting on his fishing 'tryalls':

> [In a] vessel saild from Dysart the beginning of September 1766 [mainly for herring but also] for the cod & Kerban fishery . . . of the Kerbans we got twixt Canna and Rum Seven . . . Upon tryall I found the Vessell too expensive & unwieldy for the Kerban [and] Cod . . . therefore . . . bought two small ones a sloop about 30 tons & a wherry twixt 15 and 20 tons, with these I try'd the cod and Kerban this season [.] of Kerban, twixt Canna Rum & Skye, where one was got, we kill'd 8.[29]

He ended his report on a note of pessimism, apparently believing that neither a basking shark fishery nor offshore long-line fishing were likely to be sustainable enterprises:

> On the whole my own opinion is that from the tryalls I made the Kerban & Cod & Lyng fishing will become no considerable length on this coast, without a considerable encouragement from the publick . . . The common people upon whome in a great measure the success of that scheme depends . . . are quite ignorant of the nature of fishing Cod & Lyng & the Kerban in most parts . . .[30]

Thomas Pennant, writing in 1772, considered that the Commissioners had been deceived by MacLeod who 'most shamefully abused their goodness' but this seems to have been an unduly harsh judgement by the naturalist, as something of MacLeod's character is known from Boswell's *Journal*. Seven years after the fishing 'tryalls' he impressed Boswell and Dr Johnston when they met him in Skye as 'an obliging serviceable man . . . and a good sportsman'. Even though there was a falling out over money later, the flaw seems to have been drunkenness rather than dishonesty and the quarrel was resolved.[31]

MacLeod's observation that 'a considerable encouragement from the pub-lick' would be needed, by which he meant government bounties or financial grants from bodies such as the Board of Commissioners for the Annexed Estates or the British Fisheries Society, was sound. People living at subsistence level such as those on Canna would have been unable to find the capital to buy and outfit sizeable fishing boats and obtain harpoons and lines without such assistance. As it turned out, the necessary assistance must have indeed been given as MacLeod's gloomy forecast proved unfounded. Even if he himself left the 'kerban' fishing (there is a suggestion that he had been dispossessed of his farm) the people of Canna 'quite ignorant' in 1768 seem to have quickly adopted the new techniques and persevered with them to good effect. The party of directors of the British Fisheries Society, whom we have seen taking an interest in the production of fish oil in Lewis and Canna during their 1787 travels, were impressed with the thriving fishery they later found on Canna:

> a considerable quantity of fish are actually caught here now . . . A great many sun-fish or basking sharks are taken in these seas. The liver is oily, and the only part of the fish that is made use of . . . In Cannay there are about three hundred inhabitants, all Roman Catholics, a sober, quiet industrious race, and not contemptible fishers, especially of the sun-fish.[32]

This report was printed for public interest in 1792 in an Edinburgh periodical *The Bee*, with a perceptive editorial comment on the 'sun-fish' that gave full credit to the anonymous Donald MacLeod:

> The first sun-fish that was ever caught on these coasts was by a native of Cannay, on the shore of this island, about twenty years ago. An adventurous undertaking at that time, when they were ignorant of every thing that respects this fish, but its bulk and strength.[33]

In 1768, the same year that the disillusioned Donald MacLeod was reporting to the Commissioners for the Annexed Estates, their itinerant Inspector-General, Archibald Menzies, was staying near Tarbert on Loch Fyne when a basking shark was seen and men in boats were sent after it. The next day after a 'long chase' a 30-foot basking shark was brought in and 192 gallons of oil were recovered from the liver. [34] His description of the basking shark hunt at Tarbert is so matter-of-fact in its tone that it can be inferred that capturing the basking shark in and about Loch Fyne was a commonplace activity, having gone far beyond the 'tryall' stage, and from Thomas Pennant's visit to Arran in June 1772 we know that harpooning the basking shark was a routine fishing activity there.

By contrast, a basking shark fishery in the Hebridean Islands was still being developed. In February 1777 the Commissioners for the Annexed Estates gave favourable consideration to a request from David Campbell of Shawfield, in Islay, for £200 for 'a vessel from 25 to 30 tons burden':

> Such a vessel may be employed all the year round in fishing for herring, for cod, and for cairban, which come on at different seasons.[35]

The vessel bought was the *Nancy*, a 'Cod Fishing Smack' whose master was Archibald Hamilton. In the meantime David Campbell had died and his brother Walter took over the fishing experiments but unfortunately the results are not known.[36]

In 1785, James Anderson published a massive tract promoting the cause of a herring fishery for the western coasts and as an aside noted that while whales were abundant but were 'so restless and active' that they couldn't be caught, the basking shark was a recent prey:

> It is only of late that they have found out a way of killing the basking shark . . . The oil from the liver of one fish, will sometimes sell from 20 to 30 l. sterling.[37]

It seems then that by about 1780, small-scale basking shark hunting was established both in the Firth of Clyde and in the Sea of the Hebrides. In both places these were summer activities as determined by the habits of the shark, and opportunistic ones marginal to other forms of fishing: herring in the Clyde, ling and cod in the Isles. In the Firth of Clyde the fishery was possibly a more 'settled' activity pursued concurrently with the herring fishing while off Canna and Islay it was more of an 'experimental' activity in areas where offshore long-line fishing was comparatively new.

With this picture in mind Donald MacLeod's claims can be assessed. If it is assumed that the habits of the fish have remained the same for millennia, the basking shark would have been a familiar summer sight to the earliest inhabitants of the western coasts, and MacLeod's claim 'that he was the first that ever discovered the cairban' (in the sense of something totally new) can be dismissed. However, if 'discovered' is taken, more appropriately, to mean realising the economic potential of a basking shark fishery, MacLeod's claim can be taken at face value, but only in respect of the Western Isles. A Clyde rival has an equal claim, as Archibald Menzies during his Tarbert stay in 1768 revealed that

> One Stewart at Bute . . . has been pretty successful for some years past in this Fishery with the Harpoon.[38]

It thus seems that MacLeod and Stewart and possibly others, including the Loch Fyne men, were hunting the basking shark in 1764, if not for a few years before, and MacLeod's claim to have been the first successful hunter may have been a device to forestall other requests by potential rivals for financial assistance from the Commissioners. But in the absence of evidence to the contrary, both Donald MacLeod and Stewart of Bute can be identified as pioneers of the Scottish basking shark fishery, which appears to have begun more or less simultaneously around Canna in the Sea of the Hebrides and in the more sheltered waters of the northern Firth of Clyde in or about 1764.

The steady expansion of the fishery in the 1790s is evident from the parish narratives in the *Old Statistical Account*. Out of some 175 parishes in which sea fishing is noted, ten mention the presence of the basking shark with another three giving a reference that could be the basking shark.[39] The 'occasionally' visiting basking shark was fished at Lochgilphead, Loch Fyne as well as off Kilmory in the Island of Arran, and at Ayr. In the Outer Hebrides, Harris, South Uist and Barra are mentioned as having success with the basking shark; and among the 'Small Isles' – Canna and Tiree – some of the fish taken off Canna yielding 12 barrels of oil. Two or three fishing vessels had been regularly sent from Peterhead to Barra, possibly for the previous twenty years, bringing home cargoes of dried cod and ling for export 'besides the oil from the sun-fish which they catch, which is sometimes considerable'. At Portree, Skye, however, 'Whales and cairbans, or sun-fish, come in sometimes to the Sounds after their prey, but are rarely pursued with any success.'[40] The description of taking the shark in South Uist is particularly vivid:

> [The basking shark]. . . is a stupid and torpid kind of fish; he allows the harpooner often to feel him with his hand, before he darts at him. The inhabitants to the east side of the island, (such as are able to fit out boats, lines and harpoons,) have been for some years very successful during the summer months, in this branch of business, owing entirely to the laudable exertions of the trustees for managing the fisheries of Scotland, in granting premiums to the owners of boats, that extract the greatest quantity of oil from the liver of the basking shark. The lucky adventurer in this fishing, should he chance to harpoon a large one, may have 9 or 10 barrels of liver, from which the return in clear oil is about 8 barrels.[41]

TECHNIQUES

If it is accepted that hunting the basking shark for its liver oil was indeed a novel introduction to Scotland in the early 1760's, the question arises – how did those such as MacLeod and Stewart gain their knowledge of the potential of the fishery and the method of capturing the shark. In assessing this it is useful to separate the *idea* of fishing the basking shark from the *techniques* used.

For a precedent, MacLeod and Stewart would have had to look no further than Ireland where a fishery based in several localities on the west coast appears to have been well established by 1740 as in that year contractors were selling the oil for lighting the streets of Dublin.[42] It is known that there was an intensive sea trade between the Clyde ports and Ireland in the eighteenth century and further that in the middle of that century Irish fishermen were active in South Uist, the Shetlands and very likely other localities on the western seaboard.[43] Anyone who was inclined to enquire into the Irish basking shark fishery at that time undoubtedly soon became aware that there was a government bounty on the oil.[44] This policy which provided a potent economic stimulus was later to be applied in Scotland. A Norwegian basking shark fishery using harpoons was operating by 1762, but as it may have begun more or less simultaneously with the Scottish one, it is unlikely that it directly influenced these novice basking shark fishers in the west of Scotland.[45]

If the concept of a basking shark fishery was a derived one, what can we say of the methods? In western Scotland harpooning was the technique for capturing and killing the basking shark from the beginning of the fishery with one minor but important exception which we wll consider before harpooning methods are described. The *Old Statistical Account* records that at Lochgilphead (Loch Fyne) in the 1790s:

> the sun or sail-fish occasionally visits us; this sluggish fish sometimes swims into the salmon nets, and suffers itself to be drawn towards the shore, without any resistance, till it gets near the land, that for want of a sufficient body of water, it cannot exert its strength, in disentangling itself from the net, the fishers in the mean time take advantage of its situation, and attack it with sticks and stones, till they have it secure.[46]

This appears to be the only evidence that, occasionally at least, the basking shark was despatched in a similar way to a small whale. Traditional Scottish whale catching did not involve pursuit of a whale by boats with harpoons but relied on herding groups of whales, confused by splashing and shouting, into a bay where they could be killed with knives and lances. John MacIver, a 'depute justiciary bailie over the fishers on the Northwest coast of Schotland', describes such a scene when a large number of bottlenose whales were trapped at Stornoway in 1768:

> The Method taken here to get this kind of fish into a proper place for Slaughter is as follows. When they are seen rising and blowing [off] the headlands a number of boats (from thirty to fifty often) go immediately

who have a quantity of stones from one to three pounds weight each in every boat and get with all possible speed without the whale and form a semicircle, when one of the men stands in the Bow of each Boat containualy throwing stones after the fish at the same time as they go on they endeavour to keep the Boats in this circular line. this method seldom fails in Bringing them up to the very head of the lochs when some Boat will rush in upon them to wound some who directly run ashoar and all the rest follow when Most of the Boats will pursue and the Slaughter begins . . . [in May and June] . . . above one hundred and eighty kill^d in Loch Stornoway & near it.[47]

The larger whales, such as the slow-swimming right whale and the faster sperm whale, which could have been caught with harpoons hurled from open boats, are not common in the seas around Scotland. The rorquals, which include the minke, commonly encountered in the herring fishing, are too fast and agile to be caught by this method (harpoon capture of rorquals did not come to Scotland until 1903). So beyond the herding and stabbing described for Stornoway there seems to have been no incentive for the development of indigenous Scottish harpoon whaling. Harpooning as a method of capturing the basking shark was probably adopted from Ireland where at least one early operator hunted both whales and sharks, and from the Arctic, brought back by Scottish whalers.[48]

There is only a hint of the gear used by Donald MacLeod for capturing the shark. He mentions procuring 'proper tackling and nets' with the vessel he ordered from Leith but it can be supposed that 'tackling' included a harpoon and ropes. Discussing the shadowy 'Stewart at Bute', Archibald Menzies not only notes his success with the [hand-held] harpoon but intriguingly suggests that he was a pioneer in Scotland, in 1768, of the gun harpoon, at least as far as the basking shark fishery was concerned:

> One Stewart at Bute is fitting out a Boat with a small swivel [gun] at the Bow, he proposes fixing a Harpoon to a piece of Wood which is to serve as a Wadd to the Gun. This he is to fire into the Fish . . .[49]

The probability that the gear used by Arctic whalers sailing out of Scottish ports, and presumably readily available from ship chandlers, was also used in the early basking shark fishery is strengthened by details in the accounts that were rendered to the Commissioners for the Annexed Estates by Walter Campbell of Shawfield in 1778 or 1779 in respect of the *Nancy*:

> Paid Daniel McGibbon of Greenock for Salt, harpoons, whale lines etc for [to?] accompt. £24.[50]

The type of harpoon used in this early fishery would probably have been an iron harpoon head about 60 centimetres long of a simple V-shape, the barbs lacking the backward-pointing 'stop-withers' which came later. The base of the shank is expanded in a hollow cone to accommodate a wooden shaft circa 2 metres in length. (Fig. 22) The line would have been looped around the base of the shank as a 'foreganger'[51]. It is unlikely that the harpoon was hurled any distance at the shark. The usual method, inferred from Pennant (below), called for a very close approach to the shark such that the harpoon was driven home almost vertically by the combined strength of two men. This would have required a swift retreat by the boat crew as in the turmoil of the stricken fish sounding its tail flicks could have smashed the boat. After harpooning and the long-drawn out hauling in, the exhausted shark was finished off by stabbing with a lance.

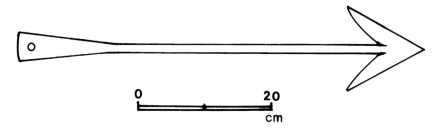

Fig. 23. The type of harpoon used in the first fishery. This specimen of an early 18th century forged iron double-barbed harpoon with plain barbs, i.e. without stop-withers, is probably very similar to the type used in the early Scottish basking shark fishery. (No 1881-641 in the Buckland Collection, Scottish Fisheries Museum, Anstruther)

A graphic description of the habits of the basking shark and its mode of capture at Lochranza, Arran, in 1772, is given by Thomas Pennant in his *Tour in Scotland*:

> They swim very deliberately with their two dorsal fins above water, and seem quiescent as if asleep. They are very tame or stupid; and permit the near approach of man: will suffer a boat to follow them without accelerating their motion, till it comes almost within contact, when a harpooner strikes his weapon into the fish as near the gills as possible: but they are often to [sic] insensible as not to move untill the united strength of two men has forced in the harpoon deeper: as soon as they perceive themselves wounded, they fling up their tail and plunge headlong to the bottom, and frequently coil the rope round them in their agonies, attempting to disengage themselves from the weapon by rolling on the ground, for it is often found greatly bent. As soon as they discover that

their efforts are in vain, they swim away with amazing rapidity, and with such violence that a vessel of 70 tuns, has been towed by them against a fresh gale: they sometimes run off with 200 fathoms of line, and with two harpoons in them; and will find employ to the fishers for twelve and sometimes twenty-four hours before they are subdued. When killed they are either hauled on shore, or if at a distance, to the vessel's side. The liver (the only useful part) is taken out and melted into oil in vessels provided for that purpose: a large fish will yield eight barrels of oil, and two of sediment, and prove a profitable capture.[52]

The accompanying plate shows a carvel-built six-oared open boat lying with its stern to the shark which is in an unlikely posture well above the sea surface. The details are somewhat obscure but two men appear to be about to thrust the harpoon into the shark's head while a third holds the coiled line. A similar boat with rowers is nearby (with a second harpoon?) and two sailing vessels are also standing by – the one to the left with square sails is possibly the *Lady Frederick Campbell*, the boat which transported Pennant.[53] (Fig. 24) A tempting

Fig. 24. Taking the basking shark at Lochranza, Isle of Arran in 1772. Two men harpoon the shark from the bow of an open boat whose rowers are ready to take the strain as the fish sounds. The shark is absurdly high out of the water. The crew of the second boat may be standing by to do further harpooning if there is an opportunity. The sailing vessel to the left is possibly the *Lady Frederick Campbell*, which was transporting Thomas Pennant. (Illustration by Moses Griffith – Pennant (1774): plate 13)

inference from Pennant's description is that cutting out the liver at sea was occasionally practised, rather than the dead shark just being towed to a beach. If so it is most probable that the dead fish was lashed to the side of one of the sailing vessels, the liver cut out, chopped up and barrelled, and the carcass released. But without obvious derricks to take the weight of the carcass it is hard to see how cutting-out could be done effectively in any but a very calm sea. Writing much later, in 1875, David Landsborough indicates that the basking shark fishery in Arran was by his time only of historical interest, but his narrative supplements Pennant's account with interesting additional details:

> A century ago there was more animated fishing at Arran than any I have mentioned – that of the basking shark, or sun fish . . . The liver of a good-sized fish yielded about eight barrels of oil, for the sake of which it was keenly pursued. All the fishermen in Arran were provided with harpoons and tackle for its capture; nor during the season of its visit did the Arran and Saltcoats Packet ever cross without them. A sharp look-out was kept, and no sooner was its well-known sail (two or three feet high) discerned than all was bustle and activity, and soon a boat was speeding toward it over the water. Four men manned a boat – two rowed, one managed the rope, and one handled the harpoon. Taking it was attended with some danger, for it is very powerful; and, like the whale, on being struck it plunges to the bottom. On one occasion the rapidly uncoiling rope caught the foot of the man who had charge of it, and in a moment he was overboard, and down into the depths. "Cut the rope," shouted the oarsmen to John McDonald, the master. "No," he replied; "the man is dead already, and the fish will do good to his widow." My informant, Mr McKelvie, the intelligent septuagenarian teacher at Little Mill, had the anecdote from the lips of John McDonald.[54]

In Orkney and Shetland, although the basking shark was taken from time to time, it seems very unlikely that any sustained hunting of it took place, as shark appearances seem to have been very erratic. The Reverend George Low, the Orkney naturalist, writing to Thomas Pennant in May 1773, describes the capture of a basking shark 'in our harbour [probably Stromness]' by 'three Highland wherries' which had put in there on the way to Shetland:

> [They] manned their boats, being provided with harpoons, and went after him; He was not in the least disturbed at the approach of the boat but suffered them to come closeup to him when two of them struck him then indeed for a little time he made the sea foam around him and after tumbling a while went to the bottom. They imagining he had been dead

wanted to drag him onshore and got the assistance of 8 or 9 boats, who, after much struggling got him from the bottom upon which one of the people wounded him with a launce. This effectually roused him and set him arunning, and, in spite of the efforts of all the people in the boats he pulled the whole after him thro the harbour till the harpoons came out of him, and he was given over for lost . . . [The shark soon reappeared] and notwithstanding of what he had met with he suffered the boats to come so near as to wound him with three harpoons; one of them near the gills which made him rage and tumble about dragging and beating the boats with his tail like as many chips; till at last [with] repeated efforts, and pierced with many wounds, he perished and was drawn ashore.

Twelve barrels of oil were extracted and 'the flesh looked partly like beef and partly like carse turbot, it was cut in pieces and much of it eaten by the poor people'.

Interestingly, Low also notes another method of taking the fish as a shark had been 'caught in a neighbouring island by the country people throwing a noose of a rope over his pectoral fins, and playing him'. These details indicate that even if the basking shark was indeed an infrequent visitor, the northerners knew how to deal with it effectively.[55]

END OF THE FISHERY

This first Scottish basking shark fishery does not seem to have survived much beyond the mid-1830s although so far no precise date can be given for its end. If a general work of the time (Webster's 1817 *Topographical Dictionary*) is to believed, the fishery was flourishing in the early 19th century:

and, besides other fish which are caught for their oil, we may mention the *cearban*, or sun-fish, the fishery of which is prosecuted with considerable success on the western coasts.[56]

However, from about 1820, the references to the basking shark become more anecdotal and it seems that while hunting of the shark still occurred, it was a very peripheral business. The Swiss traveller, De Saussure, wrote in 1822 that 'the sun-fish is sometimes pursued in the Hebrides' but he does not imply that it was of any importance in the economy.[57] A similar impression of a waning activity is given for Harris in the late 1830s by the *New Statistical Account* of 1845:

The natives occasionally capture with the harpoon the sun-fish, which loiters along the coast during the summer months . . .[58]

The *New Statistical Account* also confirms that the basking shark had been fished in South Uist, a very poor island, in the early 1800s and gives a clue to the reason for the demise of the fishery:

> About thirty years ago, there was a considerable fishing carried on in dog-fish and sun-fish or basking-shark. But since the bounty on the oil of these fishes has been withdrawn, this branch of industry has been altogether discontinued.[59]

(Another supposed description of South Uist's basking shark fishing in Forsyth's *The Beauties of Scotland* (1808) is quite deceptive as it is taken almost word for word from Pennant's 1772 account of Lochranza.)[60]

The importance of bounties and 'premiums' in sustaining the fishery is substantiated by the account book of Father Angus MacDonald, parish priest of Barra where an entry for 22 November 1818 reads:

> Competition for carban premium.
> Mary of Sandray in Barra 112 gallons
> Mary of Barra ————— 186 ditto
> [both 'Marys' were fishing vessels][61]

In 1819 the small island of Sandray, south of Barra, had three boats, of which the *Mary* was one and any bounty would have been vital for its small community.

The use of bounties to encourage trading activities the government considered to be beneficial was common in the eighteenth century and was particularly characteristic of whaling – '. . . a trade founded on bounty and nurtured by protection . . .'[62] An Act of 1799 allowed the British Fisheries Society to give rewards of not more than 'sixty pounds in one year' to deserving claimants curing fish or 'preparing soap or oil from fish' and the 'carban premium' referred to was very likely given by this Society.[63] A short-lived bounty of £3 per ton for oil extracted from whales and fish caught in Britain was instituted in 1820 but its professed object – '. . . the Further Encouragement and Improvement of the British Fisheries' soon withered under the impact of Free Trade policies and it was abolished in July 1825.[64] With the end of the Napoleonic wars and the opening-up of the Pacific sperm whale fishery, imported whale oil was readily available and this circumstance alone would have favoured ending the government bounty.

Assessing this rather tenuous evidence and noting that there is little mention of the basking shark in the nineteenth century, it is concluded that the fishery in the Western Isles came to an end in the 1830s; but while the loss of bounties was no doubt a significant factor, it is unlikely to have been the only reason. The numbers of shark may have declined in areas of former abundance and other types of fishing may have been more lucrative by this time. The onerous salt tax which crippled the development of the herring fishery in the west had been abolished in 1786 and it seems that line-fishing was quite profitable, for some at least:

> The Barra men are among the most active and industrious fishermen in Scotland. They carry on an extensive ling fishery solely by their own exertions . . .[65]

It is revealing that this quotation from a descriptive work of the 1820s makes no mention of the basking shark. And yet even an apparently successful fishing community such as this was at times existing on very small margins between subsistence and a sufficient profit to make modest capital investments. Nearly twenty years later the *New Statistical Account* was very revealing about the real state of Barra:

> The people of Barray were in former years very successful in harpooning *cearbans* or sail-fish, from which they extracted a good deal of oil, and received a premium from the Board of Trustees for Fisheries; but this productive source of wealth has been discontinued, from their inability to provide the necessary tackling; and although hundreds of these fishes appeared last season [1839] on the coast, no one was in a condition to take advantage of the circumstance.[66]

The picture for the inner Hebrides was similar. In the same work the minister of Tiree and Coll recalls eight barrels of basking shark oil being worth £25 in his youth but that the once-abundant fish had been seen little in the previous four decades. The inhabitants obtained their oil from schools of small whales which they had become expert at driving ashore with boats.[67]

The Clyde fishery seems to have waned about the same time. Discussing the fish and fishing potential of Arran at some length, J. Headrick in his *Island of Arran* (1808) states that the herring fishery 'is the only fishery in which the people here ever engage'. He does not mention the basking shark at all.[68] Another visitor, in about 1820, found a herring fleet based at Lochranza but does not make mention of the basking shark and Landsborough's 1875 dismissal of the basking shark fishery as an activity long discontinued has already been noted.[69] For Ayr on the southeastern Clyde coast the *New Statistical Account* lists the basking shark as one of the fish 'found in the bay [but] of no economic importance . . .'[70]

A northern reference is given by George Barry in his *Orkney Islands* (1805):

> The Basking Shark . . . which has here got the name of the *hoe-mother*, or *homer*, that is the mother of the dog-fish, is the most common of the

larger shark kind that is observed around these islands. He is often seen
rushing violently through the deep, and even sometimes entering our
creeks and bays. One of twenty-two feet long, and sixteen in
circumference, was about thirty years ago killed in the harbour of
Stromness.[71]

Aside from useful information on the names of the fish, it is clear that, unlike
careful observers such as Pennant and Low, Barry with his 'rushing violently
through the deep' knew little of the habits of the shark, and the mention of one
killed thirty years previously (George Low's shark?) suggests that the fish was
seldom seen in Barry's time. Certainly there was still a demand for whale and
fish oil in Orkney as many years later 'cuthes and sillocks' were abundant and
were being caught for food and for the lighting oil from their livers, as were
dogfish. The smaller whales were still customarily embayed and killed for their
oil. With the addition of cod livers, a similar situation was the case in
Shetland.[72] We may conclude that the basking shark would also have been
taken regularly had it been present in appreciable numbers.

   References to the basking shark in the writings of Scottish naturalists at this
period are uncommon. In the same volume of the *Memoirs* of the Wernerian
Society which contained John Barclay's paper on the Stronsay Monster, P.
Neill's descriptive list of fishes in the Firth of Forth gives the basking shark as a
fish which 'seldom enters the Firth' although 'common in the Scottish seas in
the summer' and notes that one was observed off Portobello in the summer of
1808. [73] A monstrously overblown 300-page 'prize essay' on the fishes of the
Forth in the same *Memoirs* twenty years later, in its two pages on the basking
shark, takes the basic description from a standard reference book; its discussion
from other authors, including Neill in 1808, and makes no reference to the
fishing of the shark which was coming to a close in the West, or to any potential
use of shark products. [74]

   The overall picture that emerges of this first Scottish basking shark fishery
which persisted for some seventy years portrays an activity which probably only
in unusual circumstances became anything greater than taking the shark as
opportunity offered: a profitable, but occasional, sideline to the normal routines
of the summer fishing in communities where fishing was principally a
subsistence activity carried out by men whose prime interest was in their
land.[75] We can imagine that intermittently, for a few seasons, stimulated
alternately by an abundance of the sharks or by some form of bounty (and
possibly these two factors coincided at times) the basking shark was hunted
intensively. This was obviously the case in the Canna of the late 1780's and is
almost certainly true of Barra.

To flourish, the emergent fishery needed powerful economic stimuli. A market short of whale oil was one and the government bounty for whale and fish oil even if short-lived was another. Even if the withdrawal of the government bounty was a profound disincentive in itself, other factors were probably more effective in causing the fishery to languish. While the annual appearance of the basking shark in early summer was predictable to within a week or so, its numbers in any one year were very variable. This of itself worked against the possibility of any sustained large scale fishery developing. By contrast the migratory routes and seasonal areas of the various large whales were fairly well known by about 1800, so that vast quantities of sperm oil were available to Britain in the early nineteenth century. Sperm oil was preferred to any fish oil and it is more than probable that its availability swamped the oil market, driving down prices and so making basking shark oil uncompetitive.

We may also assume that more profitable fishing had squeezed out the basking shark hunting in the upper Clyde region, if not further south. From the late eighteenth century until well into the nineteenth, the herring fishery became a progressively more intensive activity in Loch Fyne. The fish were plentiful, the Glasgow market was relatively close, and the farmers who fished with drift nets did well. From about 1830, those who adopted the new ring-net method did even better.[76] To these men, as to their descendants several generations later, the basking shark was merely a nuisance as it tore through their nets. In the 1840s, so the *New Statistical Account* tells us for Inveraray, the herring season lasted half the year and its commencement was signalled by 'the prolonged visit of the 'whale', as the sailfish is called'. There is no suggestion that the 'whale' itself was any longer sought.[77] Further to the west and north the intermittent, local summer fishing was beginning to be neglected in favour of regular participation in the herring fishery of the East Coast.[78] And not to be ignored were the widespread disruptions to traditional life brought about by the Clearances and emigration during the same period.

No doubt influenced by all of these factors, the basking shark fishery appears to have lapsed by the end of the 1830s. Shark oil's great competitor, sperm oil, was likewise threatened by coal-gas as an illuminant by the 1820s and although other uses sustained the market for a few decades, it was to lose its predominance when petroleum-derived products became cheap and widely available in the 1860s. When the basking shark was again hunted, in the next century, its liver oil was sought for products very much more sophisticated than a lighting fuel and a substitute industrial oil.

Notes

1. Fenton (1978): 525 & 548.
2. Shaw (1980): 127.
3. Martin (1995): 8.
4. Martin (1703): 386; Brand (1701): 197.
5. Shaw (1980): 125.
6. Dunlop (1978): 1.
7. McKay (1980): 46.
8. McKay (1980): 6.
9. Menzies (1768) 'Voyage': [67] (SRO E729/9).
10. 'Piscator' (1792) vol 9: 92.
11. Martin (1995): 11-12.
12. Campbell (1994): 120.
13. Pottle & Bennett (1963): 281. The fish were *cuddies*.
14. *OSA* vol 14: 222-223 for Nigg; *OSA* vol 15: 374–375 for Peterhead.
15. *OSA* vol 15: 159.
16. *NSA* vol 13: 12 (quotation) & 250.
17. O'Dea (1958): 27, 225 (quotation) & 227.
18. Waterer (1946): 145, for the tanning process; Cochran (1985): 66, for tanning trade; *OSA* vol 5: 525, for tanning at Stranraer; *OSA* vol 6: 20 for tanning at Ayr.
19. Singer (1957): vol 3: 35
20. McNally (1976): 8, for embrocation; Beeton (1861): 974, for leather.
21. Jackson (1978): 55.
22. Holdsworth & Lavery (1991): 8.
23. Kristjansson (1983): 396.
24. Bowen (1972): 66 for early whale bones; Wheeler & Jones (1989): 85 for denticles.
25. MacLeod (1766) 'Memorial . . .': 2 (SRO E728/13/4). This 'Memorial' is given in full at Appendix B.
26. Smith (1982): 160 for age; MacLeod 'Memorial': 3 (SRO E728/13/4).
27. Smith (1982): 160.
28. For costs of boat and crew see SRO E 727/19/8(2) & 9(1).
29. MacLeod in letter from Oban dated 11 October 1768 (SRO E727/16/3).
30. MacLeod in letter from Oban dated 11 October 1768 (SRO E727/16/3).
31. Pennant quoted in Smith (1982): 161; Pottle & Bennett (1963): 172 & 199.
32. Campbell (1986): 116 for dispossession; & 'Piscator' (1792) vol 8: 176-177.
33. 'Piscator' (1792) vol 8: 177-178.
34. Menzies (1768) 'Voyage': [20]-21 (SRO E729/9). See Appendix C.
35. Campbell's letter to the Board is dated 10 February 1777 (SRO E727/60/1). The Board's 'Observations' on Campbell's plans is dated 24 February 1777 (SRO E727/60/2). Smith (1992): 127 & 160 gives Campbell's first name as 'Daniel' – 'David' here may be an error.
36. SRO E60/3/1 & E60/3/2.
37. Anderson (1785): 15.
38. Menzies (1768) 'Voyage': [16] [20] & 21 (SRO E729/9).
39. Listed in Fairfax (1995): 71.

40. Peterhead – *OSA* vol 15: 434–435; Skye – *OSA* vol 20: 192.
41. *OSA* vol 20: 130 -131.
42. McNally (1976): 9.
43. Cochran (1985): 141 & O'Brien (1918): 168-169.
44. McNally (1976): 7.
45. O. Lindquist *pers. comm.* 1995.
46. *OSA* vol 8: 340-341.
47. MacIver (1768) 'Journal' (SRO E727/18/11(1)).
48. Fairley (1981): 122-123 & Jackson (1978): 62.
49. Menzies (1768) 'Voyage': 21 (SRO E729/9).
50. SRO E727/60/3/2.
51. D.P. Henderson *pers. comm.* 1995.
52. Pennant (1774): 169-170 & plate 13.
53. Bray (1986): 85.
54. Landsborough (1875): 95-96.
55. Low letter to T.Pennant 27 May 1773: [1-3] (WCRO CR 2017/ TP 290/4). For a literary 'improved' version, see Low (1813): 172-174.
56. Webster (1817): x.
57. De Saussure (1822): 55.
58. *NSA* vol 14, sect 1: 156.
59. *NSA*, vol 14: 187.
60. Forsyth (1808): 356-357. A similar stricture applies to Knox (1787): 37-38 & 127.
61. J.L. Campbell, Canna *pers. comm.* 21 Aug 1995.
62. Jackson (1978): 119.
63. 39 Geo 3: Cap 100 (1799).
64. 1 Geo IV Cap 103 (1820) established the bounty and 5 Geo IV Cap 64 (1824) abolished it. See also Jackson (1978): 119.
65. McCulloch (1824) vol 3: 8.
66. *NSA* vol 14, sect 1: 213.
67. *NSA* vol 7: 204 & 216.
68. Headrick (1807): 366.
69. McCulloch (1824) vol 2: 38.
70. *NSA* vol 5: 53.
71. Barry (1805): 296.
72. *NSA* vol 15, sect 3 (Orkney): 74 for 1841; & sect 3: 89, 104, 121 & 163; *NSA* vol 15, sect 4 (Shetland): 58 & 133.
73. Neill (1811): 550–551
74. Parnell (1838): 418-420.
75. Gray (1978): 101-102.
76. Gray (1978): 119.
77. *NSA* vol 7: 32.
78. Gray (1978): 108-109 & 119-120; & Sinclair (1825): 202.

Chapter Five

The Modern Fishery

AFTER THE FIRST SCOTTISH fishery came to an end there was a long period when the basking shark was an occasional object of curiosity to naturalists, but otherwise its presence does not seem to have impinged noticeably on public consciousness. Infrequent and rather cursory references to the basking shark were to be the pattern followed for most of a century. A popular journal for the amateur natural historian, *The Scottish Naturalist*, flourished from 1871 to 1964 but apart from the occasional short notice of a stranding or a sighting, specific references to the basking shark are uncommon from 1900 on.[1] In 1899, the annual report of the Fishery Board for Scotland has a few lines on an 8-foot basking shark captured off Murray's Bay, Ayrshire in September 1898. Should this, the first reference to the shark in these reports for seventeen years, be taken as a sign that it was a comparative rarity by this time? Possibly so, as Landsborough's outdated 1875 *Arran* is the only reference quoted and there is certainly no indication that there was any current economic interest in the shark.[2] A later Fisheries Board report, that of 1922, refers to damage done to the nets of Barra fishermen by the sharks, but does not suggest that the fish were being hunted at that time.[3]

To assess the level of popular interest in the shark for the early part of this century one useful gauge is the newspaper, the *Glasgow Herald*. The indexes for this, beginning in 1906, have no reference to the basking shark until 1919 when the fish were reported in Kilbrannan Sound, between Kintyre and Arran, and further references are few until the mid-1930s. In July 1934, billed as a new sport for the Clyde, a 'ketch-rigged Grimsby pilot boat' was to operate out of Greenock taking paying guests for a week of harpooning sharks.[4] Even if the sharks were appearing in reasonable numbers they were not arousing comment in the next few years. But this came to an end in September 1937 when the 'Carradale Incident' (treated in Chapter 3) turned a dramatic spotlight on the fish which remained on it until the outbreak of war made basking shark concerns irrelevant.

'FISHERMEN'S PLEAS'

For two years after the Carradale Incident the newspapers took an interest in complaints by Clyde fishermen that the exceptional number of sharks were 'infesting Clyde waters' and 'becoming an increasing menace'.[5] In June 1938, the local member of parliament asked for an 'immediate Government inquiry into the menace to fishing caused by basking and thresher sharks outside Campbeltown Loch'. The official view was that no complaints had been received from fishermen '. . . during the present year' and the request was turned down.[6] On 23 May 1939 question time in the House of Commons saw local members painting a lurid scene of fishermen 'afraid to put to sea' and bathers 'chased out of the sea by sharks' and demanding to know what action the Secretary of State for Scotland would take to destroy the basking sharks and stop their 'depredations on the herring shoals' of the Clyde. The government's view was that the Clyde fishermen were fishing as usual and that at that stage there had been no complaints of damage to gear. The Fishery Board's 'cruisers', the term used for fisheries patrol vessels, would continue to destroy sharks by 'the methods which have proved successful in the past'. This was an oblique reference to the previous year when a cruiser had killed 50 sharks by ramming them.[7] The next month the member for Greenock querulously demanded action on 'the menace of basking sharks much more obvious and much more dangerous all round the coasts' of western Scotland and Northern Ireland. The Secretary of State did not take this too seriously, asking the member to let him know the whereabouts of the sharks.[8] The basking shark 'menace' was in reality a minor consideration for governmental authorities. The relevant reports of the Fishery Board for Scotland are silent on the matter. Compensation for damaged fishing gear when it could be shown to be the result of basking shark entanglement was the most appropriate administrative redress rather than futile attempts to destroy the sharks by sending fisheries cruisers after them.

ANTHONY WATKINS – THE PIONEER

In that fateful September of 1937, Anthony Watkins, then a clerk in a London commercial office but with some experience of sharks in the tropics, had his interest in basking sharks kindled by reading accounts of the Carradale Incident. Knowing that shark oil was being imported into Britain, he decided to investigate the commercial possibilities of oil from the basking shark. After consulting a retired surgeon, Dr Seccombe Hett, who had been studying the sharks in the Clyde, Watkins invited Hett and another friend to spend two weeks of that summer shark-hunting in a converted naval patrol vessel, the *Myrtle*.[9] They made headlines when Watkins and the *Myrtle*'s deckhand harpooned a large shark from a dinghy, but being unable to subdue it were steadily towed out of Kilbrannan Sound, around the Mull of Kintyre and out into the Atlantic. The skipper of the *Myrtle*, Dan Davies, set off in pursuit of the reluctantly sea-going pair, but could not keep up with them. Not only did he have to contend with the *Myrtle's* unreliable engine, which kept breaking down, but he was additionally hampered by a fire in the engine room. Eventually he gave up the chase and the *Myrtle* limped into Campeltown. Amazingly, after a night of slow but steady dragging 'in the general direction of America' Watkins and his companion managed to haul the shark up close to the surface, and by poking at its gills with an oar Watkins made the shark turn about so that it was now towing them back to Kintyre. Many hours later they met up with the Campbeltown lifeboat which had been alerted by Davies and were taken on board after tying buoys to the shark. [10] This foolhardy escapade, farcical in the extreme, was the start of Watkins' small-scale basking shark fishery which, initially based at Carradale, continued except for the war years until 1950. Watkins continued experimental fishing in the *Myrtle* with a hand-held harpoon, arranging for the liver oil from the first shark he captured to be analysed and for the flesh and skin to be tested for marketing possibilities. The oil, found to be low in vitamin A and lacking in vitamin D but high in iodine, was valued at £25 per ton. The flesh, processed by the Glasgow fish merchant, J.M. Davidson, produced 'a low quality guano [fertiliser] which he estimated would sell for about £7 per ton' but it would not sell as food. A thin leather could be produced from the skin although the cost of making it was thought to be prohibitive. [11]

On the assumption that the sharks were kept under the surface by rough seas and therefore that wind velocity was significant, Watkins also tried to analyse the potential for suitable basking shark-fishing weather, concluding that:

> A day with a 5 m.p.h. wind I put into the category of a 'good' shark-fishing day, 10 m.p.h. was a 'possible' and 15 m.p.h. was 'bad'. I found that out of the 120 days of the season, on average one could expect 34 good days, 56 possible and 30 bad days. [12]

In June 1938 he formed a company, Scottish Shark Fisheries Ltd, with a nominal capital of £1500, and floated an ambitious and expensive proposal for a shore factory and fleet of catchers:

Shore factory	£7,000
6 Catchers, complete with guns and equipment	£6,000
Working capital	£5,000
	£18,000

but sensibly reduced this to a factory to process livers and flesh, one catcher and £300 working capital all of which could be financed from the nominal capital.[13] From the first, Watkins envisaged a mixed fishing operation: his catchers would take herring in the winter and sharks in the summer so that the factory in due course would need to be equipped to process fish meal from both. In his initial optimism Watkins seems to have neglected any consideration of the number of basking sharks that would be the potential catch in the seasons ahead and he was probably overly-influenced by the large numbers in the Clyde in 1937.

A Norwegian Kongsberg Vapenfabrikk harpoon gun was ordered and a site selected for a small factory on Forestry Commission land at Carradale, about half a mile north of Port Crannaich. A 40-ft Loch Fyne skiff, the *Dusky Maid*, was purchased for £400 at Girvan and modified to take the Kongsberg gun.[14] (Fig. 26)

The factory, a large shed, was completed at a cost of £570 by May 1939 and

Fig. 25. John Paterson, the manager of Antony Watkins' Carradale shark factory, at the bow of a shark catcher (probably the *Dusky Maid*) with a Kongsberg Vapenfabrikk harpoon gun. This photograph possibly taken in 1946 when Greenock-made harpoon heads were used with wooden shafts strengthened with a metal base. The harpoon line is attached to the harpoon by metal rings (or a shackle) and it is looped below the bow before coming up throught he fairlead. The gun with its mount appears to be of the same type as the one used by William Sutherland in the *Jessie Alice* in the 1950s which is preserved in Mallaig.
(Courtesy Isabel White, Castle Douglas)

soon equipped with its boiler and metal vats, with a local man, John Paterson, being appointed to manage it. Finding the Clyde still empty of basking sharks, Watkins began the season by taking the *Dusky Maid* north to the Minch where some time was spent experimenting with harpooning techniques. Watkins and his crew caught a number of basking sharks and were able to return to Carradale with sufficient barrelled liver to begin the oil-extraction processing.[15] For the remainder of the season they would hunt in the Firth of Clyde, the Sea of the Hebrides and the Minch as opportunity offered. At first the sharks that were caught away from the Firth were gutted on a convenient beach and the livers, in barrels, were brought to the factory for oil extraction. Sharks caught in the Firth of Clyde were lashed to the *Dusky Maid* and towed to the beach in front of the factory where the livers were removed, cut into pieces and put in barrels which were rolled up into the factory on a temporary wooden slipway. (Fig. 45) Gutting the sharks at sea was also tried and, as a modification of this to enable easier working, the shark was towed into shallower water until it grounded and then the liver was removed and the harpoon extricated.[16]

For Watkins, the 1939 season ended abruptly with his call-up for war service and it was not until the summer of 1946 that he was able to resume shark-fishing. The company, which had remained profitable during the war because the *Dusky Maid* was kept going in fishing for herring, was renamed 'Scottish West Coast Fisheries' and an additional 8500 £1 shares were created.[17] The post-war economy Watkins returned to was a straitened one: fishing vessels of any sort were much in demand and were expensive and the basic wage for a crew member had doubled to £5 per week. Watkins assembled a flotilla of sharkcatching vessels. He bought the *Gloamin'*, a 90-foot drifter, which he converted into a factory ship to replace the Carradale factory now considered to be too far from the Sea of the Hebrides and the Minch, and two 40-foot West Coast ring-net boats, the *Paragon* and the *Perseverance*, were purchased to be catchers in company with the *Dusky Maid*.[18] The crews were local ring-net fishermen who had not obtained a berth in a fishing boat.[19] Kongsberg harpoon guns were temporarily unavailable so Watkins tried the inventive combination of modified cut-down 2-pounder anti-tank guns with locally-produced harpoon heads mounted on wooden shafts.[20] To his advantage was the scarcity of tropical vegetable oils and whale oil. There was a premium on basking shark oil which was predicted to sell for as much as £100 per ton.[21]

As it turned out, however, this first post-war season in the Minch was barely successful. Even when new Kongsberg guns had been fitted in August, replacing the creative but unsatisfactory expedient of the anti-tank guns, the difficulty of developing an effective harpooning technique delayed the start of the season. Operations were further hindered when the handling of shark carcasses on

Fig. 26.   Securing the tail of a basking shark with a sling to the *Dusky Maid*, A. Watkins' catcher. The taut harpoon line is passing over the fairlead. The harpoon gun is a Kongsberg Vapenfabrikk type. (Watkins 1958)

board the *Gloamin'* proved to be more awkward than had been expected. By November 1946 Watkins had redirected his little fleet to herring fishing with the *Gloamin'* stripped of her oil-extraction plant and refitted as a fish-carrier. An intense but lucrative herring fishing effort ended abruptly when the *Gloamin'* was wrecked at Loch Boisdale, South Uist.

Shark-fishing began again in the Sea of the Hebrides in late April 1947 with another drifter, the *Recruit*, fitted out as a replacement factory ship, and the three catchers operating as before, and for the first time sharks were successfully caught in rough seas, to the east of Barra. The fleet returned to the Firth of Clyde in mid-June and did well in the shark shoals that were then off the Ayrshire coast. Radio-telephones were introduced at this time to good effect, allowing the catchers to converge as soon as one found a shark shoal. They tried netting the sharks, as an alternative to harpooning; it worked, but the nets were expensive and it was impractical unless there was a regular run of sharks in one place, which was not the case in Scotland.[22] Oil prices had remained buoyant so the company was doing well, as is shown by a week's profit and loss statement typical of this period:

Sale of Oil			£1,430
Less Wages	Basic	£84	
"	Bonus (29 sharks)	£72	
Coal		£34	
Diesel Oil		£17	
Sundry Expenses		£35	
		£242	
Trading Profit		£1,188	[23]

Watkins' own account ends on this upbeat note and the company stayed in existence until 1952 although Watkins seems to have given up an active part in the business by 1950.[24] It is known that at various times in 1948 (if not as early as 1947) he offered a scheme of 'joint development' to the ailing Isle of Soay Shark Fisheries (which was declined) and it seems that in 1950 he may have taken his vessels to western Ireland for the season.[25] Eighty-one sharks were caught in the 1947 season by the Watkins group. (As recollected by Angus Paterson, a crew member in the *Recruit*, 40 sharks were taken in the Cyde and 41 in the Minch) and as prices remained high, about £130 per ton, these should have brought a good profit.[26] But as the 1948 season had been a bad one for the Soay company, with only 42 sharks caught, compared to 166 in 1947, it is probable that low numbers also seriously dented the profits of Watkins' company in spite of the variable but still high oil prices.[27] The contracted oil price in July 1947 was up to £110 per ton; during the 1948 season the market price dropped from £135 to around £90 per ton.[28]

GAVIN MAXWELL AND THE SOAY VENTURE

Although Anthony Watkins had pioneered the modern basking shark fishery in Scotland, Gavin Maxwell anticipated him in his post-war operations by nearly two years.[29] Maxwell, a somewhat footloose Oxford-educated young man of aristocratic Scots lineage, with real expertise in outdoor pursuits such as shooting and stalking, had been commissioned into the Scots Guards in September 1939. Recurrent stomach ulcers caused him to be medically down-graded and he spent most of his war service in a training role with the Special Forces at several locations near Mallaig, the west coast fishing port. In his leave periods he sailed among the Hebridean islands and became greatly taken with the beauty of the small island of Soay off the southern shore of Skye. He decided to buy it, becoming in 1944 the owner, and the laird of its few inhabitants.[30] During the summer of that year, he was awed by the sight of his first basking shark in the Sound of Sleat and, seeing commercial possibilities in the fish, spent the last weeks of his leave attempting to harpoon one so that samples of the various potential products from it could be sent away for analysis. As the new laird of Soay, Maxwell felt under some obligation to provide paid work, even if only seasonal, for his crofters if at all possible, and the prospect of a profitable basking shark fishery could fulfil that aim. By early 1945, these two ideas had coalesced and his Island of Soay Shark Fisheries was launched with a working capital of £11,000 advanced by his mother from his potential inheritance. He later raised an additional £4500.[31]

Gavin Maxwell was an extraordinarily gifted, versatile and visionary man who involved himself intensely in his work, revelling in the sheer physicality of the open-air life that pursuit of the basking shark gave him, but with all his manifold talents he was markedly impractical and decidedly not a business-man.[32] It is only by bearing this in mind that we can understand the rise and fall of the Soay venture. He had found out what he could about the habits of the basking shark and had taken the advice of J.M. Davidson, the Glasgow fish merchant, on the on the market for basking shark products. Like Watkins before him, he had been too easily impressed by the plentiful numbers of the shark at that time, not realising quite how unsound this was as the basis for a commercial fishery.[33] Unfortunately, instead of beginning the enterprise in a small way, he did three things more or less simultaneously: £1000 was paid for an unsuitable boat, the *Dove,* a 45-year old Stornaway drifter in poor condition; the construction of a processing plant on Soay was begun; and a specially-designed custom-made harpoon gun was ordered.[34] So it was that with only a sketchy knowledge of the basking shark's habits, especially its unpredictable appearances from year to year, and minimal experience in catching it, the major part of Maxwell's capital, probably about £9000, was put into the establishment of the Soay factory with all the additional expense entailed by transporting materials to the island and building in such an isolated locality. His very first employee was J. 'Tex' Geddes, reputedly a Newfoundlander of Scots extraction, who had served with Maxwell in the Special Forces.

Maxwell began by operating his company from an office in Mallaig, which with its jetties and slipways, was the obvious home port for his vessels. The first season, the summer of 1945, was an experimental one using the *Dove* as the catcher, skippered by Bruce Watt, a Mallaig man. For the 1946 season, Maxwell was at sea in the *Sea Leopard*, a sleek 70-foot ex-naval motor launch which had replaced the *Dove* in April at a cost of £4000. Living on board and using his cabin as his office, he was unable to supervise the working of the Soay factory which was plagued by a discontented workforce and badly needed a manager on site.[35] The *Sea Leopard* was crewed by four men (skipper, engineer, deckhand and cook) with Maxwell and Geddes as harpooners. The smaller *Gannet*, Maxwell's own 30-foot lobster boat from his army days, was often towed by the *Sea Leopard* and was crewed by Geddes and the deckhand when it acted independently.[36] A motorised 15-foot lifeboat, the *Button*, bought to be used as a tender, completed the Soay fleet. Maxwell and his men ranged the Sea of the Hebrides and the Minch throughout the 1946 summer, hampered by *Sea Leopard's* unsatisfactory Oerlikon gun and the capricious, misfiring Greener gun in *Gannet*.[37] Energy and enthusiasm could not overcome their lack of experience. They were all still learning and on the whole their giant prey had the better of them – 'too many sharks were either missed outright or lost after they had been harpooned', and much time was wasted towing those sharks that were caught back to the Soay factory. Overheads at this time were £160 per week in addition to wages for the crew and factory workers.[38]

Near the end of the 1946 season the financial position of Maxwell's company looked bleak and a large injection of further capital was urgent. Through family connections, Maxwell was able to sell his company, including the island of Soay, to the Hamilton & Kinneil Estates, which administered the business interests of the Duke of Hamilton, for £13,550. This solved his financial problem, but he became merely an employee, the managing director, being required 'to devote his technical skill and knowledge to the Company's service'. The new Island of Soay Shark Fisheries Ltd was incorporated on 9 May 1947 with a nominal capital of 26,000 £1 shares and Maxwell was to be paid £600 per annum plus a commission on profits.[39]

The new season started on 5 May 1947 and by early July 86 sharks had been captured, nearly 50 of these from one shoal hunted over eighteen days. The price for the shark liver oil remained gratifyingly high at £110 per ton and fairly soon rose to a peak of £135.[40] However, operations were dogged by harpoon losses and the persisting difficulty of bringing a harpooned shark quickly alongside the catcher.[41] There were still attempts to utilise all parts of the shark, and the difficulties in operating the factory continued. With oil prices high, Maxwell's desire to concentrate on livers alone seemed vindicated and he tried to follow the Watkins' precedent by replacing the dry rot-ravaged *Sea-Leopard* with a factory ship to process livers at sea. Several ambitious schemes for factory vessels were suggested but nothing came of them, even though the parent company had acquired the drifter *Silver Darling* for conversion to a factory ship. A season of high, but still variable, oil prices did not, however, mean that the operation was profitable overall; as a report made to the company board by Maxwell in July 1947 and their records for early 1948 reveal. In July 1947 the current price for oil was £130 per ton. With the average basking shark giving 1 ton of liver which yielded 7 hundredweight of oil, this was £45 10s per shark. In respect to the sea-going part of the business:

Wages were
    skipper   = £8 per week
    mate   = £6-15
    engineer   = £6-10
    crew member = £4-15

plus a ration allowance of 15 shillings per week to the 7 to 9 crew members.

Bonuses to the crew were
    per shark   = £3
    per shark (Saturday afternoon)   = £5
    over 10 sharks in a week   = £10
    over 15 sharks in a week   = £15[42]

But, as assessed in February 1948, the loss for the 1947 season apparently amounted to £28 for each shark caught:

Costs:
    catching   = £35
    processing   = £16
    overheads   = £11

                   £62
Less sale of oil & flesh = £34
Loss per shark   = £28[43]

The two small catchers, the *Nancy Glen* and the *Maggie McDougall* that had been bought to replace the *Sea Leopard* did not do well and the 1948 season ended early with few sharks caught. The parent company was unhappy with Maxwell as managing director and by the spring of 1948, convinced of the impending collapse of the Soay company, he had distanced himself from the operation, renouncing living in the *Sea Leopard* in favour of a flat in a castle on the Clyde and going up to Mallaig occasionally.[44] For his part, Maxwell resented what he saw as indecision and indifference on the part of the directors, and in July of that year he resigned. Maxwell's successor, R. Findlay, carried on into the 1949 season, but the wreck of the *Nancy Glen* at Loch Skipport in May left the small slow *Gannet* as the main catcher. This loss of catching capacity, combined with a drop in oil price to £80/£90 per ton appears to have decided the parent company to wind up the Soay company, and its assets were sold off in May and June 1949.[45]

In his 1952 book, *Harpoon at a Venture*, Maxwell gives his version of the 'Decline and fall; 1948-9', cataloguing the problems, including the shipwreck, which underlay the final collapse.[46] Commenting on various points made in the book in a letter to Maxwell, G.L. Norris, the hard-headed legal adviser to the parent company, who of all the directors had taken the closest interest in the Soay fishery, saw things somewhat differently. He observed with real perception: 'the pursuit of natural history and writing are your true metier . . . commercial business is not your line and therein lies one main cause of the failure of the Soay venture'. He went on to note the great financial loss (circa £50,000 in total for both companies) and gave three reasons for the failure of the Soay scheme:

1. Failure of the sharks to appear or failure to find them with sufficient regularity or in sufficient numbers to make any such venture commercially possible in spite of their attractive livers.
2. Failure [with] boats and apparatus . . .
3. Failure to find really reliable captains and crews for these boats . . .[47]

Maxwell was by temperament a romantic, inclined to see the failure of the scheme in terms of defective personal relations.[48] Norris, not involved in the drama of personalities but just as concerned for its success, had coolly and quite accurately pinpointed the reasons for failure, not the least being the numbers and the habits of the basking shark itself. And his insight into Maxwell's real talents was truly prophetic: not only did *Harpoon at a Venture* go on to become a bestseller in Britain and America but, with the bitter end to the Soay venture in which he had lost all his capital well behind him, Maxwell became admired world-wide for *Ring of Bright Water* and his other otter books. Maxwell even received some satisfaction from an odd little legal sequel to the Soay episode. Angered by references to himself in P.F. O'Connor's 1953 book *Shark O!*, he successfully sued O'Connor for libel on the grounds that his integrity as an author had been attacked, and received £500 damages, costs and an apology from O'Connor and his publisher.[49]

THE LATE 1940s AND EARLY 1950s

The ignominious end of the Soay venture did not, however, signal the end of a basking shark fishery in the western seas. Over a period of some four years several individuals and at least one group of fishermen took up basking shark hunting, spurred on by the continuing comparatively high prices for oil and the knowledge most of them had of the Soay scheme's weaknesses. Without exception, all believed they could do better.[50] Rather ungenerously described by Maxwell as 'the several small freelance shark fishermen whose shoots grew seedily from the stump of my felled tree', the men concerned had different backgrounds.[51] J. 'Tex' Geddes and Harry Thompson had been employees of the Soay company while P.F. O'Connor came to shark-fishing as an outsider, getting his first taste of 'shark fever' with Thompson and his partner George Langford of Raasay.[52] The Mallaig group were a close-knit set of established professional fishermen who turned to basking shark fishing as a supplementary activity to their principal occupation – ring-net herring fishing. And near the end of this short but intense period of shark fishing (when basking sharks seemed to be especially abundant) alien competition arrived for the first time with small squadrons of Norwegian catchers fishing illegally but very effectively in the Minch.

Tex Geddes
Maxwell's most able harpooner had been his first crew-member, Tex Geddes. A tough, plain-speaking outdoorsman, he was in many ways a good foil for Maxwell – down-to-earth, practical and a much better seaman. When Maxwell resigned as managing director of the Soay company, Geddes also left its employ, to go shark-fishing independently with George Langford.[53] He arranged to sell to the Scottish Fish Meal Manufacturing Company in Glasgow not the shark oil, but the raw liver, which was to be delivered to the railhead at Mallaig.[54] Provided the price of shark oil remained competitive with whale oil, Geddes and Langford could look forward to making an adequate living. Geddes was experienced, their capital investment was minimal (a boat with two men, guns and gear) and as they did not intend to extract the oil themselves, they had no concern for either a shore factory or a factory vessel. They intended to occupy themselves in the off-season with lobster fishing.

As this small operation was getting under way the Soay company was in its final stage, and at its disposal sale Geddes obtained its two Greener guns, harpoons and other gear.[55] He and his wife also bought the island of Soay and made their home there.[56] For the 1950 season, Geddes went out on his own account, buying Langford's boat, the *Traveller*, a 34-foot Fifie fishing boat. He had its deck strengthened to take a harpoon gun and the mast re-rigged so that livers could be cut out at sea and hoisted inboard to be barrelled.[57] Geddes worked out an effective procedure for cutting out the livers with an improvised lance and hauling them on board with the aid of a brailer, a large scoop-net. With John McInerney as his deck-hand, Geddes hunted the basking sharks in the Sea of the Hebrides and in the Minch and when working off Harris and Lewis, would unload his barrels of liver at Stornoway, to be taken to Mallaig by steamer. Geddes found himself in competition not only with O'Connor and Thompson but also, by 1951, with the fleet of Norwegian boats which was systematically scouring the Minch much to the satisfaction of the Stornaway herring fishermen who viewed the basking shark as a pest.

The Norwegian competition forced Geddes to consider the scale of his operation: to compete he needed a larger, faster boat than the *Traveller*, but such a vessel would need more than two for a crew and labour costs would consequently increase noticeably. The answer was to give the *Traveller* a larger engine but the 1952 season got away to a slow start as a new propeller and shaft proved difficult to obtain. 1952 was again a season of competion with the Norwegians in the Minch and in spite of being much smaller than any of the Norwegian vessels the *Traveller* performed creditably with its new engine. A precipitate drop in the ever volatile oil prices determined that 1952 would be the last season for Geddes – £48 per ton for the raw liver suddenly became only £25 and within a couple of weeks, £15.[58]

P.F. O'Connor

Three years younger than Gavin Maxwell, like him P. Fitzgerald O'Connor inclined to the independent life-style promised by island living in the Inner Hebrides and had farmed on Coll for some years after war service in the Highland Light Infantry. He was persuaded to join Thompson and Langford in a shark-fishing scheme, bringing his own boat, the 36-foot *Cornaig Venture*. (Fig. 26) In their first season, 1950, they worked the Minch, cutting out livers on any convenient beach and sending the barrelled liver pieces to a factory in Falkirk.[59] This first, somewhat experimental season convinced them, just as Geddes had become convinced, that if a shark-fishing enterprise was to succeed, it should remain small-scale. 'Cut down handling, have good equipment, use a

Fig. 27. Harpooning a fairly small shark from P. F. O'Connor's *Cornaig Venture* in the early 1950s. The harpoon line is taut through a fairlead as the shark is winched in with the crew readying a sling to be thrown over the tail of the fish. The gun appears to be a modified anti-tank type. (O'Connor (1953))

mobile factory', could be taken as O'Connor's motto.[60] The 'factory' element
shows that unlike Geddes he intended to convert the livers into oil at sea, but
compared to Watkins with his factory ship, *Recruit*, O'Connor envisaged only a
floating processing barge towed to the operating area.[61] In preparation for the
1951 season, which was to be his last, O'Connor attempted to get outside capital
to augment his £5000. He had *Cornaig Venture* refitted, engaged a crew (J.B.
Cunningham and two others), acquired a gun and harpoons and bought a 26-
foot metal life-boat, the *Minnie*, which he fitted with a boiler and rendering
tanks, as his factory barge.[62] For the early summer, the island of Coll was
O'Connor's base with the *Minnie* moored in Arinagour Bay while he fished in
the Sea of the Hebrides. In June he shifted operations to the Little Minch and
the Minch and did the liver extraction with *Minnie* moored in a harbour on the
southern side of Scalpay. It was in the Minch that O'Connor first came across
the Norwegian shark boats and in spite of numerous requests for assistance to
the Ministry of Agriculture and Fisheries and the fishery protection squadron,
and considerable press publicity, it proved impossible to dislodge the interlopers
from territorial waters.[63]

Norwegian Shark Catchers

The Norwegian excursions into Scottish waters are not well documented, but it
is thought Norwegian shark catchers first came to the Shetlands in some
numbers immediately post-war and continued to fish to the west of Shetland
right through the 1950s and for some decades beyond that.[64] (Fig. 27) It would
have been vessels of this fleet that spead their activities to the Minch. They
engaged in line-fishing for porbeagle sharks as well as harpooning the basking
shark. Some extended their activities to the harpooning of small whales.
O'Connor describes the Norwegians as being very efficient. With the advantage
of having lookouts in the crowsnests of their vessels, they were systematically
scouring the Minch and apparently catching three or four sharks per hour.[65]
The Norwegian presence was to lead to an important innovation in harpoon
type in the Scottish basking shark fishery.

The Mallaig Group

As far as is known the last 1950s group to exploit the basking shark in the
West consisted of four professional fishermen from Mallaig, the fishing port
and railway terminus on the Sound of Sleat. James Manson, known as 'Black
Jim' or 'The Gannet' among the fishing community, was the acknowledged
leader of the group which also included his half-brother William Manson,
their brother-in-law William Sutherland, and Peter McLean.[66] They were
looking for a profitable sideline to their usual ring-net herring fishing during

Fig. 28. Norwegian shark-catchers at Lerwick, Shetland, late 1940s. These vessels are of a standardised design with their distinctive crowsnest for the shark spotter. The Kongsberg Vapenfabrikk guns, each loaded with a harpoon, are conspicuous. What appears to be a harpoon line running in the accumulator through a block slung from the mast is can be seen on H 13 V to the right. The black band on the crowsnest reputedly signified a boat licensed to take small whales as well as basking sharks. (Courtesy Shetland Museum, Lerwick)

a lean season and were stimulated to try basking shark hunting by the example of the Norwegians and by seeing Tex Geddes operating near them.

Impressed by the superiority of Norwegian techniques, they fitted Kongsberg harpoon guns to their four boats: the *Margaret Ann* (J. Manson), the *Mary Manson* (W. Manson), the *Jessie Alice* (W. Sutherland) and the *Golden Ray* (Peter McLean). For three seasons they pursued the basking shark in the Minch, the Sound of Harris and Loch Gairloch, continuing to fish for herring as well. A good day for the Manson group meant a catch of some fifteen sharks, when the livers were extracted and the carcasses abandoned; on a poor day with a small catch, the carcasses were kept after liver extraction and sent to Falkirk for processing into fish meal. At this time the shark carcass was worth £60 and the livers, £15 per ton. In their first year, 1951, they followed the usual practice of towing the sharks to a convenient shore, in this case Loch Maddy, South Uist, and butchering them on a beach. They then changed to cutting out the livers at sea to save time, and even tried rendering at sea, using a boiler bought from P.F. O'Connor. This was found to be impractical and the Mansons reverted to the practice of bringing the unprocessed livers back to the Mallaig railhead. Looking back to that period, William Manson admitted that their shark hunting efforts were never really profitable; and that it was more the anticipation of rewards rather than the actual returns which kept them going. In the 1952 season he operated alone for some months when the other boats trawled for white fish (i.e. not herring). His efforts did not pay, with the expenditure on harpoons, powder and tackle outweighing the return from shark livers.

Shetland

In 1952 in Scalloway, Shetland, father and son, Archibald and John Fullerton, who operated a 40-foot seine-net boat, the *Britannia*, took note of Norwegian success in what seems to have been an exceptional season for basking shark numbers around the islands and decided to try hunting the shark for themselves. They bought a Kongsberg gun and were able to catch twenty sharks in the summer of 1953, but they too stopped when they found that the price for the livers would do no more than cover their expenses.[67]

The downward trend of basking shark liver oil prices, which probably reflected the effect of abundant oil from the resurgent Antarctic whaling operations, brought about the end of the 1950s fishery. It is possible that the Norwegian incursion had depleted the numbers of basking sharks, but there is no clear evidence for this and it does not seem likely that Norwegian competition, unwelcome as it was, had any significant effect. Later in the decade, there were occasional references to the basking shark, suggesting that there was some rather desultory official interest in promoting a renewed fishery, and later still the biologist F.C. Stott wrote articles for *Fishing News* analysing Norwegian, Irish and French shark hunting with the aim of stimulating commercial interest in the fish in Britain. Nevertheless, it appears that Scottish fishermen, no doubt well aware of the real pitfalls of trying to get a consistent living from the basking shark, remained uninterested and it seems that the sharks were left alone until the 1980s.[68]

THE RENEWED CLYDE FISHERY

It is interesting that at no time during the 1950s had there been any whisper of criticism of the hunt for the basking shark. Capture of the fish provoked no public outrage. But when the basking shark was again hunted in Scotland thirty years later the fishery was conducted in the shadow of increasing public interest in marine conservation issues. In 1982 Howard McCrindle began a small operation which was to last just over a decade. This was dogged by controversy from the very beginning and the struggle between shark-fisher and conservationist must inevitably colour any assessment of it. McCrindle, who was then based at Girvan, Ayrshire, began fishing the basking shark system-atically in the Clyde and the northern part of the Irish Sea in the *Franleon*, a 65-ft Peterhead-built seiner, as a summer alternative to prawning.[69] (Fig. 28) His interest in the basking shark had, however, been sparked earlier, in the winter of 1978-1979, when he was carrying out mid-water trawling in deep water to the north of Arran for the first time. There he found his efforts 'plagued by basking sharks' in the net – some of them lively, others torpid. Of these, four were caught and processed. For the summer of 1982 he tried a locally-made hand harpoon before obtaining a Kongsberg gun from an Irish source, and one shark was caught on 1st August. In 1983, in the *Franleon II*, a 48-ft MacDuff boat, he continued with the Kongsberg gun and imported Norwegian 'pencil' harpoons and in 47 days fishing caught 122 sharks to make a very successful season.

McCrindle set a self-imposed limit, deciding that a 6-metre (20-ft) shark was to be the smallest size he would harpoon. This nod in the direction of the conservationists and animal welfare groups did not save him from threats to his life and property, as later in the year he received an anonymous telephone call that his home would be petrol-bombed, and an underwater saboteur attempted to disable his trawler by drilling holes through the hull.

Ninety-two sharks were taken in 1984 and 40 in 1985. The 1986 season, a short one with only 14 days of fishing, was his poorest one up until that time, but even so, 38 sharks were killed.[70] In 1987, plankton was sparse (a circum-stance attributed to radioactive fall-out from the 1986 Chernobyl disaster) and only one shark was caught. His shark hunting continued in tandem with his prawn fishing in a variety of boats: the *Girl Avril* in 1988 (15 sharks taken), the *De Aston* in 1989, the *Delvan* in 1990, and the *Star of David*, a 50-ft Campbel-town boat, in 1991 and 1992. Twenty sharks were taken in 1988 to 1990, one in 1991 and nine in 1992.[71] There was no shark fishing in 1993 when the *Star of David* was decommissioned under a government scheme, but to the fury of conservationists, who were vocal in the press, McCrindle had another successful season in 1994 in a new boat, the *Provider*, a 50-ft Eyemouth trawler, with nine sharks taken.[72] McCrindle has not fished the basking shark since, and, with efforts to totally protect the basking shark on the brink of success, he may achieve a place in fishing history as the last Scottish basking shark hunter.

The physical remains of the Soay venture testify to the scale of failure caused by unrealistic levels of investment in a highly uncertain enterprise, and in retrospect it is clear that those who hunted the shark with minimum capital investment in their vessels and gear, with small crews and hence low labour

Fig. 29.   Howard McCrindle in shark-hunter pose at the bow of the *Star of David* in 1992. The gun is a Kongsberg Vapenfabrikk 50mm: a larger calibre than the earlier types, and protruding from it is a 'pencil' harpoon (brugdespyd) of the type with two holes. The trace attaching the harpoon to the coiled line hangs from the gun. (Photograph, J. McLean (*Scotland on Sunday*) 12 Jul 1992)

costs, and with the flexibility to take on other forms of fishing, have done the best in a fishery that for all operators was notoriously unpredictable in its rewards. They also optimised their efforts by concentrating only on raw livers, avoiding the complications of processing. In the gear used, especially the guns and harpoons, the modern fishery was unique within the wider sphere of fishing in Scotland, and this gives it a significance beyond its relative economic unimportance.[73]

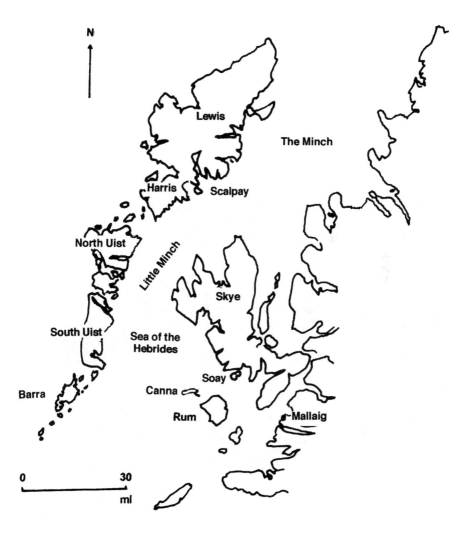

Map 4. The Sea of the Hebrides & the Minch.

Notes

1. The earlier title was *Annals of Scottish Natural History*. For basking shark references see Taylor (1900).
2. Scotland – Fishery Board (1900): 291
3. Scotland -Fishery Board (1922): 18.
4. *GH* 13 July 1937: 9d.
5. *GH* 25 Sept 1937: 10 & 27 Sep 1937: 11
6. PD (HC) vol 337, 1937-38: 1928.
7. PD (HC) vol 347, 1938-9: 2088 & 2089 & *GH* 24 May 1939: 7.
8. PD (HC) vol 348, 1938-9: 180-181.
9. This account of Watkins' fishery is based almost entirely on his own book – Watkins (1958).
10. Quotation -Watkins (1958): 55; *GH*, 20 Sept 1937: 11e & 12.
11. Watkins (1952): 96-98.
12. Watkins (1952): 98.
13. The company was incorporated at Edinburgh on 11 June 1938 and the name was changed to 'Scottish West Coast Fisheries' on 11 April 1946. It ceased business in 1952 (SRO BT 2/20465). For table of costs – Watkins (1952): 99. For Memorandum of Association see SRO BT 2/20465 or extract in Fairfax (1995): 72-73.
14. *Dusky Maid* – Olsen's (1940): 504, (1948): 501 & (1950): 506
15. Paterson – Watkins (1958): 120.
16. Watkins (1958): 152.
17. Watkins (1958): 169 and 'Special Resolutions' of 11 April 1946 (SRO BT2/20465).
18. *Gloamin'*- Olsen's (1940): 517; *Recruit* – Olsen's (1950): 568; *Perseverance* – Anon (1995b).
19. A. Paterson *pers. comm.* 1995.
20. Watkins (1958): 175-177.
21. Watkins (1958): 167.
22. Watkins (1958): 233 & 235.
23. Watkins (1958): 239.
24. The rear of the dust-jacket of Watkins, *Hunting Ground*, states, 'He sold his fishing interests in 1950' but he wrote to the Companies Registration Office in 1953 *re* Scottish West Coast Fisheries Ltd: 'not now carrying on his business, the last of its assets having been disposed of last year [1952]' (SRO BT2/20465).
25. Minute of 30 Oct 1948 (HKIS1); G.L. Norris letter of 22 Jan 1948 (HKIS2); Watkins to Norris 2 Sept 1948 (HKIS2) & Ireland – O'Connor (1953): 27.
26. Angus Paterson *pers. comm.* 1995
27. G. Maxwell 27 & 28 Nov 1956 (HKIS5).
28. Minute of 12 July 1947 (HKIS1); Maxwell v. O'Connor 28 Nov 1956 (HKIS5).
29. This section is based upon Gavin Maxwell's own account – Maxwell (1952) and the biography of Maxwell by his friend Douglas Botting -Botting (1993).
30. Maxwell(1952): 19 & 24.
31. Botting (1993): 74.
32. Botting (1993): 74.
33. T. Geddes *pers. comm.* 1995

34. Maxwell (1952): 39, 40, 42.
35. Botting (1993): 85. *Sea Leopard* – Olsen's (1948): 565 & (1950): 578.
36. Botting (1993): 81.
37. Botting (1993): 85
38. Quotation – Botting (1993): 90 & 85.
39. SRO BT2/25375 or extract in Fairfax (1995): 74-75.
40. Botting (1993): 100.
41. Maxwell report 12 July 1947 (HKIS1.).
42. Minutes 12 July 1947 (HKIS 1).
43. Minutes 21 Feb 1948 (HKIS 1).
44. Botting (1994): 105.
45. R. Findlay letter to H. Thompson 9 August 1949 (HKIS3).
46. Maxwell (1952): 216-228.
47. G.L. Norris to Maxwell 2 July 1952.(HKIS 5).
48. Maxwell letter to Norris 12 July 1952 (HKIS 5).
49. *T* 27 Nov 1956: 5f & 13 Dec 1956: 2f.
50. This section is based on Geddes (1960), O'Connor (1953) and discussions with J. 'Tex' Geddes of Soay and William Manson of Mallaig.
51. Maxwell (1952): 227.
52. O'Connor (1953): 23–25.
53. Geddes (1960): 33-34; & Hutchinson (1998) (Obit.).
54. Geddes (1960): 34.
55. Geddes (1960): 33-36
56. Minutes 10 Nov 1952 (SRO BT2/25375); & MacDonald (1992): 21-25.
57. Geddes (1960): 55-57.
58. Geddes (1960): 133 & 155.
59. O'Connor (1953): 29.
60. O'Connor (1953): 41.
61. O'Connor (1953): 29 & 42.
62. O'Connor (1953): 83.
63. O'Connor (1953): 178.
64. Berry & Johnston (1980): 93; & Goodlad (1971): 32.
65. O'Connor (1953): 234-235.
66. This section is derived almost entirely from the recollections of William Manson of Mallaig, and thus all detail is W. Manson *pers. comm.* 1995. For anecdotes of the group, especially J. Manson, see Ralston (1995): 70-75.
67. Nicolson (1992).
68. Rae (1956); Stott (1967 & 1974).
69. Cramb A. (1987). This section is based principally on discussions with Howard McCrindle *pers. comm.* 1995, 1997, 1998.
70. Cramb (1987).
71. McLean (1992).
72. Hancox (1994).
73. The basking shark fishery was generally ignored in official reports. See *Report on the Fisheries of Scotland 1939–1948* (1949), Edinburgh, HMSO, which does not mention the basking shark, even though Watkins, Maxwell and O'Connor were actively fishing it at the time.

Chapter Six

Harpoons and Guns

IN RETROSPECT, it seems rather odd that hand-darted harpoons were used at
the beginning of the modern basking shark fishery, even if such an anachro-
nistic technique was in the main limited to the first, experimental, stage of the
Carradale and Soay operations. Both Watkins and Maxwell were surely well
aware of the existence of gun-fired harpoons in whaling, so their use of hand
harpooning merely indicates that both men were at first spurred by curiosity.
They wanted samples from the carcasses to send away for chemical analysis and
commercial assessment and with this as the sole aim the tedious procedure of
hand-harpooning was of no particular moment. Both men were independently
investigating the possibilities of a commercial fishery (Maxwell in 1944
apparently unaware of Watkins' 1930s work) and their initial grasp of the
detailed requirements of such an undertaking was decidedly incomplete.

HAND-DARTED HARPOONS

The harpoons they used were of two types. In 1937 Watkins bought two toggle
(swivelling-barb) harpoons from a London firm for £2. 10s. each, and had ash
shafts made for them (0.9 metre harpoons with 1.83 metre shafts). Finding that
they were unbalanced when he first used them, he hollowed out the shafts for half
their length and filled them with lead shot.[1] (Fig. 29A) Later, in 1944, Maxwell
began with a double-shanked gun harpoon ('the old type of whaling harpoon')
which he lashed to a boathook.[2] For the 1945 season he changed to a toggle
harpoon forged by a Mallaig blacksmith and had the barb made 'flattened and
slightly "scooped" ', claiming to have invented this type, although it was in fact
just a variety of the toggle harpoon which had been used in whaling since at least
the 1840s. The toggle harpoon has a head with a simple point and rear barb,
which swivels on the shank. Initially, the head is kept lying parallel with the shank
by a wooden peg which plugs holes drilled through the rear of the head and
through the shank. After the harpoon pierces the fish, the strain on the line causes
the peg to shear and the swivelling head turns at a right angle to the shank, thus
giving greater holding power as the shark struggles.[3]

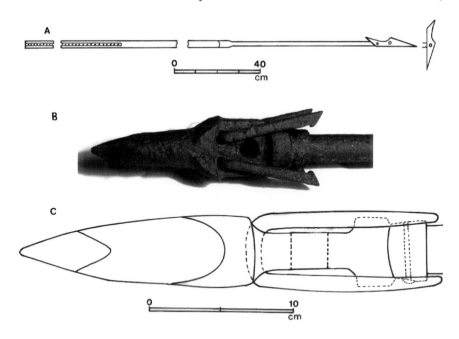

Fig. 30. Harpoons I. **A.** Hand-darted toggle harpoon used by Anthony Watkins 1937. Length 2.7 metres; rear half of ash shaft filled with lead shot to balance the harpoon (Watkins (1958): 9, 10 & opp. 58). **B.** Head of A. Watkins forged steel 'Carradale-type' harpoon. Overall length = 111.2 cm. **C.** Diagram of the same head. (**B** & **C** harpoon presented by N. McDougall, Carradale, in Campbeltown Museum & courtesy A. Martin. Photograph, B. J. Fairfax)

In his trials in the Clyde in the *Myrtle* in September 1937, Watkins used his toggle harpoon with 439 metres of manila line (5 centimetre 4-strand manila in 2 coils of 120 fathoms), attached to the harpoon by a looped 'foreganger'. The length of the line had been calculated to allow the stricken shark to sound and touch bottom.[4] In spite of a successful strike the first shark escaped as the harpoon pulled free after the *Myrtle* had been towed for several hours. Thinking that the mass of the *Myrtle* had put too much strain on the line, Watkins' solution was to try harpooning from an eight-foot dinghy in the belief that a lighter boat would lessen the strain. In the event the first strike from the dinghy was immediately followed by a fouled line and the boat was pulled under. It was later recovered but in the process the harpoon pulled out of the shark. At the second attempt the dinghy was towed out into the Atlantic. A third attempt, using a line with three buoys, ended successfully but not until after the usual hours-long tow had exhausted the fish.

Maxwell had similar experiences with his hand harpoons. The gun-harpoon which he had lashed to a boathook was discarded after it pulled out when the shark dived and rolled on it. Seeking more length to allow the toggle harpoon to be thrust deeper into the shark, he fitted it into one end of a 4.5 metre steel tube, which formed a detachable shaft which would remain in the harpooner's hands. When they first used this type, Maxwell decided to join two harpoons by a Y-shaped wire trace so that they could be jabbed in vertically, simultaneously. The results were mixed, however: the harpoons came away from the steel shafts satisfactorily, but after several hours of playing the shark one harpoon snapped and the other pulled out.[5] Such were the limitations of hand-harpooning and this technique was soon abandoned.

Any method of capturing the basking shark has to take account of its behaviour when struck by a harpoon. After a short flurry at the surface, propelled by great sweeps of the tail, it sounds, rolls on the sea bed, if possible, to rid itself of the intrusive weapon and, if that manoeuvre fails, swims at some depth seemingly with inexhaustible stamina, towing its captor's vessel behind it. To counter this, harpoons need to have substantial barbs and the strain on the line has to be taken up by a powerful winch so that the shark's resistance can be progressively overcome. Harpooning by hand – 'hand-darting'-, is particularly difficult because of the need to get above the shark so that the harpoon can be driven home from a vertical position, otherwise it is unlikely to go deeply enough to hold. In practice this means that hand-harpooning is only likely to succeed in very calm conditions.

THE KONGSBERG GUN AND OTHER TYPES

Watkins ordered a harpoon gun as soon as he had formulated his intial concept of the Carradale operation. The gun he chose was a small (37 millimetre) weapon made by Kongsberg Vapenfabrikk, a major Norwegian manufacturer of whaling guns.[6] The gun itself, breech-loading for the charge and with a recoil action, cost £90 and by the time a set of twelve 17lb twin-barbed harpoons and the required ammunition were added, together with freight charges and import duty, the total cost was double this. The Kongsberg gun was mounted on a four-legged stand placed well forward in the bow of the *Dusky Maid,* bolted through the deck timbers with an extra cross-beam fitted underneath the rear legs to give additional strength.[7] A 4-inch (10 centimetre) manila line was attached to the harpoon by a short wire loop – the 'trace' – but it was soon found that a line of this weight directly connected to the harpoon caused it to deflect when it hit the water (the shark's dorsal surface was about two feet below) so other sizes of line were tried. After experiments with 3½, 3, 2½ and 2-inch manila lines (all 120 fathoms long) Watkins in time established that the

2½-inch (6.4 centimetre) line both allowed the harpoon to strike accurately and, used with a winch, was strong enough to hold the shark. When the fish was finally subdued it was lashed to the samson-post by a 4-inch (10 centimetre) manila rope around its tail. Also, Watkins found that deflection was less of a problem after he had learned to fire only when the fin was at least half-exposed.[8]

The Kongsberg harpoons were found to be satisfactory. Unlike the earlier hand-darted harpoons, their expanding 15-centimetre barbs ensured that they did not pull out and, indeed, they often proved difficult to remove from the carcass as they were so deeply buried. The velocity of the strike was such that the harpoon was known to go right through the fish on occasion.[9]

Modified Anti-tank Guns
When Watkins returned to shark-fishing in 1946 he was unable to use his Kongsberg gun as its ammunition and harpoons had disappeared. The factory's inability to supply replacements until the end of the summer led to his choice, as a temporary expedient, of several Army-surplus two-pounder anti-tank guns. These were of similar bore to the Kongsberg gun and were modified by having the barrels shortened and the mountings altered.[10] Iron harpoon heads cast in Greenock were used with wooden shafts that had been strengthened with a metal base. The wooden shafts proved to be unsatisfactory as even with the metal reinforcement they kept splintering and so Watkins tried various metal shafts, finally achieving an all-metal harpoon with an increased range 'infinitely superior to the original Norwegian ones I had used before the war'. The harpoon would penetrate a shark so far under the water that the harpooner could 'only just see it' and it usually bored right through a fish that was higher up in the water.[11] It is probable that the harpoon with quadruple barbs in the Campbeltown museum is an example of this type. (Fig. 30 B & C)

In his early search for a suitable harpoon gun, Gavin Maxwell does not seem to have considered the products of Kongsberg Vapenfabrikk, perhaps because he knew they would be unobtainable in 1945. His first gun was constructed by a private gun-maker (probably H. Leyton Greener, a director of the W.W. Greener firm of Birmingham) around a 20 millimetre Oerlikon barrel and was mounted on a steel tripod with a circular base. (Fig. 31) It came supplied with a hollow tubular harpoon which fitted over the barrel. Maxwell was sceptical of this type of harpoon, 'barbless and to my mind innocuous', which, in its operating principle, was the same as the Norwegian 'pencil harpoon' used later in Mallaig by the Manson brothers and also by McCrindle.[12] The trials with the new gun were unsuccessful possibly because the charge was too small and thus the muzzle velocity was too low to fire the harpoon with sufficient force to stop it deflecting when it hit the water (in the words of Maxwell's gunner, Tex

Fig. 31.   Harpoon gun. Modified Oerlikon type used in the Soay fishery before the Greener guns. The hollow harpoon fitted over the barrel. (Courtesy D. Botting)

Fig. 32.   Greener harpoon gun. Gavin Maxwell (left) and T. Geddes adjusting the firing mechanism. The 'seal's-tail' stock has been cut down to take a bicycle grip Bowden triggering device and the brass casing over the powder nipples can be seen by Maxwell's fingers. The gun sits in a steel crutch passing through the sloping plate of the armourplate steel gun mounting. An early form of the 'Soay-type' harpoon is loaded. A wire trace looped through the base of the harpoon connects it to the heavy harpoon line. The barbs of the harpoon are tied together, and to the gun sight, with light cord. This both kept the harpoon from falling out of the barrel when the gun was depressed and, after firing, kept the harpoon head compact until it entered the shark. When strain came on the harpoon line, the cord snapped and the barbs expanded. The vanes on this type of harpoon were found to deflect it under water and were cut off. (Hulton Getty Picture Collection)

Geddes: 'Useless – no puff!') and Maxwell reverted to the hand-darted harpoons previously described.[13] The bow of the *Dove* was so high (10 feet) that it was difficult to get an accurate aim, but with this gun transferred to the much smaller *Gannet* and with new double-barbed harpoons supplied by the Greener company several successful kills were made by the time the experimental 1945 season had finished.[14]

THE GREENER GUN AND HARPOONS

For the 1946 season, Maxwell persisted with the Oerlikon gun which he took off the *Gannet* and fitted to his new catcher, the *Sea Leopard*, obtaining an old-style muzzle-loading whaling gun from W.W. Greener for the *Gannet*.[15] The Greener gun, of a classic design which would have been quite familiar to an early-nineteenth century Arctic whaler, was to become the standard type of gun for the remainder of the Soay fishery, and after that was also used by Tex Geddes. Two of these Greener guns still exist, but with steel stocks with oval grips and a Martini-Henry action rather than the original 'seal-tail' wooden stocks with cap and hammer action and brass cover-plate as they were originally supplied. Each is 1.3 metres long, of which 99.5 centimetres is the steel barrel which has a bore of 4.3 centimetres. (Fig. 33) To align the gun more easily and speedily, Maxwell had the stock of the first Greener modified to take a pair of motorcycle handlebars with a Bowden clutch-grip trigger release.[16] (Fig. 32)

The harpoon heads, of mild steel and with four expanding barbs, also made by the Greener company, were the same for both guns. However, while the harpoon shaft for use with the Oerlikon was still a steel tube fitting over its barrel, the shafts to be used with the Greener gun were substantial rods turned from hickory and reinforced with metal bands, with a socket to accommodate the loose-fitting separate harpoon head.[17] Maxwell claimed that this four-barbed harpoon head was of his own design – 'harpoons made this time specifically and undeviatingly to my own drawings' – but it was just a refinement of the two-barbed expanding design supplied from the Greener factory.[18] In its earliest form the head of this type of harpoon bore four flanges in front of the expanding barbs. These flanges, however, were soon sawn off when it was found they deflected the harpoon under water, and if they did strike, such a large hole was made that the harpoon pulled out.[19] (Fig. 35) To load the Greener gun a measured charge of black powder was poured down the barrel, two felt wads (Fig. 34A) were rammed home and the socketed harpoon shaft followed, sticking slightly out of the muzzle where the harpoon head was slotted into it. The harpoon barbs were tied together with string and similarly, the head itself was usually tied to the gun barrel to stop it sliding out before firing.

Basking Shark

Fig. 33. Composite photograph of 'Sugan', the Greener harpoon gun used by J. T. Geddes. It has the Martini-Henry firing mechanism and a loop-type steel stock which replaced the original cap nipples under a brass cover and the wooden 'seal-tail' stock. Overall length = 1.3 m. Length of barrel = 99.5 cm. Bore 4.3 cm. (Courtesy J. T. Geddes, Soay)

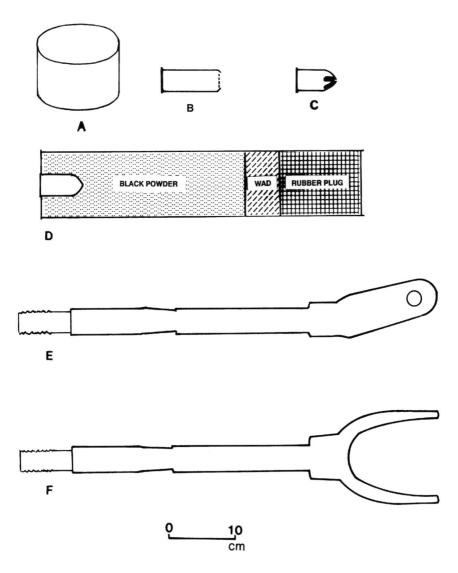

Fig. 34. **A.** Wad used in Greener harpoon gun. 4 cm diameter. **B.** .38 cal. blank cartridge used in the Martini action of Greener harpoon gun. 2.9 cm long. **C.** .38 cal. cartridge used to fire Mallaig group's Kongsberg guns. 2 cm long. **D.** Diagram of brass cartridge used in Mallaig Kongsberg guns with .38 blank in position. Not to scale. **E & F.** Steel crutch used for Greener harpoon gun in the *Sea Leopard* and the *Traveller.* (**A, B, E & F** courtesy J. T. Geddes, Soay. **C & D** courtesy W. Manson, Mallaig)

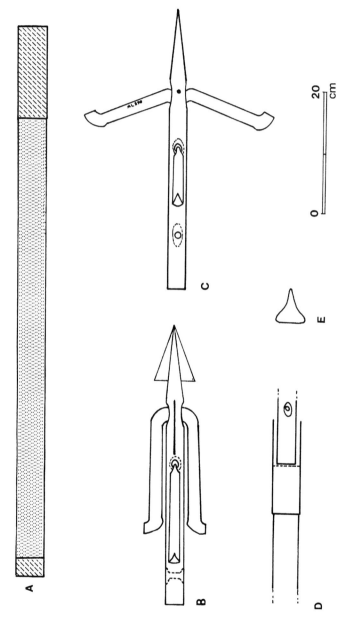

Fig. 35. Harpoons 2. **A**. Harpoon shaft of turned hickory reinforced with a steel ring at each end for 'Soay-type' harpoons. **B**. Early Soay-type – continuous head and shank with quadruple swivelling barbs, forward barbs apparently longer than rear ones. Two vanes on head and two (at right angle) behind. **C**. Later Soay-type – as for type **A** but without vanes, just pointed head. Barbs of equal length. **D**. Shank of a Soay-type harpoon sloting into hickory shaft. **E**. Cross-section of barb of Soay- and Mallaig-type harpoons. Each nickel-chromium barb has the inscription 'M L 270' cast on it. (ML probably stands for 'muzzle loading' in Greener factory number). (**A** ANSFM 1995/216/5 & **C** ANSFM 1995/216/1 in Scottish Fisheries Museum, presented by J. T. Geddes. All to scale indicated except **B** & **E**. **B** drawn from a photograph but probably of similar size to **C**. **E** cross section = 2 cm.)

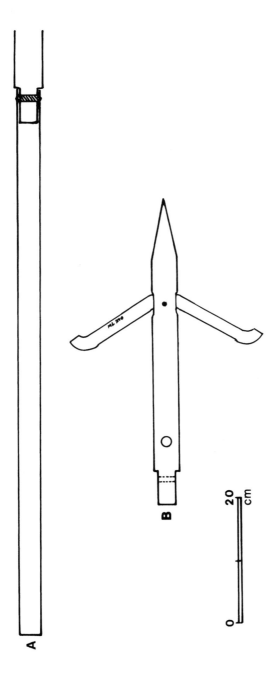

Fig. 36. Harpoons 3. **A**. Shaft for 'Mallaig-type' harpoon – a hollow steel tube with harpoon shank fixed in the open end by a steel pin. **B**. 'Mallaig-type' harpoon. Similar to 'Soay-type' with continuous head and shank but with hole for steel pin in shank and twin swivelling barbs only. (Courtesy Mallaig Heritage Centre)

In May 1946, even with the new Greener gun and new harpoons, the early operations of the season were dogged by failure. The Greener kept misfiring, the harpoons fired by the Oerlikon in the *Sea Leopard* continued to be deflected when they hit the water and when the harpoons were hand-darted, the barbs bent backwards and pulled out as the steel of which they were made was apparently too soft to hold its shape under strain. The Oerlikon-type gun and the tubular harpoons were abandoned, and, in late 1946, a second Greener gun was bought for the *Sea Leopard*.[20] The harpoon barbs described as 'folding back like the ribs of an umbrella' were replaced by tough cast nickel-chromium steel ones.[21] Given the working conditions, damp powder was often the reason for the Greener misfires and in the *Sea Leopard*, a measured powder charge was kept dry and ready for use in a warm space above the galley. The guns were proofed for seven drams of powder. The misfires which had crippled the harpooners' efforts for two seasons were eventually ended by converting the Greener firing mechanism from one using two percussion caps struck by a hammer to a Martini-Henry action in which a .38 blank cartridge was the detonator. The old curved 'seal's tail' wooden stock was replaced by new steel stock with a large end-loop as a grip.[22]

It is not clear exactly what type of gun O'Connor used initially but there are some clues that it could have been a remodelled anti-tank gun fitted with a recoil action and a handlebar grip firing mechanism, and mounted on a heavy iron tripod. The harpoon appears to have been of the double-barbed Mallaig type.[23] Later, O'Connor obtained Kongsberg guns of 40 millimetre bore.

Geddes continued to use the Greener guns as described above with the hickory metal-reinforced harpoon shafts and the quadruple barbed harpoon heads. One of his surviving guns 'Sugan' is shown in Figure 33. The gun was supported in a steel crutch (Fig. 34 E & F) and in the *Gannet* with its 3-foot high bow, the gun in its crutch was positioned just above deck level with the crutch passing through a sheet of armour plate lying above the deck timbers. Geddes aimed and fired the gun lying full-length on the deck.[24] In the *Traveller* he used the armour plate gun-mounting first made for the *Sea Leopard*, which still survives on the Soay factory site (Fig. 52D). This mounting was bolted to the strengthened deck timbers through a cut-down lorry tyre which acted as a shock absorber, and was positioned such that its obliquely-placed top plate faced to starboard.

THE 'PENCIL' HARPOON

To set up their operation, the Mallaig group bought two Kongsberg guns from Watkins, and two more, for the Manson brothers themselves, were imported from Norway through the Leith-based whaling company, C. Salvesen. The group also bought some of Watkin's quadruple-barbed 'Carradale-type' harpoons, but these were too heavy, so they lightened them by removing the steel shaft and replacing it with steel tubing butted at the end. Even after this modification they still affected the recoil of the gun. The group also used a form of harpoon with twin expanding barbs, the mild-steel head being riveted to a similar tubular shaft. The head, a slim pointed rod, is identical to the type used by Maxwell and Geddes except that it has only two barbs, not four. Like the barbs of the Soay type these are stamped 'ML 270' which indicates a common origin (the Greener harpoons were supplied with spare barbs). It is thought that William Sutherland bought several of these 'Mallaig-type' harpoons from O'Connor. (Fig. 36)

Impressed by the success of the Norwegian catchers in the Minch, the Mallaig men soon abandoned these barbed harpoons in favour of the barbless Norwegian 'brugdespyd' –which they called a 'pencil' harpoon from its strong resemblance to that object.[25] The distinctive pencil-harpoon, quite different from any barbed harpoon in form and function, originated in Norway as a specific weapon for use with the basking shark. A typical example is a substantial steel shaft about 1 metre long with a prominent groove on each side from the point back to about halfway along its length where there is a hole for the wire trace. There is a usually a second hole very near the point. The two sides of the trace loop lie in the groove when the harpoon is inserted into the gun (Fig. 37).

The operating principle of this type of harpoon is radically different from that of the barbed harpoons which hold the shark by becoming embedded in it. Fired into the shark, the pencil harpoon acts as a giant steel skewer, passing right through the fish and when strain comes on the line, turning at right angles to the trace and so holding the fish. Unlike the barbed types which tended to become hooked in parts of the cartilaginous skeleton and often had to be chopped out, this harpoon is easy to extract. Once the shark is secured, the trace is unshackled from the line and the harpoon is gripped, either right where the trace is attached to it, or by hooking it through the second hole. The harpoon is then pulled away and the trace follows, passing out through the body of the shark.

The surviving Mallaig example, 91.5 centimetres long with only a central hole, is case-hardened steel and is from a batch made by a Sheffield firm.[26] (Fig. 36A) Compared to Norwegian-made harpoons the British ones were found to be unsatisfactory because after one successful shot the harpoon would bend and could not be straightened to be used again. Norwegian examples were made from mild steel and while they also would bend, they could be hammered

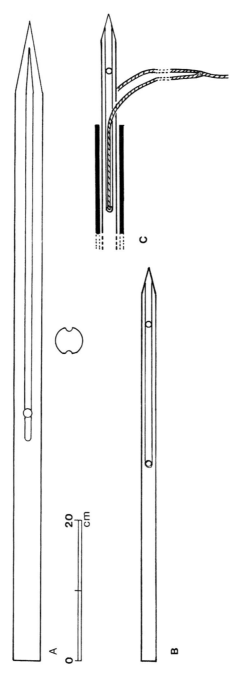

Fig. 37. Harpoons 4 – 'Pencil harpoons' (brugdespyd). **A.** Central hole type used by Mallaig group, with cross-section. **B.** Two-hole type used by H. McCrindle. Not to scale. Length = 1.25 m. **C.** Diagram of pencil harpoon and trace in the gun barrel. (**A** Courtesy D & R McMinn, Mallaig)

straight. A striking example of efficiency of the pencil harpoon is recalled by David McMinn, who was hunting the basking shark in the 1950s with his father-in-law William Sutherland when a large shoal was sighted off Neist Point in northern Skye. When they fired at a shark on the surface the harpoon passed successively right through three of the fish.[27]

The charge for the Kongsberg guns was contained in a brass cartridge case and, as used initially on the Mallaig vessels, was 2 ounces of cordite. Replacement cordite was not easily available and the Mansons replaced it with a 'large spoonful of black powder'. The charge in the cartridge was held in by a wad and a rubber plug and was fired by a .38 calibre blank of a smaller type than that used with the Greener gun[28] (Fig. 34C & D).

Howard McCrindle began in 1983 with a 'home-made' hand-harpoon comprising a steel head with welded-on barbs fixed into a 12-foot length of 1¼-inch pipe by a wooden peg. The trace and line were secured directly to the head through a welded flange. With the harpoon jabbed into the shark from above, the wooden peg broke and the barbed head trailing the 80-fathom line attached to two 40-gallon drums and a dahn buoy went with the plunging fish. A light rope attached to the inner end of the pipe and tied to a cleat on the boat allowed it to be recovered. McCrindle speedily abandoned this technique, adopting a Kongsberg gun but in this case one of a larger calibre, 50 millimetre, apparently manufactured for harpooning Minke whales as well as basking sharks. In each of his boats the bow was strengthened and a steel plate was fitted to take the gun mounting and stanchions. As the gun was fitted with dampeners there was no recoil. The pencil harpoon he used was again a longer type at 1.25 metres, costing £110. (Fig 37B) The charge initially supplied for this gun was 50 grams of explosive in total, necessary for the type of harpoon used to kill Minke whales. A small linen bag contained 10 grams of black powder in its sealed base and 160 in squares of a grey slow-burning Nobel plastic explosive. The charge was held in the brass cartridge with compressed cardboard wadding and a rubber disc and was detonated by a .38 cartridge. The recommended charge for the pencil harpoon was 30 grams (achieved by reducing the numbers of the squares of explosive from 160 to 80) which in practice would not drive the harpoon right through the shark. After some experiment, McCrindle found that 100 squares giving a total charge of 35 grams proved very satisfactory.[29]

Notes

1. Watkins (1958): 10 & 58.
2. Maxwell (1952): 33.
3. Maxwell (1952): 36. For toggle harpoons, see Lytle (1984): 28-29; & Henderson (1972): 38, n5.

4. Watkins (1958): 11.
5. Maxwell(1952): 57-60.
6. Watkins (1958): 102, 108-109 & 143.
7. Modifications to *Dusky Maid* – Watkins (1958): 108-110.
8. Watkins (1958): 133-135 & 140-141.
9. Watkins (1958): 143 & 152.
10. Watkins (1958): 174-175 & 192.
11. Watkins (1958): 176-177 & 191-192.
12. Maxwell (1952): 40 & 52.
13. T. Geddes *pers. comm.* 1995; Maxwell (1952): 52-54 & 57.
14. Maxwell (1952): 73-75 & 85.
15. Maxwell (1952): 89 & 91. For early use see Greener (1910): 514-517; & Singer (1958): 59.
16. Maxwell (1952): 158.
17. Maxwell (1952): 103
18. Maxwell (1952): 89.
19. T.Geddes *pers. comm.* 1997.
20. Maxwell (1952): 102-103.
21. T. Geddes *pers. comm.* 1995.
22. Maxwell (1952): 100, 102-104 & 147.
23. O'Connor (1963): 72 & 77.
24. T. Geddes *pers. comm.* 1995.
25. Myklevoll (1968): 59.
26. In possession of D. & R. McMinn, Mallaig.
27. D. McMinn *pers. comm.* 1997.
28. W. Manson *pers. comm..* 1995.
29. H. McCrindle *pers comm.* 1995.

Chapter Seven

Catching and Processing

THE SIMILARITY in size between a large basking shark and the smallest rorqual, the minke whale, combined with the theme of guns and harpoons in the last chapter may suggest that the pursuit of the basking shark was another form of whale-hunt. The minke, like the shark, is drawn to the plankton of the western Scottish seas in the summer, so both may be found feeding in the same general area at the same time. Moreover, Norwegian catchers operating in the west of Scotland were equipped to take the smaller whales (minke and bottlenose) as well as the basking shark. But in spite of the similar technology of guns and harpoons, there were significant differences between whaling and shark hunting.

The whale, a mammal, must come to the surface at regular intervals to breathe air and the spouts have always betrayed it to pursuers. Even when harpooned and mortally wounded, the whale must still surface to breathe, exposing its body to further harpoon strikes. The shark, having gills, has no such dependency on air and comes near to the surface because it is feeding in the upper plankton layers. The exposure of the massive dorsal fin which gives away its presence is an incidental feature and as the shark continues to swim on constantly changing its distance from the surface the emergence of the fin may be only a fleeting occurrence. Basking shark hunting has always been a very hit-and-miss affair, usually requiring the search of a vast area of sea to find a shoal.

FINDING THE BASKING SHARK

To locate the basking shark, its hunters systematically cruised the sea-lochs and bays known to be the fish's favourite haunts, at the same time trying to question other fishermen and lighthouse keepers about possible shark sightings, an intelligence-gathering process made significantly easier by the introduction of radio. When nearing an area of sea in which he anticipated sighting the shark, the shark-hunter took note of various clues which pointed to concentrations of fish, especially the particular signs that indicated the likely presence of herring. As herring and basking sharks share the same planktonic food, any sign of a likely herring school is a pointer to the possible appearance of basking sharks. One of these signs is an 'oiliness' of the water, indicating a heavy concentration of planktonic animals at the surface. Another sign is the behaviour of diving birds. A gannet dives vertically when feeding on herring but diagonally from a lower height when taking mackerel, so in the right conditions the characteristics of gannet diving were keenly analysed.[1] Experienced herring fishermen had a considerable advantage over those who had not come from a fishing back-ground. James Manson of Mallaig, well-known for his exceptional eyesight and hearing, could see gannets plunging at a great distance, hear herring shoals 'playing' and detect from afar the changes in sea colour which denoted plankton-rich areas.[2] On occasion, the presence of the sharks could even be smelt in a calm sea, as Anthony Watkins recalled:

> [with no sharks visible] "I can smell shark," said Alec . . . I sniffed
> unbelievingly, and immediately I got it, a distinct and quite
> unmistakable whiff of shark. They must be very close, I thought. Water
> acts as a complete barrier to the human nostril. What we were smelling
> was slime from their bodies which must have drifted to the surface and
> come into direct contact with the air.[3]

The sharks were then seen feeding ahead of the *Dusky Maid* and soon broke the surface.

Particular locations thought to be favoured by the basking shark were those where strong tidal streams concentrated the plankton masses, an effect intensified by strong winds. In a southerly wind the Mallaig men would go to the outer headlands of Loch Bracadale and Loch Dunvegan in western Skye, while if the wind was strong from the northeast, they would cross Cuillin Sound to Stac rock (Iorcail?) off Canna.

By the time of Howard McCrindle's operations it was possible to locate basking sharks in the Clyde by echo-sounder down to a depth of 190 metres and late in the season he was catching them in a mid-water trawl, often in deep water to the north of Lochranza. He found that for every two sharks that escaped the net, one was entrapped with its head in the narrow cod-end. They were hauled up, lifted bodily onto the deck and then cut up.[4]

HARPOONING

Even when a shark was seen under water, generally nothing could be done until it rose within a few feet of the surface so that its first dorsal fin appeared and the depth of water over the back of the fish was minimal, thus lessening the chances of harpoon deflection. To seize the brief opportunity before the shark submerged and ensure a successful harpooning, a speedy coordinated action by the crew of the catcher was essential. By the late summer of 1946, as they progressively eliminated the problems with the guns, Maxwell and his men in the *Sea Leopard* had refined a procedure for responding rapidly to a shark sighting before the fins vanished. An alarm buzzer was sounded from the bridge, waking off-watch members of the crew, and within three minutes all would be on deck, the gun would have been fired, and every man was in position for the task of hauling in and securing the shark. Maxwell describes jumping out of his bunk, donning overalls (with boxes of Greener percussion caps in the pockets), running to the gun at the bow, grabbing as he went a harpoon-stick, wads and a dry charge of powder thrust at him from the wheel-house window. Three coils of line with harpoons and traces attached were routinely kept ready for use near the gun.[5]

In the Scottish fishery, the conversion of the various types of fishing boats that were used as shark catchers was an ad-hoc business with few changes made other than the strengthening of the foredeck to take the gun mounting. By contrast, the Norwegian shark catchers seen in Scotland had been designed for the task with many of the features that were standard in the larger whale catchers, notably a crowsnest for the lookout and an elevated platform leading from the bridge to the gun platform. In general, harpooning of the basking shark took place at very close quarters, from 4 to 6 metres – possibly 8 metres was the maximum. The gun therefore had to be in a position to fire downwards at a sharp angle, and to give a clear line of fire it was mounted as far forward as could be managed, right at the bow or close to the gunwale on the starboard side. The alternating appearance and submergence of the shark combined with its erratic course made it a difficult target for the novice harpooner in spite of its slow speed, and there was a period of trial and error for all before regular, successful strikes were made.[6] To keep the vessel aligned on the shark, skilful cooperation, which also had to be learned, was necessary between the helmsman and the harpooner. (Fig. 38) With slight variations, the aiming point for all operators was usually just behind the prominent first dorsal fin – 'you aim for just aft and slightly to one side of the dorsal fin.'[7] (Fig. 39) Tex Geddes tried to get a view of the nose and tail before firing to determine the size of the shark and, firing at an angle of 30 degrees, aimed behind the dorsal fin but low enough to put the harpoon under the vertebrae to save the labour of cutting it out later.[8] The Mallaig men had some initial difficulty at Loch Boisdale in accurately aiming their guns and H. Leyton Greener came up from Birmingham to help them to do this. Trial shots were made at a floating tea-chest resulting in the gunsights being adjusted by raising them a half-inch. Greener also tried to paralyse a basking shark by firing a curare arrow into it from a .303 rifle but this unlikely killing method had no discernible effect on the shark.[9]

Fig. 38. Action on the foredeck of the *Sea Leopard.* Gavin Maxwell at the gun, with Dan McGillivray (looking to the rear) and Tex Geddes (right) ready to throw a coil of harpoon line and a barrel float overboard. (Maxwell (1952))

All accounts of capturing the shark from either the old or the modern fisheries report the same pattern of behaviour by the stricken fish. As soon as the harpoon strikes and strain comes on the line, the shark sounds, diving steeply to the sea bed where it rolls in an attempt to dislodge the harpoon. But as this is seldom succesful, it then swims steadily out into deeper water, in earlier days often towing an open boat for many hours before it tired sufficiently to be hauled close up and lanced to finish it off. In the modern fishery, the existence

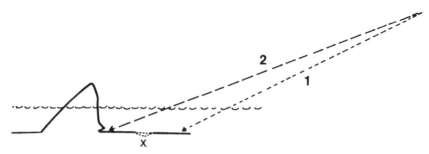

Fig. 39. For all operators the aiming point was just behind the first dorsal fin. H. McCrindle's technique to counter the distortion caused by refraction was to aim at a point about 30 cm behind a white patch (X) commonly found to the rear of the fin. This line of aim (1) gave a resultant line of fire (2) which planted the harpoon just behind the fin. Not to scale.

of the powered winch changed this and considerable mechanical strength rather than human muscular effort was now deployed against the shark. However, even with the equipment of the 1940s and 1950s the strain on the line was considerable and some 'playing' of the fish was usually necessary to overcome its resistance. Like the whale catchers from which their design derived, the Norwegian shark boats were routinely fitted with an 'accumulator' a device like a giant spring which allows the harpoon line to be played without excessive strain on the winch. The Mallaig group made one for their vessels from three large lorry tires lashed together and secured to a thwart at the stern.[10]

As the harpoon line dragged the shark up to the catcher the crew prepared to lassoo the lashing tail. It was then secured by a sling and hauled right out of the water, thus depriving the shark of its motive power. Either a second sling was put around the head, or a rope or 'Grinda-hook' was inserted through the jaw to hold the fish to the side of the vessel.[11] P.F. O'Connor practised stabbing the brain at this point with a lance made from a long knife bolted to a 6-foot pole, but none of the other operators seems to have bothered with this procedure.[12] For lassoing it was important to have a strong line that was also light. Tex Geddes used a loop of stretched seine net rope thrown away by Mallaig fishermen with metal ball-races attached to give some weight to it.

By the end of the 1946 season, Watkins' catching methods had been refined by trial and error such that a basking shark was played for about 15 minutes, compared to an hour or so in 1939, before being winched up to the surface.[13] The Kongsberg harpoon guns with good traversing and elevating qualities also allowed sharks to be taken even in rough weather with 'an average of nine sharks for every ten rounds fired.'[14] Even though the shark usually put up a good struggle as it was hauled up to the boat, aggressive behaviour beyond tail lashing seems to have been very rare. Archie Paterson, at the time a young crewman with Watkins in the Minch, recalls only one instance of atypical behaviour. They had harpooned a large shark which did not sound in the usual way but stayed at the surface with its tail lashing. Then it turned and came back at the boat flailing it with its tail. Lassoing this shark proved so difficult that a second boat had to come alongside to assist with the task.[15]

After much experimentation, Maxwell had evolved a rather different harpooning technique by the middle of the 1946 season which markedly improved his catch rate. The *Sea Leopard* and the *Gannet* would cruise in company searching for a shoal of sharks. To avoid the lost opportunities brought about by the need to haul in and secure each fish as it was caught, each harpooned shark was left dragging a marker buoy so that it could be retrieved later while the catchers went off in pursuit of the other sharks. The buoy was a 40-gallon steel paraffin drum attached to the end of the harpoon line. On the *Sea Leopard*, the

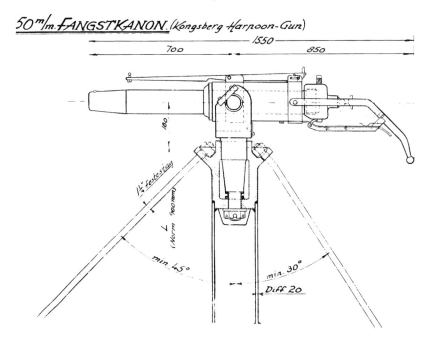

Fig. 40. Kongsberg 50mm harpoon-gun. (Courtesy H. McCrindle)

18-foot (5.48 metres) steel wire trace attached to the harpoon hung down over the side of the boat with the first coil of the harpoon line just below the gun. The remaining coils were tied with light cord to the outside of the starboard railing. As strain came on the line, the cord snapped, the coils of rope paid out and the barrel was thrown overboard. The arrangement in the *Gannet* was slightly different in that the line was coiled in the hold. This method of working with buoys depended on the depth of sea being less than the length of the harpoon line. If the shark went into deeper water, not only did the barrel disappear but a great burst of air coming to the surface showed that the barrel had imploded with the pressure and a shark worth £100 disappeared with £15 worth of gear.[16]

The Mallaig group found that the harpooning operation took about 20 minutes. As the harpoon struck, the boat went 'slow astern' tautening the 3½-inch nylon harpoon line and then quickly 'full astern' to stop the shark swimming. With the accumulator taking the strain, little winching was required. The boat then went 'ahead' to bring the tail of the shark alongside. The tail was lassoed with a wire sling and the rope from this was taken forward and put through the same lead as the harpoon rope so that the tail could be brought to the bow and held there. Going 'slow ahead' brought the shark alongside. The trace was then unshackled from the harpoon line and the harpoon caught up with a sling. As the harpoon was brought on board the 18-foot wire trace followed, being pulled out through the shark's body. The shark's head was gripped with two hooks on either side and the animal turned belly-up, ready for gutting.

Sometimes, in very favourable conditions, many sharks were caught in a very short time. Early one morning in Loch Bracadale, Skye, the crew of the *Mary Manson,* responding to a cry of 'sharks galore' from their cook, harpooned 13 sharks before breakfast. They used 40-gallon drums on 20-fathom lines to buoy many of the sharks, since after shooting three in quick succession, the boat had a shark lashed on either side and one astern.[17]

McCrindle found that if the harpoon missed striking behind the dorsal fin but entered near the head, the shark often reacted by spinning vigorously, rolling the trace and the line around itself 'like a giant yo-yo' such that it crashed against the side of the boat. It then spun away, unravelling the line while leaping out of the water. This violent display did not last long as McCrindle's harpooning technique was to start the winch immediately the gun fired, and within a few minutes the shark was hauled in and hoisted up, the tail was cut off, and the tail-less shark left secured to a dahn buoy for later recovery.[18]

CUTTING OUT THE LIVER

Whether on a beach or at sea, there were fairly standard methods for cutting out the liver of the shark. A typical gutting scene on the beach in front of the Carradale factory shows the liver being cut out, chopped into pieces and the pieces put into barrels. It seems that with the fish on its side the opening of the shark's belly was done by making two vertical cuts, one next to the pectoral fins and the other on the inner side of the pelvic fins, followed by a longitudinal cut along the top side. This gave a large flap which flopped down, allowing the liver lobes to bulge out.[19] (Fig. 41A) Sometimes this was followed in gutting at sea, provided the fish could be turned onto its side and held in that position. This was the method used by the crew of the *Recruit,* but it was more usual to gut the shark at sea with the fish floating on its back. A transverse cut would be made next to the pectoral fins, followed by a longitudinal cut along the middle of the belly from the pectorals to the cloaca. (Fig. 41B) The liver lobes floated out as the eviscerated body of the shark, deprived of its flotation, began to sink. Their internal attachment was cut and the lobes were caught up in a brailer, winched onto the deck and then chopped up. The gutting method varied slightly from one operator to another. Among the Mallaig group, with the tail of the shark

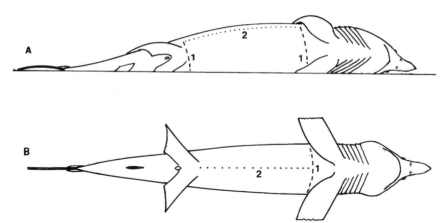

Fig. 41. Opening the belly of the basking shark to extract the liver. **A.** In a fish lying on its side on a beach, a large flap is cut which opens from the top. **B.** A shark at sea, on its back, with a 'T' cut in the ventral surface so that the liver lobes can float out. For both, 1 = first cut(s), 2 = second cut. Not to scale.

held up tightly to the bow and the head secured amidships by hooks, the first transverse cut was made with a 3-metre lance, a modified bayonet blade on a wooden handle. A second tool, with a more easily sharpened scythe blade, was used to make the longitudinal cut. The liver was flipped out of the belly at the tail end and the head was dropped to speed up the release of the lobes. McCrindle made the first transverse cut a deep one to sever the base of the lobes so that they floated out completely free of the carcass.[20]

DISMEMBERING THE CARCASS AT SEA

The Mallaig Group from time would be able to sell shark flesh and if the shark fishing was rather slow it was worthwhile to utilise the carcass as well as the livers. After taking out the liver, the carcass was towed to shallow water, most often in Loch Bracadale and in calm water the tail was heaved to the peak of the boat's derrick. Two sets of hooks were then put into the body as far down as possible and made fast to the stringer. The carcass was now held vertically and it was cut through horizontally so that the upper segment could be lowered onto the deck and dragged aft for cutting-up. The remaining half of the shark, held by the hooks, was in turn heaved up and more hooks were again put further down in the body, nearer the head. Another horizontal slice was made just above the level of the gills and the second segment of the shark was hauled away to the afterdeck. The unwanted third segment, the head and gills, was abandoned and left to sink. (Fig. 42)

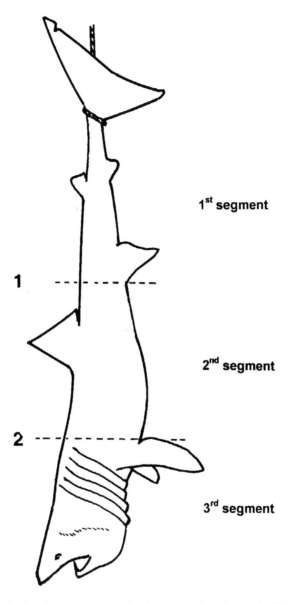

1st segment

2nd segment

3rd segment

Fig. 42. Dismembering the carcass at sea after liver extraction. As practised by the Mallaig group, the shark was progressively hoisted with the derrick and held to the gunwale by hooks. 1 = the first horizontal slicing. 2 = the second slice. The 1st and 2nd segments were cut up into chunks and barrelled; the 3rd segment (head and branchial region) was abandoned. As practised by H. McCrindle, the tail was cut off while the shark was still in the water and then with hooks inserted in the body near the anal fin the shark was hoisted out and dealt with in a similar way to that described.

These large slabs of the shark were cut into pieces that could be easily handled, with an axe being used to chop through the cartilages. The chunks of flesh with skin attached were put straight into 40-gallon drums and taken to Mallaig from where they were railed to Davidson's fishmeal works in Falkirk. For a short time the pancreases were salvaged and preserved with ice in drums and also sent to Davidson's.[21]

Howard McCrindle dismembered the carcasses at sea in a very similar manner to the Mallaig group but before the head was discarded the pectoral fins were cut off. If the flesh was not required, the shark was left in the water and slicing off the dorsal and pectoral fins was done from a rubber dinghy with the shark being turned as necessary by rope loops.[22]

FACTORY VESSELS

Shark-hunters such as Geddes and the Mallaig group, who kept their operation simple by going no further than barrelling raw liver, could cut out livers on a convenient beach or at sea. Their choice depended on the size of their vessels, where they were working, and the nearness of a railhead from which barrelled liver could be sent to the buyer. As noted earlier, the Mallaig group began by cutting out the livers on beaches but soon changed to cutting out at sea. Rendering the livers on board one boat for a brief period was found to be impractical and was quickly discontinued. The others who aspired to processing oil from the livers (Watkins, Maxwell and O'Connor) were faced with either having to have suitable shore facilities and a staff to run them, or, to avoid the necessity of bringing shark carcasses or livers back long distances, equipping floating factories like the whaling factory ships.

Very early in their respective schemes Watkins and Maxwell had built land-based processing plants, but in time both men became converted to the idea of a factory ship. In late 1945 considering the Carradale factory to be too far from the fishing area in the Minch, Watkins had the *Gloamin'* fitted with a wooden gutting deck and a steam liver-processing plant. He found, however, that although steam extraction of the oil worked well, lifting the sharks on board the vessel and getting the gutted carcasses off was too hazardous in rough weather. Two members of the crew had to stand on the shark's floating and often still twitching body to get slings around it so that it could be hoisted on board, and sharks swaying at the end of the derrick required very careful control by the winchman to avoid an accident or damage to the boat. With the *Recruit*, the successor to the *Gloamin'*, the sharks were held alongside in slings and were gutted by two men working from a dinghy.[23] (Fig. 43)

For most of the Soay company's existence, sharks were towed to the Soay factory, the carcasses that were awaiting processing being kept floating in the harbour inflated with compressed air if they could not be handled quickly. It was only late in the last full season (1948) that gutting sharks at sea became the practice and it was taken to be a major advance, as Maxwell's successor wrote to a director – 'The main step forward is that we can now liver at sea in five minutes!'.[24]

Neither under Maxwell nor his successor did the Soay Company acquire a factory vessel, even though two proposals for factory ships were entertained. The first, the *Silver Darling* a 120-foot drifter with a 60-foot hold, was bought for £12,000 and conversion to a factory ship was mooted in June 1948. A two-framed steel structure was proposed for bringing the sharks on board. The top frame, supporting a ramp with rollers, was to slide out over the lower frame and the captured shark would be winched up the ramp. The estimate for the conversion, £6000, was considered to be excessive and the naval architect who assessed the *Silver Darling* had doubts about its suitability for conversion as its hold capacity and deck space were too small. Nothing came of the proposal and the parent company sold the ship.[25] A second project in the same year was altogether more ambitious, although at an estimated cost of £5000, somewhat cheaper. A large ex-naval Landing Craft (Tank) was looked at and tentative plans were drawn up by which it could be modified. Maxwell's views were ambivalent; he favoured obtaining a 'LCT Mk IV' but later observed that 'all landing craft were junk' so one can doubt that he had any clear idea of a suitable factory vessel.[26] (Fig. 44)

PROCESSING

The processing of the basic basking shark products was fairly uncomplicated and required only a boiler and a number of metal tanks.[27] Oil was separated from the raw livers by steaming. Pieces of liver were put into open vats, steam was passed through and the oil, floating on top of the mixture, was run off into settling tanks. The remaining liver tissue ('foots') was then run out of the boiling tanks which were hosed down and filled again with fresh pieces of liver.[28] This 'gravity settling 'method, used both at Carradale and at Soay, was the least efficient of several possible techniques for extracting liver oil. Fine mincing of the liver and centrifuging of the steamed mass, as practised in the United States, gave a higher yield. At Soay the shark flesh, low in fat, was minced, cooked with steam and then dried for fish meal. Fins could be left in the open air for skin to come off the thin cartilaginous rays and vertebrae could similarly be left out in the open to dry.

Fig. 43.   Liver extraction. A basking shark on its side next to A. Watkins' factory ship the *Recruit*, receiving the first cuts to open the belly. The fish will be turned onto its back to complete the extraction of the liver. (Watkins (1958))

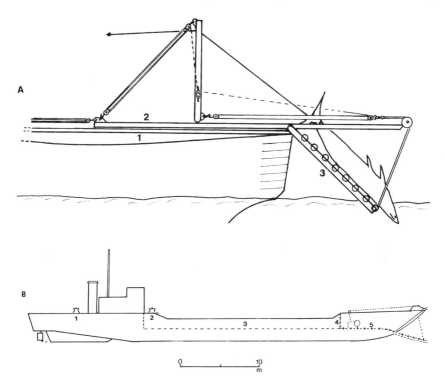

Fig. 44. Factory ships for the Island of Soay Shark Fisheries Company. **A.** Proposed modifications to the stern of the *Silver Darling*. A framework of steel girders (1) secured to the deck supported a moveable frame (2) which could be extended over the stern, dropping a ramp equipped with rollers (3) up which the basking sharks would be dragged. The line from the sling holding the tail of the shark went forward to the winch. **B.** Adapted Landing Craft (Tank), probably the 192-ft, 640-ton LCT Mk III type built between 1941–1944. Sharks were to be hauled on board over rollers in the bow ramp and forward well (5) into the well-deck (3). New watertight doors were to be fitted (4) and the capstan (1) shifted forwards (2). (**A** redrawn from original; **B** redrawn from original by G. L. Watson & Co, Glasgow naval architects, 20 Feb 1948. Both in HKIS 4, courtesy Duke of Hamilton, Lennoxlove)

The Carradale factory

In selecting a site for his factory, Watkins needed one which was within his fishing area, near a village so that there would be an assured labour supply and yet far enough away from the village to minimise the nuisance of the smells emanating from the processing operations. Convenient fresh water would be required for the boiler and the location had to be accessible for bringing in such items as boiler coal and barrels and also near a transport system to take the filled barrels to their market.[29] As built, the Carradale factory consisted of a small oil-

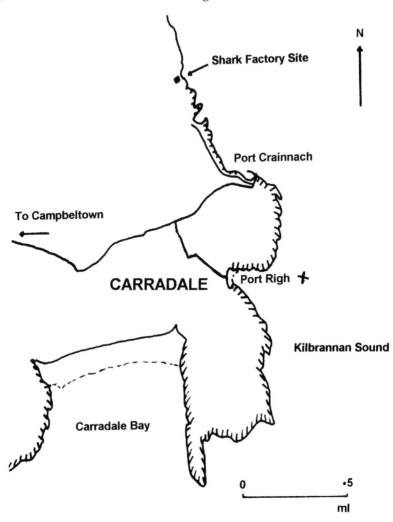

N

Shark Factory Site

Port Crainnach

To Campbeltown

CARRADALE   Port Righ ✛

Kilbrannan Sound

Carradale Bay

0   •5

ml

Map 5.   Carradale, Kintyre. Shark factory site is indicated. X marks the position of the 1937 'Carradale Incident' when three people were drowned in an encounter with a basking shark.

extracting plant in a large shed. Even though a temporary wooden slipway was constructed for rolling the barrels of liver up from the beach, the projected fish meal plant, permanent slipway and a jetty never materialised for the war intervened, and on resumption of the fishery in 1946, Watkins changed from shore-based to ship-based processing.[30] There was no road to the site so the lighter pieces of equipment such as small galvanised tanks and pipes were manhandled along the beach, while large storage tanks and the boiler were floated to the site, towed by a dinghy. (Figs. 45 & 46 & Maps 5 & 6)

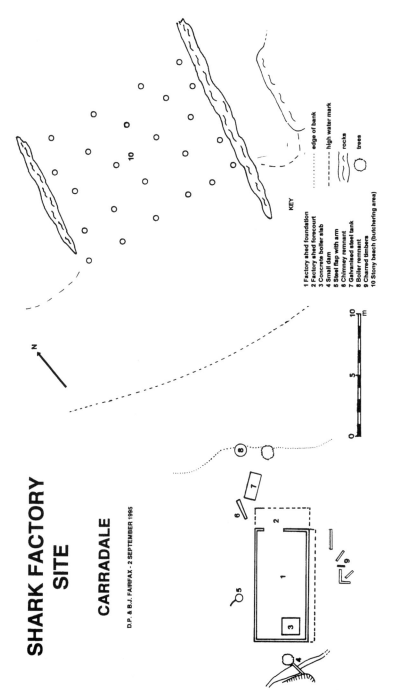

Map 6. Plan of Shark Factory Site, Carradale.

The Soay factory

Like Watkins in Carradale, Maxwell set up a processing factory as an integral
part of his shark-fishing scheme, locating it at Soay for several reasons: the island
was near the main shark grounds; there would be no rental and minimum
difficulty with official planning procedures as he owned the island; and its
existence would fulfil the obligation he felt as Soay's laird to provide some
employment for the crofters.

For the factory site Maxwell chose a rocky shelf on the northeastern shore of
Soay's small tidal harbour which had been the site of a modest herring station in
the early 19th century. A derelict stone salt store still existed as a relic of that
earlier 'Soay venture'. But while it is an idyllic spot for the naturalist and lover of
the outdoor life, Soay was totally unsuited to be the base for even a small
industrial enterprise. All the building materials and the equipment for the
factory had to be transported across from Mallaig on the deck of the *Dove* and
the heavier items such as the locomotive boiler and firebox which was to be the
factory's steam plant had to be winched and levered up a steep slope to their
final positions. Contractors and some of the factory staff had to be ferried in and
accommodated in a small barrack block, an old Army hut, which had been
brought over in sections and reassembled behind the factory. When the factory
became operational coal had to be brought in for the boiler with the processed
oil and other products making the return journey to Mallaig, the railhead.
Water was pumped from a small loch into a large galvanised water tank on the
bank behind the factory.[31] (Figs. 47–52 & Maps 7 & 8)

Fig. 45. Watkins' Carradale shark factory under construction 1939. Foundations are being laid.
The boiler (no 8 on plan) and small galvanised tank (no 7) are still on site. (Watkins (1958))

Fig. 46. Gutting basking sharks on the beach in front of the Carradale factory. The liver is being removed from the shark in the foreground and slices of liver can be seen between the legs of the worker. The liver pieces were put into barrels and manhandled up to the factory door. (Watkins (1958))

The Soay factory was considerably larger than the Carradale one, producing oil, dried flesh, fish meal, skins and dried fins. The shark carcasses were hauled up a steep slipway on trucks that ran on a small marine railway and then were winched sideways onto the concrete stance where they were skinned and dismembered. A mobile crane with a nominal lift of one ton was on the site but turned out to be unreliable in use as the weight of a shark's head being lifted off the stance would overbalance it.[32] The locomotive boiler produced steam for the winch which hauled the railway trucks as well as the steam for the liver reduction process. Steam was introduced into vats via a flexible pipe and a perforated tube and broke down the chunks of liver. The resulting oil was run off, filtered and put into drums. Maxwell estimated that a large shark gave a ton of liver, from which 7 hundredweight of oil could be extracted (ie 3 sharks to give a ton of oil). In practice the yield of oil was rather less than this.[33] The flesh of the shark was cut into pieces and taken to the mincers in open boxes. After passing through the coarse and fine mincers it was put into metal trays on a conveyor belt set up in a tunnel for 'cooking' by the forced draught from the brick furnace built behind the old stone store. The shark fins and the vertebrae were spread on the heathland behind the factory and left to dry. A brick ice house proved to be unsuccessful and, with the door sealed up, it was converted

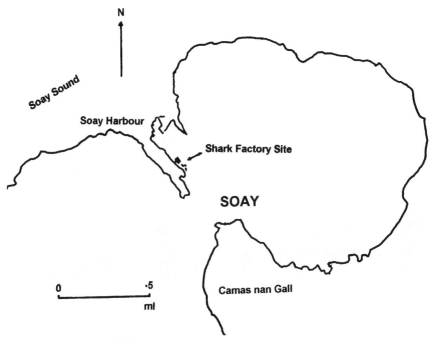

Map 7. Island of Soay. North-eastern corner showing shark factory site.

to a brine tank with shark flesh being dropped down through the hatch. This experiment was also a failure – a spectacularly disastrous one when sixteen tons of putrefying flesh had to be disposed of.[34]

The factory was probably the one single element in the Soay venture which did most to bring it to ruin. It was an over-ambitious concept and it was in decidedly the wrong location. Its working did not run on an even course: the workmen were often disaffected and it needed a resident manager to make it operate efficiently. Maxwell admitted as much: 'The Soay factory was the narrow channel through which nothing ever seemed to run smoothly, and to which the greater part of our losses could be traced.'[35]

BASKING SHARK PRODUCTS

Throughout the term of the modern fishery marketing of the oil, flesh and other products of the basking shark has been a particularly uncertain business, characterised especially by wildly fluctuating prices for the oil. The importance of basking shark oil must not be exaggerated. As in the time of the first fishery it was but one of many animal and vegetable oils utilised by industrial processes and as before, demand for it was closely related to the availability of whale oil.

Fig. 47. View of the Soay factory in operation in 1946 with the Cuillin mountains of Skye in the background. The icehouse is at far right. Lying against it are planks down which discarded shark heads were slid, to be towed away by the motor boat in the foreground. The tall chimney marks the locomotive boiler which provided steam for winching the sharks up onto the stance, and for steam extraction of oil from livers. The smaller chimney indicates the position of the mincers and shark flesh was dried in the roofed conveyor tunnel running from the mincers to the furnace behind the old stone store. Boxes for shark flesh are piled against the wall of the store. The *Sea Leopard* is visible to the left, having jsut towed in sharks. (Courtesy Hulton Getty Picture Collection)

By 1900 illuminants and most lubricants had long been derived from petroleum, but the industrial economies of the early 20th century still required vast quanties of animal and vegetable oils for new products: margarine as a cheap substitute for butter, soap, a variety of pharmaceutical and cosmetic goods and, especially important in wartime, glycerin for nitroglycerine. The fundamental chemical process which enabled large-scale production of these commodities from the raw oils is 'hydrogenation' (invented in 1903) by which hydrogen is passed through the 'unsaturated' oils under pressure converting them into the 'saturated' form. A hydrogenated oil has a higher melting point, so it is semi-solid at room temperature, and its better resistance to oxidation means it deteriorates much more slowly.[36] The advent of hydrogenation greatly increased the demand for whale oil and other natural oils, such that Antarctic whaling flourished from the early 1920s until the early war years.

The availability of natural oils and fats remained diminished for some years

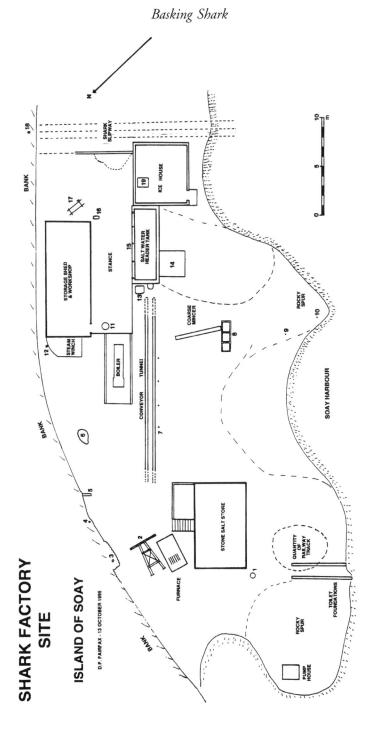

Map 8. Plan of Shark Factory Site, Island of Soay.

KEY TO PLAN OF SHARK FACTORY SITE, ISLAND OF SOAY

Unless otherwise indicated, all structures were part of the shark factory.

L = length W = width H = height D = diameter

A. Named Structures and Features.

PUMP HOUSE. Brick foundation with corrugated iron sides. L = 1.83m. W = 1.55m. H = 1.62m. Built by T. Geddes for lobster rearing scheme.

TOILET FOUNDATIONS. Concrete with beach pebbles. Left hand foundation L = 6.3m. Right hand foundation 5.7m

QUANTITY OF RAILWAY TRACK. Light railway, gauge c. 0.62m. Rail, H = 0.6m.

FURNACE. Triple brick foundation with grate. Produced hot air for conveyor tunnel. L = 3.67m. W = 2m.

CONVEYOR TUNNEL. Two rows of double brick foundations. L = 18.8m. Each row W = 0.27m. Dried shark flesh passed along this tunnel in slotted metal trays.

COARSE MINCER. Steel Archimedes (?) screw inside casing. L = 4.8m. W = 0.47m. H = 0.37m.

BOILER. Old railway locomotive boiler with firebox. L = 4.42m. H = 1.56m. D = 0.84m. On concrete foundation with brick edges.

STEAM WINCH. L = c. 2.5m. On concrete foundation.

STORAGE SHED & WORKSHOP. L = 11.9m. W = 4.79m. H = 2.58m. Built on stance by T. Geddes for lobster rearing scheme.

STANCE. Concrete surface used for cutting up basking sharks.

SALT WATER HEADER TANK. Brick. L = 7.97m. Depth = 1.4m. Built by T. Geddes for lobster rearing scheme.

ICE HOUSE. Brick. L = 5.88m. W = 6.42m. H = 4.1m at south corner. After use as ice house, door sealed and building used as tank for salted shark flesh. Later had concrete pens built inside by T. Geddes for lobster rearing scheme.

B. Numbered Structures

1. STEEL GEAR WHEEL. D = 0.61m. Not part of shark factory.
2. SUPPORT FOR AN OVERHEAD CONVEYOR BELT. W = 3.24m. across top plank.
3. WINCH BLOCK. Set in formed concrete. H = 0.29m.
4. STEEL ROD. Set in rock.
5. SMALL CONCRETE FOUNDATION (?)
6. BOULDER. Hole bored in it for winch block (?)
7. ROW OF STEEL RODS. In concrete footings. Supported the roof over the conveyer tunnel.
8. SETTLING TANK FOR SHARK OIL. Brick. L = 3.25m. W = 0.94m. H = 1.1m.
9. STEEL MOORING RING.
10. STEEL MOORING RING.
11. STEEL GUN MOUNTING. Ex *Traveller* (and *Sea Leopard*) H = 0.55m. D = 0.7m.
12. STEEL WINCH BLOCK. See 3 above.
13. FINE MINCER. H = C. 1m. Steel with 2 Archimedes (?) screws.
14. CONCRETE SLAB. L = 3.55m. W = 2.65m. Possibly not shark factory.
15. FENCE. To stop cattle falling into salt water header tank. Built by T. Geddes.
16. JAW OF GRINDER.
17. GRINDER MECHANISM. L = 1.98m. W = 0.58m.
18. STEEL SPIKE. H = 0.85m. 'F171' stamped on top.
19. HATCH OF ICE HOUSE. L = 1.06m. W = 0.9m. Single brick combing.

Fig. 48. A view of the Soay factory from behind. The boilerhouse encloses the locomotive boiler with its tall chimney. The 'bone-yard' in the foreground has numerous vertebrae and fins drying in the sun for conversion into fish manure. (Maxwell (1952))

Fig. 49. Soay factory. A shark on the bogie of the slipway being readied for hauling up to the concrete stance where it will be cut up. (Maxwell (1952))

Fig. 50. Soay factory. A basking shark being skinned on the stance. Some of the workers are wearing the armoured gloves provided by Maxwell; others are not. (Maxwell (1952))

after the Second World War and the demand for basking shark oil in this period can probably be attributed directly to the fact that Antarctic whaling, which had resumed in 1945, could not supply all the requirements of the resurgent postwar economy. For a few brief years the shark oil was both available in quantity and close to the home market. By the early 1950s peanut oil, from tropical regions, was becoming available as another, cheaper alternative to shark oil.[37] At this time, the bulk of Scottish basking shark oil probably ended up as margarine, but the active constituent of shark oils, the lipid squalene, has always been in demand for more advanced products than a culinary spread.

Fig. 51.   Soay factory. A discarded one-ton shark's head being taken by the mobile crane to the edge of the ice-house where it would be slid down planks into the harbour and then towed out into the deep water. (Maxwell (1952))

Squalene

Squalene ($C_{30}H_{50}$), a terpenoid hydrocarbon found widely in many animal and vegetable oils, is present in high concentrations in the livers of deepsea sharks. The liver oil of the basking shark has a high squalene content, nearly 50% (which may be a clue to its winter habitat).[38] Being unstable and unsaturated, squalene is usually used in its hydrogenated form, squal*a*ne (perhydrosqualene, $C_{30}H_{62}$) which unlike other hydrogenated substances is a liquid oil, stable, inert, colourless and odourless. Squalane has many applications in the manufacture of cosmetics and pharmaceuticals as a moisturiser and has been used as a specialist precision lubricant, especially for low temperatures.[39] It has other uses as a surfactant, and as a constituent of dyes, artificial silk and perfumes. Like many other natural products however, shark oil derivatives have been largely replaced by synthetic substitutes, although certain deepsea sharks are still being fished for their squalene-rich livers.[40] In the 1940s there was considerable interest in shark liver oil as a source of vitamins, especially vitamin A. Although the livers of some shark species have a high percentage of this vitamin, up to 175,000 vitamin A units per gram, the percentage in the basking shark liver is

A
B
C
D

Fig. 52. Soay factory site 1995. **A.** Locomotive firebox and boiler in foundation of the boilerhouse. **B.** The coarse mincer. **C.** The fine mincer (no 13 on plan). **D.** The gun-mounting (no 11), made from armour-plate steel, used in the *Sea Leopard* (Maxwell) and then in the *Traveller* (Geddes).

very low indeed at 300 units per gram. Vitamin A could be synthesised from 1947 onwards, so the interest in shark livers for this purpose ended.[41] There was also, briefly, some interest in other potential medicinal products from the shark. Pancreases from Soay were sent away to have insulin extracted, but again, synthesised insulin soon replaced the natural product.[42] Over the years the oil remained in demand for specific non-industrial uses. It was still prized by some as an ointment for injured animals and lighthouse keepers valued it as a lubricant for the fine mechanisms in their charge.[43]

At Soay the vertebrae were converted to fish meal but in later years there was a small demand for cartilage as a catalytic starter in the process of biochemical polymerisation.[44] In recent years, because sharks as a group are remarkably free of cancers there has been much interest in studying substances in the cartilage that might be useful in treating cancer in humans. One experiment using an extract from basking shark fin and vertebral cartilage found that it inhibited the growth of new blood vessels around tumours in rabbits thus slowing the growth of the tumours.[45] Shark oils in general (with squalene as the essential

Fig. 53. Basking Shark fins on sale in Singapore. Mr Robert Chan of the Top of the Plaza restaurant poses with basking shark fins, known as *tin kow*. About 500,000 kg of shark fins are eaten annually in Singapore and the most expensive of all is basking shark fin, costing about $ Singapore 400 per kilogram. It appears to be supplied mainly from Norwegian sources. (Lum (1996) and courtesy the *Straits Times*)

constituent) are now in some demand in capsule form as strengtheners of the immune system.[46]

Fins and Skin

Dried shark fins have always been a choice item in Asian cuisines, and possibly an aphrodisiac in some cultures, and in the later years of the fishery the fins have become the most lucrative product of the shark. (Fig. 53) The Soay company obtained a price for fins at £1000 per ton and sold some of the fin cartilage to a firm in Cairo for use as an aphrodisiac, but it may be doubted that there was a consistent market for it. [47]At one point in the 1970s the liver of the shark fetched £550 per ton and the fins brought £3000 per ton; by the early 1990s livers were being dumped as the price had dropped to £250 and in the middle of the decade the value of the fins had climbed to £20,000 per ton. During this period the first and second dorsal fins, the pectorals and the bottom half of the caudal fin from a large shark yielded 92 kilograms of saleable product.[48] The skin has from time to time been made into leather, but although durable it is a product with a limited market much subject to the vagaries of fashion. At Soay it was found that there was no quick way of skinning the shark carcass and at 6d per square foot the price offered was too low anyway.[49]

Flesh

In the late 1940s Maxwell sold at least one consignment of pickled basking shark flesh to the United Nations Relief and Rehabilitation Agency for distribution as a food item in war-ravaged European countries. McCrindle also found a market, sending shark flesh to Billingsgate in the late 1970s and during the 1983 season to a Girvan fish and chip shop which had some success with 'shark suppers'.[50]

However, this does not add up to a consistent market for basking shark meat as human food. Nor, for that matter, has the flesh been very successful as an animal food – one consignment sent from Soay to the London Zoo as food for the lions apparently made them sick![51] All shark flesh contains high levels of urea which soon produces ammonia and if it is not being dried or salted it has to be refrigerated quickly to prevent spoilage.[52] Although the meat from pelagic sharks such as the porbeagle is now in some demand as a delicacy, the more mundane product from dogfish, sold as 'rock salmon' in Scotland and as 'huss' in England, is not popular and the flesh of the basking shark would these days be considered too coarse in texture to be promoted by a fishmonger.[53] In Maxwell's time if there was no market for it as human food, it could be ground up as fish meal for cattle and that would probably be its fate now if it were to become available.

Notes

1. Geddes (1960): 61.
2. W. Manson *pers. comm.* 1996.
3. Watkins (1958): 149.
4. H. McCrindle *pers. comm.* 1995.
5. Maxwell (1952): 119.
6. Watkins (1958): 193-194.
7. Geddes (1960): 61.
8. T. Geddes *pers. comm.* 1997.
9. W. Manson *pers. comm.* 1995.
10. W. Manson *pers. comm.* 1995.
11. Geddes (1960): 66.
12. O'Connor (1953): 129.
13. Watkins (1958): 192.
14. Watkins (1958): 218-223 & 226.
15. A. Paterson *pers. comm.* 1995.

16. Maxwell (1952): 159-162.
17. W. Manson *pers. comm.* 1995.
18. H. McCrindle *pers. comm.* 1997.
19. Watkins (1958): 155; & Maxwell (1952): 205.
20. W. Manson *pers. comm.* 1995; & H. McCrindle *pers. comm.* 1995.
21. W. Manson *pers. comm.* 1995.
22. H. McCrindle *pers. comm.* 1995.
23. Watkins (1958): 193.
24. R. Findlay letter to G.L. Norris, 27 Jul 1948 (HKIS2).
25. G.L. Norris undated memo (HKIS2); & J. Dick memo 9 June 1948 (HKIS4).
26. G. Maxwell letter of 8 Apr 1948 (HKIS2).
27. See Tressler & Lemon (1957): 466 & 503; & Cutting (1955): 326.
28. Watkins (1958): 156 & 157.
29. Watkins (1958): 110-111 & 116-119.
30. Watkins (1958): 178.
31. T. Geddes *pers. comm.* 1995.
32. T. Geddes *pers. comm.* 1997.
33. Maxwell v O'Connor 28 Nov 1956 (HKIS5).
34. Maxwell (1952): 216-217.
35. Maxwell (1952): 181.
36. Riepma (1970): 30.
37. W. Manson *pers. comm.* 1995.
38. Karnovsky *et al* (1948): 1-2.
39. Anon (1996).
40. Buranudeen & Richards-Rajadurai (1986): 42; & Clover (1997).
41. Tressler & Lemon (1957): 495-496.
42. T. Geddes, *pers. comm.* 1995.
43. T.Geddes *pers. comm.* 1995.
44. H. McCrindle *pers. comm.* 1995.
45. Lee & Langer (1983).
46. Cambi (1996): 13.
47. T. Geddes *pers. comm.* 1995; & Maxwell v. O'Connor 28 Nov 1956 (HKIS5).
48. H. McCrindle *pers. comm.* 1995.
49. R.Findlay letter 18 Feb 1949 (HKIS3).
50. H.McCrindle *pers. comm.* 1995.
51. T. Geddes *pers. comm.* 1997.
52. Rose (1996): 37.
53. D. Pieroni *pers. comm.* 1997.

Chapter Eight

Conservation

[The substance of this Chapter was written before the basking shark was given full protection in United Kingdom waters.]

UNTIL RECENTLY the idea that sharks were a legitimate concern of marine conservationists would have been considered laughable; have not sharks been feared and detested since classical times? Yet the most feared of all, the great white, the very incarnation of the shark as an enemy of humankind, is now legally protected in several Australian states and in South Africa, the Maldives and California. Recently-formed scientific groups such as the European Elasmobranch Association and its national branches, such as the Shark Trust in Britain, have conservation as a principal objective and there are now other organisations in a number of countries devoted specifically to the conservation of sharks.[1] This change in the general view of sharks, which beyond their horrific reputation were previously mainly of interest to trophy fishermen and a few ichthyologists, is undoubtedly a beneficial result of the numerous television documentaries on marine life which have been pervasive in their influence on popular attitudes. The basking shark has shared in this. If we seek a definite turning point from comparative public indifference to a recognition as an interesting animal worthy of protection it is probably the early 1990s when Howard McCrindle's activities were being publicised. The moves to protect the basking shark are based not only on a changed public attitude but also on the undoubted fact that there appear not to be many of them around, and because they have been fished intensively and a quota still exists it is convenient to blame the fishery for the decline in the numbers of sharks seen in recent years. In the words of a Scottish newspaper 'the years of shark hunting have taken their toll'.[2] About 1100 sharks were taken by Scottish vessels in 1946 to 1953 and 351 were captured in 1978 to 1994. However, it has to be noted that some biologists have doubted a direct link between the catches in the modern fishery and the falling numbers.[3] Total basking shark numbers, or perhaps just the numbers of sharks appearing at the surface, may be subject to a long-term cycle possibly related to changes in the global climate which bring variations to ocean temperatures and consequent alterations in plankton intensities at different levels in the ocean. The apparent decline may well owe more to these dimly understood factors than to any human impact.

NUMBERS

It is possible to look at basking shark numbers from a historical perspective which even though imperfect and unscientific can still show the general trend of an alternation of periods of prolific numbers and leaner times. The earliest record of large numbers and indeed of fluctuations is in Pennant's 1769 *British Zoology* :

> These are migratory fish, or at lest it is but in a certain number of years that they are seen in multitudes on the Welch seas, tho' in most summers a single and perhaps strayed fish appears. They visited the bays of Caernarvonshire and Anglesea in vast shoals, in the summers of 1756, and a few succeeding years . . . [and then in a footnote] 'Some old people say they recollect the same sort of fish visiting these seas in vast numbers about forty years ago.' [ie circa 1725].[4]

Given that the Scottish fishery began about 1760, we must believe that the sharks were reasonably numerous as there would have been little point in chasing after an uncommon fish, and the abundance reported by Pennant for the Welsh coast can be assumed to have extended well north for a period of some years. As it is known that the Norwegian fishery was flourishing at the same time, large numbers of basking sharks were also present across the northeast Atlantic seaboard. How long did this period last? The *Old Statistical Account* reference for Lochgoilhead, Loch Goil, with its reference that the basking shark '. . .occasionally visits us' hints that numbers may have decreased substantially in the Clyde by the 1790s.[5] In the *New Statistical Account* the minister of Tiree and Coll, probably writing in 1839 or 1840, remarks that the basking shark 'was formerly pretty often seen on this coast, but seems for the last thirty or forty years to have entirely disappeared' and since that time he had seen only one of them.[6] This observation is not as definitive as one might hope as directly across the Sea of the Hebrides in Barra 'hundreds of the fishes appeared last season [1838] on the coast'.[7] We know that the shark was still being taken off Barra in 1813 so perhaps the two statements are best interpreted by assuming a lean period in the early 1800s with another peak beginning in the late 1830s.

Later nineteenth century evidence is even more tentative. In one reference, the heyday of basking shark hunting off Arran is given as the 1770s and, referring to the 1870s, the narrator states 'now it is seldom seen'.[8] But by the late 1930s the numbers in the Clyde were 'unprecedented' around Carradale and 'more numerous at Girvan [in 1937] than for the past 40 years'. Knowing that the numbers remained considerable until the early 1950s, a tentative timeline could be constructed for two and a half centuries to show a cycle where a period of high numbers of sharks lasting, perhaps, a decade is followed by a lean period thirty to forty years long. If this crude analysis has any validity, another period of comparative abundance should have begun about the mid-1990s and the very recent report of 500 sharks being seen off Cornwall may signify the beginnings of the next peak in the cycle.[9]

If, as is surmised, the basking shark has few natural enemies, the adults could be expected to live out their normal lifespan, subject to sufficient food being available. It has recently been discovered that the whale shark has hundreds of free-living embryos per reproductive cycle, but probably few survive, in a pattern described as 'high birth rate, low reproductive output'.[10] While it is possible that the basking shark follows a similar pattern to the whale shark, it seems unlikely, given that the only evidence currently available suggests that basking shark pups are over a metre long at birth. What is more likely is that the basking shark has a low birth rate and thus any culling of the sharks which claimed mostly the females (as in the Scottish fishery) could be expected to have a drastic and possibly long term effect on shark numbers. Much has yet to be learned about the detail of the plankton that the shark feeds on but while there are annual fluctuations in plankton abundance, there has been no suggestion that there was insufficient plankton for a large number of sharks, so it is not likely that the decline in numbers is caused by shortage of food. Because so little is known about the reproductive biology of the basking shark, conservationists believe that exploitation of the shark cannot continue to coexist with an apparent decline in numbers. They support the application of the 'precautionary principle' of giving total protection from human interference without waiting for definitive scientific evidence of a decline.

FISHERY QUOTA

A European Community annual quota for 100 tonnes of liver, taken up by Norwegian fishermen in return for a British white fish quota in Norwegian waters, still allows basking sharks to be captured in the Exclusive Economic Zone of the United Kingdom. Applying a unit value of 4.5 tonnes (= the estimated average weight of the sharks in the fishery) and accepting the proposition that the weight of the liver is equal to one quarter of the body weight, this quota represents a potential take of some 90 sharks. Even if the proportional weight of the liver is revised upwards to be one-third of total body weight, the quota still potentially allows the taking of up to 70 sharks, a significant number given the apparent decline over the last forty years.[11]

The figure expressing the proportional relationship between the weight of the liver and the total body weight in the basking shark has fundamental implications for the regulation of catches, as it is used as an index for assessing the numbers of sharks that may be caught. If a quota is expressed in tonnes of liver, and the weight of the liver in an average shark is considered to be a high proportion of the total weight, fewer sharks can be caught than if the liver is taken to be a lower proportion of total weight. Another consequence of a quota defined by tonnes of liver is that more individuals are likely to be taken in the years when only small sharks are present.[12] The determination of the average weights of different sizes of basking shark also needs much more attention. The weight of 4.5 tonnes that is commonly accepted is taken from a calculation by Matthews and Parker for an 8.8 metre fish based on a formula applied to the known weights of two large sharks in the United States. Their one personal assessment of total weight (which gave the much higher figure of 6.6 tonnes) was done by weighing a liver and then adding up estimates of the weights of the remaining bits and pieces of the shark.[13]

Even when the basking shark is not fished, other human activities take their toll. Entanglement in gill-nets kills a significant number of basking sharks in Ireland and this no doubt occurs in other parts of the world as well.[14] Recreational activities can disturb the sharks when motor boats and jet-skis are in a feeding area. Sharks have been washed ashore in Britain badly mutilated by propellors and it has been suggested that on occasion such injuries may have been caused by deliberate harassment.[15]

CONSERVATION MEASURES

Conservation measures in British waters can be considered as four parallel strands of action: lobbying the government to give legal protection to the shark; the promotion of recording schemes involving members of the public; pre-senting the basking shark positively in the media to promote a greater public awareness of its plight, and promotion of the scientific study of the sharks at sea. At the highest level, a coalition of the statutory conservation agencies and conservationist organisations, among them English Nature, the Marine Con-servation Society, Scottish Natural Heritage and the Scottish Wildlife Trust, continuously urges ministers and officials of the Department of the Environ-ment, Transport and the Regions and the several Fisheries Departments to have the basking shark protected by statute, that is placed in schedule 5 of the Wildlife and Countryside Act 1981 as a totally protected species within the territorial waters of the United Kingdom. The first recommendation for protection, made in 1986 during the first quinquennial review of the Act, was turned down and another approach was made in 1991. In spite of having the support of the Joint Nature Conservation Committee, another body which advises government on nature conservation, it still failed as fisheries considerations, which have implications beyond the United Kingdom, outweighed the claims of conservation. Ostensibly the reason for declining to give official protection to the basking shark was the lack of scientific evidence that it was in fact endangered. A similar official response was given in a Commons debate on the status of the basking shark in early 1997. The only part of Britain in which the basking shark is so far totally protected is within the territorial waters of the Isle of Man under section 5 of the Manx 1990 Wildlife Act. It is also protected in the island of Guernsey.[16]

As the stocks of the bony fishes diminish, so the fishing industry increases the harvest of cartilaginous fishes, to the detriment of many shark species, including the basking shark. Because so little is known about the fundamental biology and ecology of the basking shark, it is easy for those opposed to its protection to argue that there is a lack of hard evidence for a decline in numbers. Conversely, conservationists advocate full protection ahead of stock assessment precisely because gathering the necessary scientific data will take many years and it may then be too late to remedy the effects of exploitation. The basking shark has been given a 'vulnerable' status in the Red List of threatened animals issued by the International Union for the Conservation of Nature, and full protection by the United Kingdom would give a powerful encouragement to international efforts to protect the shark or, at the minimum, regulate its fishery in the Exclusive Economic Zones of European Union states and on the high seas.

As the name of the Marine Conservation Society indicates, it has a much wider remit than just the basking shark, but nevertheless it has run a special 'Basking Shark Watch' project since 1987. The first general objective of the project is to increase public awareness of the existence of the basking shark as a fish which deserves to be protected and to give people an understanding of the likely consequences of allowing a fishing quota for the shark to continue. Secondly, the Society actively encourages the collection of scientific data on the shark so that submissions to official agencies will steadily become more soundly based on evidence which is convincing to the government's own scientific advisers. These data will be used to draw up a management plan for the basking shark.

There are two dimensions to the gathering of data. On the broad scale, the Marine Conservation Society's sightings scheme encourages people who see basking sharks to send in a record of each observation using a specially designed form with details of the number seen, their sizes and their behaviour. These sighting records (about 1800 to date, covering 6000 sharks) are used as the raw material for a computer database which has improved the understanding of national, regional and local distribution patterns. More narrowly focussed, a migration monitoring programme centred on the waters around the Isle of Man, which ran from 1989 to 1991, was set up to identify individual sharks by skin scars and other distinctive marks such as disfigured dorsal fins.[17] This particular scheme is now continued separately by The Basking Shark Society (formerly the Isle of Man Basking Shark Project). 'Project Maximus' is the name given by the Scottish Wildlife Trust to its sighting scheme which, established in 1996, covers the Scottish coast and complements that of the Marine Conservation Society. Data are exchanged between both groups and, by incorporating old records, the span of the Trust's database has been extended by observations dating back to 1898. A distinct decline in sightings in Scottish waters from 1990 onwards has been noticed.[18] (Fig. 54)

More generally, there are now worldwide efforts being made to regulate, if not restrict, the trade in shark products even as the demand for many of them strengthens. International exports in shark fins, for example, doubled between 1980 and 1990 and further growth in this trade will continue to place pressure on the basking shark, whose large fins are highly prized.[19] Inclusion of the basking shark in the Convention on International Trade in Endangered Species of Wild Fauna and Flora CITES would offer some measure of protection to the shark in those parts of the world where its fishery is at present unrestricted. In early 1997 conservationists in the United Kingdom unsuccessfully asked the government to propose the inclusion of the basking shark in the CITES.

The final strand of this conservation impetus is active observation and study of the shark at sea by scientists. This is an expensive activity and requires much preparation for each season, as exactly where the sharks might appear or whether they might be present in any numbers is always unpredictable. To gain accurate knowledge of the environmental biology of the shark these field studies need to be carried out in successive seasons over a number of years. Unfortunately, as funding for them (in common with so much academic research) is usually from a system of uncertain annual grants, the financing necessary for a long-term project is not guaranteed.

Much work has been done around the Isle of Man and the results of a period of intensive field research carried out by the University of Wales at Bangor from 1987 to 1992 have appeared in theses and in a special report.[20] A project at the University of Plymouth is currently investigating the shark in the English Channel.

BASKING SHARK SIGHTINGS
MAY-OCTOBER 1985-1997

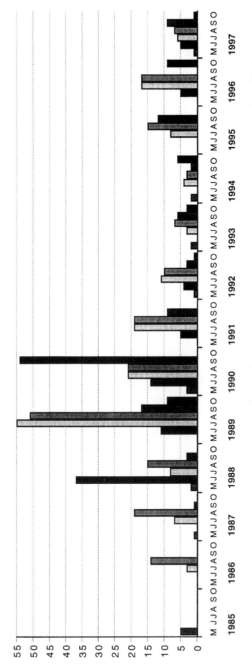

Fig. 54. Basking shark sightings in Scotland, May–October 1985 to 1997. (Courtesy D. Wilson & Scottish Wildlife Trust)

TAGGING

It is of great interest to biologists to be able to identify individual sharks so that their social interactions can be investigated and the important question as to whether the same sharks frequent a given area year after year can eventually be answered. The distinctive fin shapes and skin patches of the fish can be recorded and photographed and individuals can be tagged. The usual form of a tag is just a robust plastic label, serially numbered, with an address on it for its return if found.(Fig. 55) The label is linked to a small stainless-steel anchoring piece by a short wire. While these simple traditional tags have the great merit of cheapness, their use does not really provide much information of importance unless very large numbers of the fish are tagged at once and a significant number of these move into waters where they will be seen. Given the small numbers usually encountered, this cannot be the case with basking sharks. This form of tagging, relying very much on fishermen to return the tags from captured fish, is really most applicable to sharks which have a regular fishery, or are taken by sea anglers, so that a useful proportion of the tags is returned. Scientists require information about the behaviour of fish between the time of tagging and the time of capture when the tag is removed. The traditional methods cannot supply this.

Fig. 55. A plastic basking shark tag made for a tagging project attempted by biologists from University College, Cork. It is not known if any were successfully implanted. Tag is 20 × 5 cm. (Courtesy Dr Simon Berrow)

Attention is now focused on newer tagging devices which will record and store much more sophisticated data. Archival tags, which are minicomputers attached to the fish, can record data on time, depth, temperature, and, if light-sensitive, longitude and latitude for many years. They provide a continuous record of long-distance movements, the depths that the fish habitually lives at and, for some species, its feeding behaviour.[21] A data logger, a comparatively cheap device, has pressure and temperature sensors and records data which are particularly useful for determining the vertical movements of fish. Devices that signal information to satellites are the most promising as the data can be relayed more or less at the same time as they are being processed. Data recovery is thus not dependent upon having the transmitting equipment found and returned. A very promising development, which seems to be especially suited to large sharks, is the attachment of a video camera in a streamlined casing – the 'Crittercam' – which is towed by the shark for several hours before it is jettisoned, rising to the surface and being retrieved by boat.[22] While it can be anticipated that electronic tags of various types will be used more widely, it must be noted that some people are opposed to tagging on ethical grounds, believing that it is wrong to interfere with a fish in this way, and they prefer to study the basking shark by direct observation only.

SATELLITE TRACKING IN THE FIRTH OF CLYDE

The concept of tracking marine animals by acoustics or by radio transmissions is not new, but it was not until satellites became available for civilian scientific use that a method of long term tracking could be devised which overcame the disadvantages of previous methods. Acoustic signals have a short range and to monitor a moving animal the vessel receiving the signal has to stay close to it. While signals from radio transmitters attached, for example, to the fins of whales can be received over much greater distances, they cannot be monitored beyond the horizon, and as they indicate only the direction of the animal from the receiving vessel they need to be triangulated to establish its exact position. The ship receiving radio signals cannot be too far from the transmitting animal and even though this range is greatly improved by using an aeroplane, obviously this is an expensive and short-term solution. An orbiting satellite which can locate a transmitter anywhere on the globe and track many transmitters at the same time solves the problem of limited human monitoring, even if the basic physical constraint of absorption of radio waves underwater still applies: signals can only be received by the satellite when the transmitter is out of the water.[23]

Early Experiments

In 1978, funded by a grant from the Natural Environment Research Council, Dr I.G. Priede of the University of Aberdeen conducted a trial programme of tagging basking sharks with satellite transmitters, successfully using a long probe to implant four sharks in the Firth of Clyde with stainless-steel darts, each of which anchored a towed buoy linked to a fibreglass 'pod' containing a data collection platform transmitter. (Figs. 56 & 58A) The transmitter was to send a signal to the Random Access Measurement System (RAMS), in a United States NASA NIMBUS satellite. The objectives of this experiment (pioneering as far basking sharks were concerned) were to gain experience in satellite tracking in the investigation of the shark movements in summer feeding and, more hopefully, to find where the sharks went in winter.

Fig. 56. Tagging the basking shark in the Firth of Clyde 1978. Sketch by I. G. Priede showing the technique for approaching the shark and the getaway route immediately the fish has been tagged with the lance. (Courtesy Prof.. I. G. Priede, Aberdeen)

In the northern Clyde, once feeding sharks were seen, the final approach was made parallel to a shark in an inflatable rubber dinghy in which the exhaust pipe had been modified to minimise underwater noise. With the pod lowered into the water alongside the dinghy, the 'harpooner' jabbed the probe into the back of the fish at the base of the first dorsal fin and pulled it back sharply to disengage the dart. A second man held the coiled line at the side. The third man, controlling the motor, was ready to speed the dinghy away at a sharp angle as the shark reacted to the insertion of the dart, for a slap from the tail of the aroused shark could have easily disabled the dinghy and endangered its crew. On one occasion a blow from a shark's tail flattened one side of Priede's dinghy. As the air burst out through the stripped bung-hole the dinghy was lifted into the air, hurling two of the crew into the water. Fortunately for them, the third man managed to stay on board the sagging craft and was able to rescue them.

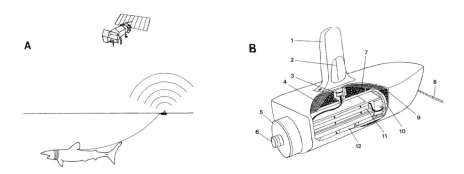

Fig. 57. Satellite tagging of the basking shark in the Firth of Clyde. **A.** The buoyant platform transmitter terminal (PTT) tends to stay on the surface sending a signal to the satellite passing overhead. If the shark dives deep, the transmitter is towed under and contact is lost. **B.** Cutaway view of the PTT 'pod'. 1. Polyethylene fin enclosing the antenna. 2. Antenna ¼ wavelength monopole. 3. 'O' ring seal coupling. 4. Antenna ground plane. 5. Access hatch. 6. Pressure switch. 7. Buoyancy. 8. Towline. 9. GRP skin. 10. Aluminium alloy transmitter casing. 11. Transmitter unit. 12. Batteries (Priede 1984)

Hopes of tracking the shark's movements were not fulfilled, however, as a fault in the design of the pods allowed leakage which ruined the transmitters. More positively, the method of attaching the equipment to the sharks proved successful as, of the three pods retrieved, one had remained attached for two months.[24] A return trip to the Clyde in 1979 with a mark 2 NIMBUS was unsuccessful as the data collection platform pods were too large and did not remain attached to the sharks.

Ailsa Craig 1982
In 1980 the Nimbus RAM system was fading and no satellite tracking was possible, so that year was spent designing an improved pod and investigating an alternative satellite system.(Fig. 57) A redesigned pod housing more sophisticated equipment was ready for the 1981 season, but the basking sharks did not oblige as none could be found off Arran. It was thus not until June and July

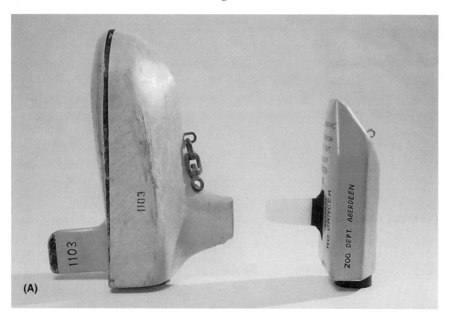

Fig. 58. Fibreglass transmitter floats ('pods') used by I. G. Priede in the Firth of Clyde. **A.** (Left) the Mk 2 NIMBUS pod used with the NASA satellite system of that name in the 1979 season. It was found to be unsuccessful as it was too large and failed to remain attached to the tagged shark. Length = 1.25 m. The ARGOS PTT (right) used in 1982 was considerably smaller (66 cm) and one remained attached to a shark for several weeks. **B.** Another view of the Argos PTT. (Courtesy Prof. I. G. Priede, Aberdeen)

1982 that Priede and his team were able to conduct another substantial tagging investigation in the Clyde. As in the earlier trial a 70 millimetre stainless steel dart was fired into the back of the shark to be the anchorage for 10 metres of steel towline connected to a strong plastic float containing the ultra-high-frequency (UHF) radio transmitter – the Platform Transmitter Terminal (PTT). The PTT was powered by Lithium batteries and had a potential life of 180 days. To lengthen the life of the batteries, a pressure switch deactivated the transmitter below a depth of 5 metres. The transmitter float (pod) was designed to sit low in the water when the fish was one to two metres below the surface. When the shark came near enough to the surface, the fin of the float was exposed and signals were transmitted from the aerial in the fin to a polar-orbiting US earth resources satellite. The data collection and location system used was ARGOS, a joint US-French system administered from Toulouse. In this system, signals could only be received if the transmitter was on the surface when a satellite was passing directly overhead, so continuous tracking was not possible. Owing to its polar orbit the number of passes made by the satellite diminished from the Pole to the Equator giving the Clyde (at latitude 55 degrees North) up to twelve locations per day. The transmitted data that was recorded by the satellite was retransmitted to a ground station, relayed from there to Toulouse and was available to the user a day later by telex.

The cost of the equipment meant that there was only one PTT available and the success of the experiment obviously depended on a reliable towline. The targetted shark was tagged north of Arran on 27 June but was next located five days later 55 miles south near the island of Ailsa Craig. Its exact position was recorded as often as it coincided with a satellite overpass and it was found to be at or near the sea surface most days in the two weeks it spent circling Ailsa Craig. There was only one sunny day in an otherwise cloudy fortnight, and on that day the shark stayed at the surface for a long time when it appeared to be feeding in a mass of warmer water. During this day its swimming speed was quite slow, being generally less than one knot. Premature breakage of the towline terminated the experiment on the seventeenth day. Overall, the feasibility of tracking the movements of a basking shark by satellite had been satisfactorily demonstrated even if the period of the experiment was too short to make any significant deductions about basking shark behaviour. The attachment of a transmitter float to a shark had not been found to be a difficult manoeuvre, although it had to be done with great care given the potential danger of placing a light rubber dinghy close to a large, unpredictable fish equipped with a powerful tail. Towing the transmitter float did not appear to hinder the fish in swimming.[25]

Isle of Arran Basking Shark Project

After the pioneering work of Priede and his associates, there was a gap of fourteen years before further satellite tracking of basking sharks was attempted in the Firth of Clyde. In 1996, Dr Mark O'Connell, a biologist from the University of Durham, spent several weeks in Arran with his colleague, Dr Tim Thom, searching for sharks to tag with a satellite device. 1996 was their experimental season and for 1997 they had refined both their project organisation and their search and tagging methods. (Fig. 59C) This Arran basking shark project, funded by Scottish Natural Heritage for 1997, depends for its success on having a large number of volunteer observers (some recruited by the Scottish Wildlife Trust) to assist the two scientists and consequently a large team has to be accommodated, fed and transported while the project is running. The need to combine an area where sharks might be reasonably expected with one where the logistical requirements of a large team could be met led O'Connell to decide on the eastern coast of Arran, north of Brodick, the main settlement and ferry port.

The principal aim of the project was to tag sharks with satellite transmitters and the quest for sharks to tag was pursued systematically. The ten-mile stretch of coast from Corrie to Lochranza was divided into five sections. Every day from 06.30hrs to 20.00hrs in each section a pair of observers equipped with a mobile telephone would constantly scan the Firth through binoculars, searching for the tell-tale shark fins but also noting other interesting marine life such as gannets, seals, dolphins and minke whales. O'Connell and Thom, with two volunteer crew, would cruise slowly along the coast in a motor yacht taking plankton samples at regular intervals while waiting to be telephoned with the news of a sighting. They would then proceed to the area where the shark had been seen and when they had located it transfer to a rubber dinghy. In this final approach they found the sound of the motor would cause the shark to stop feeding, but as they slowly came up to the fish, it would 'look up' at the boat, swim around it and then resume feeding. While they always took care to avoid the tail they were gratified to find that the dinghy could drift onto the shark and even bump against it without causing obvious alarm. (Fig. 59 & Map 9)

The tagging method used by the Durham team was similar to that of Priede. The shark was struck at the base of the first dorsal fin with a 9-foot (2.7 metres) probe which pulled away leaving the stainless steel dart embedded, but in contrast to the earlier efforts with one transmitter float, an array of equipment bobbed behind the shark as it sounded. The first item attached to the two-metre steel towline (trace) was the buoyant satellite tag with its VHF transmitter and aerial. The satellite tag recorded sea surface temperatures and, by its pressure sensor, the depths the shark reached and the dive sequences.

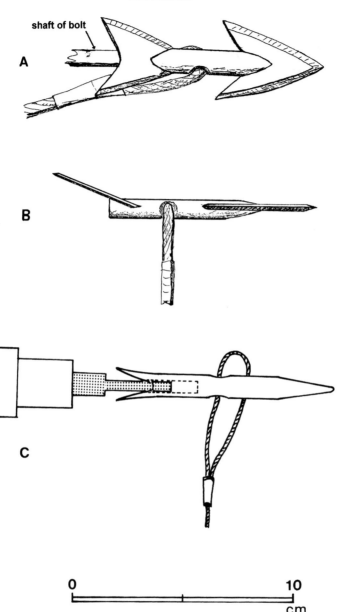

shaft of bolt

A

B

C

0   10
cm

Fig. 59. Tagging darts. **A**. Dart used by I. G. Priede in 1977–1978. **B**. Side view of the same.
C. Stainless steel dart used by M. O'Connell and T. Thom in 1996–1997 in position on the
'bolt' of the lance. In both cases, the dart was forced into the shark's back by a long lance.
The dart came away from the lance, turning side-on to the tagging line in the same manner
as the head of a toggle harpoon. (**A** & **B** Priede (1978): Fig. *3*. **C** courtesy Dr M. O'Connell,
Durham)

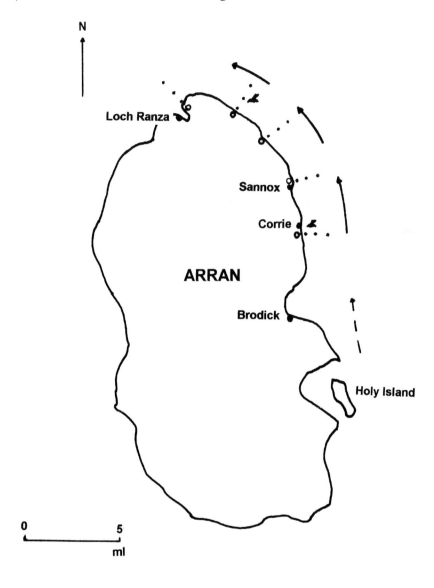

Map 9. Island of Arran. 'Basking Shark 97' project.

Fig. 60.   Mark O'Connell and T. Thom approaching a basking shark (its fin is circled) off the Isle of Arran in July 1997. Thom is holding the 2.7m tagging lance. (Photograph, Alexander Cooke, Kew)

This was the only item intended to stay with the shark so the line joining it to the others had a ferrous-magnesium alloy link which would in time corrode. The remaining pieces of equipment were a data-logger to record fine-scale temperature, depths and water speeds; a one-second repeater pinger for hydrophone location and tracking; and at the end of the line the buoyant acoustic tag containing a transmitter for short-range VHF signals. These short-range signals could be picked up by a hand-held antenna and, in theory, by this means a feeding shark could be followed around the coast.

A programme of systematic plankton sampling was carried out twice a week, based on transects from the five stations. In each transect samples were taken at 185 metres offshore (to obtain a minimum depth of 10 metres), 926 metres and 1852 metres. At each of these positions a horizontal surface tow was made at about 1 knot (the presumed feeding speed of the shark) and the top 10 metres of the water column were sampled. Weather conditions were noted to correlate plankton abundance and composition with sun or cloud and the presence or absence of basking sharks. In the first days of the study, the weather was fine and sunny with large jellyfish very conspicuously feeding in the surface waters and sharks present, but later, with similar weather, the jellyfish were much fewer and sharks were seldom seen. Over the 1997 season 35 sharks were sighted.

Two of these were tagged, but only one successfully as the stainless steel wire trace in the second shark snapped when the shark sounded.

If long-term funding can be sustained, the project will carry on from year to year, with constant technical updating and elaboration of the equipment. The various floating tags are very expensive and their recovery is a high priority. Of particular interest is the development of transmitter packages which by inbuilt timed release would detach from a shark in the depths and on arrival at the surface beam a signal announcing their location. Such devices would be invaluable in solving the mystery of the basking shark's winter location.[26] The probe used in Arran could be fitted with a hollow biopsy tuber so that a small piece of flesh could be taken from the shark for analysis of the DNA in studies of basking shark population genetics, especially important in helping to solve the intriguing question as to whether there is one North Atlantic stock or isolated local breeding populations.

PUBLIC AWARENESS

Public awareness of the basking shark has been helped immeasurably by the videotapes which have been taken by divers swimming with it and clips from these regularly feature in television natural history documentaries. The implied comparison with a whale in that the shark is large and harmless is given expression when the 'rescue' of a stranded shark is attempted. In one such recent example, Welsh volunteers 'worked for nearly six hours to help the creature stranded by the low tide'. As nothing is known about whether basking sharks can recover from strandings, perhaps the good intentions had some point although in the end this particular exercise was unsuccessful.[27] An educational pack has been produced by Scottish Natural Heritage for use in schools in Argyll. Entitled 'Boats, Barnacles and Basking Sharks', it promotes awareness of marine environmental issues in a region historically important for the basking shark fishery and where a large number of school pupils should, with luck, be able to see the living shark. Education is also a prime function of the Marine Conservation Society which issues 'Factsheets' on sharks from time to time.[28] Popular articles on the basking shark are fairly frequent in natural history and diving magazines.[29] The basking shark now features in the publicity for at least one Scottish 'whale watching' activity, which like similar schemes across the world invites the participants to observe many forms of marine life besides the whales themselves.[30] A similar combination of summer holiday and participation in observations of the shark with an avowedly scientific purpose is offered under the auspices of The Basking Shark Society, a small charity which, with minimal funding, has conducted regular observations of the sharks in Manx waters since 1982.[31]

There has been no hunting of the basking shark by a British vessel since 1994 and with the massive fish now routinely perceived as the 'gentle giant' of British seas, the momentum of the conservationist campaign for its full protection will soon overpower any consideration of fishery quotas for either British fishermen or outsiders. It can be confidently predicted that even if not this year, the name 'basking shark *Cetorhinus maximus*' will soon be gazetted as an addition to schedule 5 of the Wildlife and Countryside Act. When this happens, a minor but unusual fishery with many points of real interest for the student of Scottish sea fisheries, which persisted for over two hundred years, will finally have been brought to a close.

PROTECTION

While this book was in press, Michael Meacher, the Minister for the Environment, announced that as from 16 April 1998, the basking shark would be added to Schedule 5 of the Wildlife and Countryside Act. The full protection afforded under the Act would make intentional killing of the shark or injury to it illegal and prohibit disturbance of the fish on the sale of products from it. The Minister hoped that this protection of the fish in United Kingdom waters would be 'exemplary considering the threatened status of the basking shark elsewhere in the world'.[32]

Fig. 61. This classic photograph by the naturalist F. F. Darling shows two basking sharks (female in front, male behind) feeding at the surface close to the shore of one of the Summer Isles, Wester Ross, in June 1943. (Darling (1947): 220)

Notes

1. Shark Trust (1997); & *Shark News*, no 9, June 1997: 13.
2. Kibby (1996).
3. Kunzlik (1988): 17-18; shark numbers – 1946–1953, Kunzlik (1988): 13; 1978–1994, H. McCrindle *pers. comm.* 1998.
4. Pennant (1769): 78-79.
5. *OSA* vol 8: 340.
6. *NSA* vol 7 :204.
7. *NSA* vol 14, sect 1: 213.
8. Landsborough (1875): 96.
9. Quotation – *GH* 2 Sept 1937: 9c; Cornwall – Clover (1998b).
10. Joung *et al* (1996).
11. Pollard (1997): 2.
12. I.G.Priede *pers. comm.* 1997.
13. Matthews & Parker (1952): 256.
14. Berrow & Heardman (1994): 104.
15. Wagner (1995).
16. HC:PD:WH no 1748: 445; Act of Tynwald – *Wildlife Act* 1990 Schedule 5; S of G: I. of G: Ord. no 25, 1 Aug 1997 (w.e.f. 1 Nov 1997).
17. Mar Con Soc (1994): 3.
18. D. Wilson *pers. comm.* 1997.
19. *Shark News* no 5, Oct 1995: 4; & Lum (1996).
20. Earll & Turner (1992).
21. Stevens (1996).
22. Fergusson (1996).
23. Priede (1984): 201-202.
24. Priede (1978): 1.
25. Priede (1984): 206-207.
26. Anon (1995a).
27. *T* 10 June 1996: 8.
28. Donovan & Black (1996); Mar Cons Soc (1994).
29. Examples are: Earll (1990), Grange (1992),Tennyson (1992), Tyler (1992), Deas (1993), Anon (1995) & Wilson (1996).
30. *Geog Mag* April 1997: 64.
31. *T* 3 Sept 1996: 15; & K. Watterson *pers. comm.* 1997.
32. Dept Env Min Statement 26 Mar 1998.

Appendices

A: POPULAR NAMES FOR THE BASKING SHARK

GAELIC

cearban	= 'sharp/cutting one' from *cearb* = 'keen, sharp, cutting'? Or from Latin *carcharus* = dogfish?
	Variants: *cairbean, cairbhean, cairbein*[1],
seoldair	= sailor[2]

SCOTS

brigdie[3]	From Old Norse *bregðá*[4].
	Variants: *bregdie*[5], *brigde*[6], *brugda*[7], *bragda*[8], *brygde*[9].
carbin	From Gaelic *cearban*.
	Variants: *cairban, carfin*[10], *carbane*[11] *kerban*[12].
hoe-mother	Orkney. Literally 'mother of the dogfish'.
	Variant: *homer*[13]
muldoan	Origin not known – possibly 'a corruption of Gaelic *maol dobhran,* the otter, transferred in sea-taboo language to the shark'.[14]
pricker[15]	
sailfish[16]	
sunfish[17]	
'whale'	Local – Inveraray, Loch Fyne, 1840s[18]

NORN

brigda, brigdi	From Norse *brugda, brygda, brigde*[19]
sulbrigda, sulbrigdi	Originally *sol-brogða – sol-brygðá*[20]

ENGLISH

basker[21]
basking shark[22]
sailfish[23]
sunfish[24]

DICTIONARY REFERENCES

(For other references, see Bibliography)

Forbes, A.R. (1905), *Gaelic Names of Beasts (Mammalia), Birds, Fishes, Insects, Reptiles, Etc . . .* Edinburgh, Oliver & Boyd.

Grant, W. & Murison, D. (eds.) (1931-), *Scottish National Dictionary*, vol 2 (1941), vol 6 (1965), vol 7 (1968). Edinburgh, Scottish National Dictionary Association.

Highland Society of Scotland (1828), *Dictionarium Scoto-Celticum: a Dictionary of the Celtic Language . . .* 2 vols. Edinburgh, W. Blackwood.

Jakobsen, J. (1928), *An Etymological Dictionary of the Norn Language in Shetland. pt 1.* London, D. Nutt (A.G. Berry).

Jamieson, I., (1879-), *An Etymological Dictionary of the Scottish Language . . . New Edition . . .* vols 1 & 2 (1880); vol 3 (1880); vol 4 (1882). Paisley, [?]. (1st Edition 1808).

Kynoch, D. (ed) (1996), *A Doric Dictionary: Two-Way Lexicon of North-East Scots.* Edinburgh, Scottish Cultural Press.

Macleod, I. *et al* (1990), *The Scots Thesaurus.* Aberdeen, Aberdeen University Press.

MacLeod, R.D. (1956), *Key to the Names of British Fishes, Mammals, Amphibians and Reptiles.* London, Pitman.

Robinson, M. (ed) (1985), *The Concise Scots Dictionary.* Aberdeen, Aberdeen University Press.

Simpson, J.A. & Weiner E.S.C. (eds) (1989), *Oxford English Dictionary*, Oxford, Clarendon Press (2nd ed) vols 1, 14 & 17.

Notes

1. Derivation from *cearb* – D Thomson *pers. comm.* 1997. Other derivation and variants from Forbes (1905): 40, who gives *cairbean* as the main spelling. The scientific name is given as *Canis carcharias* in Highland Society of Scotland (1828): 207. [The editors of this Society were obviously careless with their scientific names.]

2. Used in the Tarbert (Loch Fyne) area c. 1950. (A. Paterson, *pers. comm.* 1995.)

3. Jamieson, vol 1 (1879): 299. MacLeod (1990): 25, for Shetland, Orkney and northern Scotland – not 20th century. [In fact, still used in Shetland – Nicoloson (1992): 5–8.]

4. Derivation – Robinson (1985): 65.

5. Grant & Murison, vol 2 (1941): 270.

6. This variant in Jamieson, vol 1 (1879): 299.

7. This variant in Forbes (1905): 385–386.

8. This variant in Forbes (1905): 385–386.

9. Goodlad, C.A., (1971): 32.

10. Jamieson, vol 1 (1879). Robinson (1985): 80 gives *cairban* as late 18th-early 19th century.

11. Menzies, A., (1768) 'Voyage through the Western Isles . . .': [20] (SRO E729/9).

12. In letter of Donald MacLeod 1768 (SRO E727/16/3).

13. Jamieson vol 2 (1880): 601.

14. Grant & Murison, vol 6 (1965): 358. MacLeod (1990): 26, for Aberdeen and Argyll only. Kynoch (1996): 61, for north-east Scotland. According to G. Maxwell the 'fisherman's

name for the [basking] sharks' -Maxwell (1952): 125. From *Muldoanich* 'an island in the Barra group where they [basking sharks] are fairly common . . .' (Hillaby (1946): 8.

15. Jamieson, vol 3 (1880): 546, for Peterhead 'From its projecting back fin.' Grant & Murison vol 7 (1968): 242.
16. Jamieson, vol 4 (1882): 91; references from *OSA* reports, for Argyll and South Uist. Used in Carradale, Kintyre, until recent times. (A Paterson, *pers. comm.* 1995.) OED vol 14: 374 – gives as earliest reference, Scotland 1808.
17. Jamieson vol 4 (1882): 462. OED vol 17: 196 – Ireland 1746. *OSA* has *sunfish* used as often as *sailfish*.
18. *NSA* vol 7: 32.
19. Jakobsen (1928): 73.
20. Jakobsen (1928): 73 – '. . . because the shark usually basks in the sunshine on the surface of the sea.'[An independent Norse concept or a derivation from Pennant (1769) ?]
21. Grange (1992): 58 & 60. Not in OED. Colloquial. Possibly mainly in use by scientists studying the fish at sea.
22. OED vol 1: 987 quotes Bingley (1802) who, following Pennant, states that the name came from the 'propensity to lie on the surface of the water as if to bask itself in the sun'. (Bingley (1804): 212.) Pennant, noting that *sunfish* was in use 'from its lying as if to sun itself on the surface of the water' invented *basking shark* as *sunfish* was used for other fish. (Pennant (1769): 154. 'Basking' in the modern sense of 'sunbathing' itself only dates from 1697 (OED vol 1: 987.)
23. See as for SCOTS above.
24. See as for SCOTS above.

B: MEMORIAL OF DONALD MACLEOD, CANNA, 1766

(SRO E728/13/1-5)
A three-page manuscript in an unidentified hand signed by Donald MacLeod. Contractions have been written in full and the initial capitals of the original have generally been eliminated.

Memorial with regard to the Cairban Fishing for Donald McLeod [sic] Tacksman of the Island of Canna, To the Right Honourable the Commissioners of Annexed Estates.

Humbly sheweth

That the memorialist having attempted this new species of fishery upon the west coast and isles, Doctor Walker in his tour through those parts, after conversing with the memorialist upon the nature of this fishery, advised him to apply to the Honourable Board for an aid towards enabling him to prosecute the said fishing in a proper manner: and the Doctor drew up a memorial and presented the same to the Board wherein the nature of his fishing and the memorialist's method of prosecuting the same are particularly described, to which the memorialist begs leave to refer.

That the memorialist came up to Edinburgh in hopes of receiving such aid from the Honourable Board, in consequence of what Doctor Walker had set forth in the said memorial; but the Board though disposed to assist him that time had no fund which they could bestow for that purpose.

That the memorialist under this difficulty was directed by some of the Honourable Commissioners to get an estimate made up of the expence of building a wherry etc for the cairban fishery that the Honourable Board might thereby judge what sum to apply for, to His Majesty as an aid; and the memorialist after conversing with various tradesmen at Leith presented to the Board such estimate amounting to £247 in consequence whereof the Honourable Board applied for leave to bestow the sum of £250 for promoting the cairban fishery which soon after obtained His Majesty's approbation.

The Secretary by order of the Board having informed the memorialist of His Majesty's gracious approbation, but that the Board rather inclined to freight a vessel than build one. The memorialist would humbly beg leave to observe, that the sum granted by His Majesty would soon be expended in freighting a vessel, and in the tackling proper and necessary for this fishing without obtaining the end proposed by Doctor Walker's memorial. An hired vessel and the hands therein must be under the management of the master, not the freighter, who may often thwart if not entirely disappoint the freighter in his attempts of killing the cairban; whereas a vessel built for, and entirely under the management of, the memorialist, with hands of his own breeding, will leave him at liberty to pursue his own methods of fishing, will last a great number of years and will enable him to make this fishing become of more general benefit by breeding a number of fishers upon the coast, which the memorialist presumes was the object the Honourable Board had greatly in view when they applied for power to bestow said sum of £250 for promoting it; and this was what Dr Walker had also in view as will appear from his memorial.

The memorialist being informed of His Majesty's approbation as above mentioned, came up to Edinburgh a second time, but proved unluckily too late as the Board had adjourned. However, he waited upon some of the Honourable Commissioners and explained the injury he would sustain if another season was lost without his being provided in a vessel, and they gave it as their opinion that he might in the meantime contract with a carpenter for building a vessel and be preparing his nets etc and that when the Board met in June, he would then receive the aid granted by His Majesty.

Accordingly the memorialist agreed with a ship carpenter in Leith for building a vessel proper for cod, lyng & herring fishing, as proposed by Dr Walker, as well as for the cairban, which with proper tackling and nets, will cost betwixt £500 and £600; but this additional expence the memorialist is to pay himself. That the nature of the agreement with the carpenter is, that two thirds of the price is payable about this time and the other one third at the finishing of the ship.

The memorialist begs leave to add that he was the first that ever discovered the cairban and proved successful in killing them; and that he has instructed several people on the west coast in the method of catching them.

That the necessary attendance he has been obliged to give at Edinburgh during the two last seasons of the cairban fishery has proved a very considerable expence to him besides his loss of time; he therefore humbly flatters himself the Honourable Board upon considering these and the other circumstances sett forth in his memorial will be pleased to grant him the encouragement applied for by the Board and approved of by his Majesty, agreeable to the estimate made up and presented by the memorialist eighteen months ago.

The memorialist is willing to come under such conditions and regulations for carrying on the said cairban fishery as shall seem proper to the Honourable Board; and shall at the end of every fishing season transmit to the office an exact account of his proceedings and of the number and size of the fish killed by him, in order that the Honourable Commissioners may be able to form a judgement of his diligence & success in this new branch of fishery. He will also transmit at the same time an account of his proceedings in the cod & lyng fishing.

Donald MacLeod

[On outer side] Memorial for Donald MacLeod Tacksman of the Island of Canna 1766 *[and in another hand]* Read 30th June.

C: REPORT BY COMMISSIONER ARCHIBALD MENZIES, 1768

(SRO E729/9)
Archibald Menzies of Culdares was appointed General Inspector to the Board of Commissioners for the Annexed Estates in 1764.[1] *In 1768 he undertook a* 'Voyage through the Western Isles and west coast of Scotland to . . . report the present State of . . . Farming Manufactures and . . . fisherys upon these Coasts.' *His report to the Commissioners includes this account of capturing a basking shark. [Punctuation has been inserted where necessary.]*

Whilst at Barmore [near Tarbert, Loch Fyne] we saw a large Carbane or Sail Fish in the Bay we sent some Boats in quest of it. [16] Next day we returned to Tarbert. Upon our ar[r]ival we found the Boats return'd that had gone in quest of the Carbane or Sail Fish which they had caught after a long Chase, The Fish measured 30 feet from the Head to the Root of the Tayl ten feet broad at the thickest part, has a long fin on his Back which with the Tayll he uses as a saill from whence he has his namme there are two lesser fins under his Belly. The Head resembles a Shark and is reckon'd of that tribe. Pontopidon mentions them in his History of Norway[2] – This Fish had about 10 Barrells of Liver which produce'd 6 Barrells of Oyll 32 gallons to the Barrell a Barrell is worth from 50Sh to £3 – the Oyll is reckoned superior to any other for the currying of Leather & is much esteem'd by the Clothier as it is easily discharg'd. This Fishery might turn to great account if properly follow'd as they appear in these seas in great Quantitys from the Month of June to the month of October – Sometimes the Fish appairs in Pairs at other times in Sholes when they have a Leader, as it is a sluggish Fish they are easily harpoon'd. One Stewart at Bute is fitting out a Boat with a small swivel at the Bow, he proposes fixing a Harpoon to a piece of Wood which is to serve as a Wadd to the Gun. This he is to fire into the Fish whether or not this will answer Experience will only show. Stewart has been pretty successfull for some years past in this Fishery with the Harpoon. [20]-21.

Description of fishing boats at Campbeltown:
. . . their Boats . . . are generally about 18 feet Keel 7 feet Beam and four feet hold. [30]

Notes

1. Smith, A. *Jacobite Estates of the Forty-five.* Edinburgh, John Donald, 1982: 48. For a wider discussion of Menzies' reports see Smith, A. *passim* and Wills, V. *Reports on the Annexed Estates 1755-1769* . . . Edinburgh, HMSO, 1973: xii.
2. Erik Pontoppiddan (1698-1764), Bishop of Bergen, author of the widely-read *Natural History of Norway* (1755).

Bibliography

A ARCHIVES

Scottish Record Office, Edinburgh (SRO)
  (i) Exchequer: Inventory of Forfeited Estates Papers 1745–1824. [Unpaginated typescript.]
 (ii) Forfeited Estates Papers: E727/16/1–6; E727/18/1–49; E727/19/8; E727/60/1–3; E728/13/1–5 & E729/9.
(iii) Island of Soay Shark Fisheries Limited. File BT2/25375.
 (iv) Scottish West Coast Fisheries Limited. File BT2/20465.

Hamilton & Kinneil Estates, Lennoxlove, Haddington, East Lothian.
Island of Soay Shark Fisheries Limited. Five folders of papers [assigned the prefix HKIS and a number for the purposes of the present work]:
  HKIS1. Minutes & agenda.
  HKIS2 Charges made out to 9.10.48.
  HKIS3 Charges made out to 10.11.49.
  HKIS4 Documents.
  HKIS5 Notes on libel action Maxwell v. O'Connor and Another.

University of Edinburgh Library (EU)
Papers of Rev Dr John Walker: Dc. 2. 39/1 (Papers on Agriculture, Natural History, etc) & La III 352/1 (Correspondence).

Warwickshire County Record Office, Warwick. (WCRO)
Fielding Papers: Correspondence of Thomas Pennant (1726–1798): CR 2017/TP 290/1–20 (Letters from Rev George Low).

B THESES

Fairfax, D.P., (1995) Aspects of the Basking Shark Fishery in Scotland circa 1760 to 1994. Unpublished MLitt dissertation, University of St. Andrews.

Farmery, J.S.P. (1992), Zooplankton Analysis with Reference to the Feeding Behaviour of *Cetorhinus maximus* off the Coast of The Isle of Man. Unpublished BSc project, University of Wales (Bangor).

Lindquist, O., (1994) Whales, Dolphins and Porpoises in the Economy and Culture of Peasant Fishermen in Norway, Orkney, Shetland, Faeroe Islands and Iceland, ca 900–1900 AD, and Norse Greenland, ca 1000–1500 AD. Unpublished PhD thesis, University of St. Andrews.

McLachlan, H., (1991) An Analysis of the Sightings of the Basking Shark, *Cetorhinus maximus*, in British Coastal Waters from 1987–1990, and Behavioural Observations of Sharks in the Waters around the Isle of Man in the Summer of 1990. Unpublished MSc dissertation, University of Wales (Bangor).

Stagg, A.E., (1990) A Study of the Behaviour and Migration of the Basking Shark, *Cetorhinus maximus* (Gunner), in British and Irish waters. Unpublished MSc dissertation, University of Wales (Bangor).

Strawbridge, J. (1992) The Behavioural Ecology of the Basking Shark *Cetorhinus maximus* in Inshore Waters off the Isle of Man. Unpublished MSc dissertation, University of Wales (Bangor).

Strong, P.G., (1992) Basking Sharks in Relation to Stratification and Phytoplankton around the Isle of Man, Summer 1991. Unpublished MSc dissertation, University of Wales (Bangor).

C STATUTES & STATUTORY INSTRUMENTS

(a) United Kingdom

An Act to Revive and Continue . . . an Act for the More Effectual Encouragement of the British Fisheries . . . (12 July, 1799). (39 Geo III: Cap 100.)

An Act for the Further Encouragement and Improvement of the British Fisheries (24 July 1820). (1 Geo IV: Cap 103.)

An Act to Amend the Several Acts for the Encouragement and Improvement of the British and Irish Fisheries (17 June 1824). (5 Geo IV: Cap 64.)

The Wildlife and Countryside Act 1981 (30 Oct 1981) & Wildlife and Countryside (Amendment) Act 1991

Wildlife and Countryside Act 1981 (Variations of Schedules 5 and 8) Order 1998 (1998/878) (20 March 1998)

(b) Isle of Man
The Wildlife Act 1990 (20 Feb 1990)

(c) States of Guernsey
Island of Guernsey, Ordinance of the States, no XXV: The Fishing Ordinance 1997 (1 Aug 1997)

D PARLIAMENTARY & OFFICIAL PAPERS

Department of the Environment, Transport and The Regions.
Meacher Moves to Protect More British Species (235 Env. 26 March 1998) [Ministerial Statement].
House of Commons – Debates
Parliamentary Debates (House of Commons) vol 337, 1937–38 (337 H C Deb 5s) 29 June 1938 ; vol 347, 1938–9 (347 H C Deb.5s) 23 May 1939 & vol 348, 1938–9 (348 H C Deb.5s), 6 June 1939.
House of Commons: Parliamentary Debates: Weekly Hansard, no 1748, 10–14 February 1997.
House of Commons – Reports of Committees
Third Report from the Committee, Appointed to Enquire into the State of the British Fisheries, and into the Most Effectual Means for Their Improvement and Extension. (14 July 1785)
Further Report on the State of the British Herring Fisheries. (27 June 1798)

E. HYDROGRAPHIC CHARTS

Great Britain, Hydrographic Department,
2131 Firth of Clyde & Loch Fyne.
2503 Approaches to Kinlochbervie.

F. BOOKS, ARTICLES AND REPORTS

Anderson, J., (1795) An Account of the Present State of the Hebrides and Western Coasts of Scotland . . . Edinburgh, C. Elliot.
Anon (1808) Proceedings of the Wernerian Natural History Society. *The Scots Magazine and Edinburgh Miscellany,* vol 70, Nov 1808: 805
Anon (1809a) [Proceedings of the Wernerian Natural History Society] *The Scots Magazine and Edinburgh Literary Miscellany,* vol 71, Jan 1809: 5–6;
Anon (1809b) [Proceedings of the Wernerian Natural History Society] *The Scots Magazine and Edinburgh Miscellany* vol 71, Feb 1809: 117.

Anon (1937a) The Sharks. *The Times*, 14 Sept 1937: 13d.

Anon (1937b) Sharks Attack Ships: Large Numbers Reported Causing Havoc in Scottish Waters. *New York Times*, 30 Sept 1937: [?]

Anon (1938) A Gallant Girl and Four Gallant Boys. *The Life-Boat*, April 1938: 429–430.

Anon (1995a) Satellite Tagging of Basking Sharks. *Society for Underwater Technology News*, no 39: 5.

Anon (1995b) A Story of Perseverance. *Fishing Boats* (40 + Fishing Boats & Friends Association Newsletter), no 1, Apr 1995: 6.

Anon (1996) Robane: Suprane. New York, Robeco Inc.

Barclay, [J.] (1811) Remarks on Some Parts of the Animal that Was Cast Ashore on the Island of Stronsa, September 1808. *Memoirs of the Wernerian Natural History Society*. vol 1: 418–444.

Barnard, K.H., (1937) Further Notes on South African Marine Fishes. *Annals of the South African Museum*, vol 32, pt 2, Mar 1937: 41–67 + 3 pl.

Barry, G., (1805) History of the Orkney Islands. Edinburgh, the author. (Facsimile edition. Edinburgh, James Thin, 1975.)

Beeton, I., (1861) Mrs Beeton's Book of Household Management . . . London, Chancellor Press, 1982 (Reprint of 1st edition).

Berrow, S.D. & Heardman, C., (1994) The Basking Shark *Cetorhinus maximus* (Gunnerus) in Irish Waters – Patterns of Distribution and Abundance. *Biology and Environment: Proceedings of the Royal Irish Academy*, vol 94B, no 2: 101–107.

Berry, R.J. & Johnston, J.L., (1980) The Natural History of Shetland. London, Collins.

Bettany, G.T., (1885) Barclay, John (1758–1826), Anatomist. In *Dictionary of National Biography*, vol 3: 166–167.

Bettany, G.T., (1887) Couch, Jonathan (1789–1870), Naturalist. In *Dictionary of National Biography*, vol 12: 323–324.

Bettany, G. T., (1891) Home, Sir Everard (1756–1852), Surgeon. In *Dictionary of National Biography*, vol 27: 227–228.

Bigelow, H.B & Schroeder, W.C., (1948) Sharks. In Tee-Van, J. *et al* (eds) Fishes of the Western North Atlantic. *Memoirs of the Sears Foundation for Marine Research*, no 1, pt 1: 59–546.

Bigelow, H.B. & Schroeder, W.C., (1953) Fishes of the Gulf of Maine. *Fishery Bulletin of the [United States] Fish & Wildlife Service*, vol 53. (1st revision).

Bingley, W., (1804) Animal Biography, or Authentic Anecdotes of the Lives, Manners and Economy of the Animal Creation . . . vol 3. London, R. Phillips. (2nd edition.)

de Blainville, H., (1811) Memoire sur le Squale Pelerin. *Annales du Museum D'Histoire Naturelle* . . . [Paris]: 88–135.

de Blainville, M.H., (1816) Prodrome d'une Nouvelle Distribution Systematique du Regne Animal. *Bulletin des Sciences par La Societe Philomatique de Paris*, 1816: 113–124.

Bland, K.P. & Swinney, G.N., (1978) Basking Shark: Genera *Halsydrus* Neill and

Scapasaurus Marwick as Synonyms of *Cetorhinus* Blainville. *Journal of Natural History*, vol 12: 133–135.

Botting, D., (1993) Gavin Maxwell: the Life of the Man Who Wrote *Ring of Bright Water*. London, Harper Collins.

Boulger, G.S., (1909) Walker, John (1731–1803). Professor of Natural History . . . In *Dictionary of National Biography*, vol 20: 531.

Bowen, E.G., (1972) Britain and the Western Seaways. London, Thames & Hudson.

Brand, J., (1701) A Brief Description of Orkney, Shetland, Pightland-Firth and Caithness. Edinburgh, G. Mosman

Bray, E., (1986) The Discovery of the Hebrides: Voyages to the Western Isles 1745–1883. London, Collins.

Browne, T., (1902) Notes and Letters on the Natural History of Norfolk from the MSS of Sir Thomas Browne . . . (Notes by T. Southwell). London, Jarrold & Sons.

Buranudeen, F. & Richards-Rajadurai, P.N., (1986) Squalene. *Infofish Marketing Digest* no 1/86: 42–43.

Cambi, M., (1996) Costa Rica's Shark Fishery and Cartilage Industry. *Shark News* (Newsletter of the IUCN Shark Specialist Group), no 8, Dec 1996: 12–13.

Campbell, J.L., (1994) Canna: the Story of a Hebridean Island. Edinburgh, Canongate Press. (3rd edition, first published 1984.)

Carmichael, A., (1941) Carmina Gadelica . . . Collected in the Highlands and Islands of Scotland. vol 4. Edinburgh, Oliver & Boyd.

Clarke, R., (1956) Sperm Whales of the Azores. *Discovery Reports*, vol 28: 237–298 + 2 pl.

Clover, C., (1997) Fishing Free-for-all is Putting the 'New' Deep-water Species at Risk. *Daily Telegraph*, 18 Aug 1997: 8.

Clover, C., (1988a) Shark Can Bask in Safety as it Joins New Protected List. *Daily Telegraph*, 27 Mar 1998: 12.

Clover, C., (1998b) Record 500 Sharks Seen off Cornwall. *Daily Telegraph*, 16 May 1998: 7.

Cochran, L.E., (1985) Scottish Trade with Ireland in the Eighteenth Century. Edinburgh, John Donald.

Compagno, L.J.V., (1984) FAO Species Catalogue: vol 4 Sharks of the World . . . pt 1 – Hexanchiformes to Lamniformes. (FAO Fisheries Synopses) Rome, FAO.

Couch, J., (1825) Some Particulars of the Natural History of Fishes Found in Cornwall. *Transactions of the Linnean Society of London*, vol 14, pt 3: 69–92.

Couch, J., (1862) History of the Fishes of the British Islands. vol 1. London, Groombridge. [Later edition with same text, London, G. Bell, 1877]

Cramb, A., (1987) Scotland's Lone Basking Shark Hunter under Attack. *Glasgow Herald*, 3 Mar 1987: [?]

Cust, L., (1890) Griffith, Moses (fl. 1769–1809), Draughtsman and Engraver . . . In *Dictionary of National Biography*, vol 23: 235.

Cuthbert, O.D., (1995) The Life and Times of an Orkney Naturalist: Reverend George Low, 1747–95. Kirkwall, Orkney Press.

Cutting, C.L., (1955) Fish Saving: a History of Fish Processing from Ancient to Modern Times. London, Leonard Hill.

Cuvier, G., (1817) Le Regne Animal Distribue d'apres son Organisation. tome 2. Paris, Chez Deterville Libraire.

Daily Record & Mail, (1937) 2 Sept: 1; 3 Sept: 2 & 16.

Daniel, J.F., (1922) The Elasmobranch Fishes. Berkeley, University of California Press.

Darling, F.F., (1947) Natural History in the Highlands and Islands. London, Collins.

Day, F., (1884) The Fishes of Great Britain and Ireland. vol 2. London, Williams & Norgate.

Deas, W., (1993) In Search of the Basking Shark. *Scottish Diver,* vol 31, Nov 1993: 54–58 & vol 32, Jan 1994: 89–91.

van Deinse, A. B. & Adriani, M.J., (1953) On the Absence of Gill Rakers in Specimens of the Basking Shark, *Cetorhinus maximus* (Gunner). *Zoologische Mededelingen . . . Leiden,* vol 31, no 27: 307–310.

Donovan, T. & Black, B. (1996) Boats, Barnacles & Basking Sharks: Marine Environmental Education in Argyll: a Teachers' Pack. [Edinburgh] Scottish Natural Heritage.

Dunlop, J. (1978) The British Fisheries Society 1786–1893. Edinburgh, John Donald.

Earll, R., (1990) The Basking Shark: Its Fishery and Conservation. *British Wildlife Journal,* vol 1, no 3, Feb 1990: 121–129.

Earll, R.C. & Turner, J.R., (1992) A Review of Methods and Results from a Sighting Scheme and Field Research on the Basking Shark in 1987–92. (Unpublished Report). Peterborough, Joint Committee for Nature Conservation.

Edmondston, A. (1809) A View of the Ancient and Present State of the Zetland Islands, vol 2, Edinburgh, J. Ballantyne.

English, S. (1996) Satellitcs Will Keep Watch on Secret Life of Basking Shark. *The Times,* 20 Aug 1996: 8.

Fairfax, D.P., (1998) Man and the Basking Shark in Scotland. In Lambert, R.A., (ed) Species History in Scotland: Introductions and Extinctions since the Ice Age. Edinburgh, Scottish Cultural Press: 93–106

Fairley, J., (1981) Irish Whales and Whaling. Belfast, Blackstaff Press.

Fenton, A., (1978) The Northern Isles: Orkney and Shetland. Edinburgh, John Donald. Reprinted (1997) East Linton, Tuckwell Press.

Fergusson, I. K. (1996) Tracking Sharks by Videocamera – *Crittercam:* the Video Parasite. *Shark News* (Newsletter of the IUCN Shark Specialist Group), no 7, June 1996: 5.

Fleming, J., (1828) A History of British Animals . . . Edinburgh, Bell & Bradfute.

[Fleming, J.], (1830) Ichthyology. In Brewster, D. (ed) The Edinburgh Encyclopaedia, vol II, pt 2. Edinburgh, W. Blackwood: 657–719.

Forsyth, R., (1808) The Beauties of Scotland . . . vol. 5. Edinburgh, Constable & Brown.

Fowler, S., (1996) Status of the Basking Shark *Cetorhinus maximus* (Gunnerus). *Shark News* (Newsletter of the IUCN Shark Specialist Group), no 6, Mar 1996: 4–5.

Francis, M., (1996) Observations on a Pregnant White Shark with a Review of Reproductive Biology. In Klimley, A.P. & Ainley, D.G. (Eds) Great White Sharks: the Biology of *Carcharodon carcharias*. London, Academic Press: 157–172.

Geddes, [J.]T., (1960) Hebridean Sharker. London, Herbert Jenkins.

Geographical Magazine, April 1997: 64.

Gervais, P. & Gervais, M., (1876) Observations Relatives à un Squale Pèlerin . . . *Journal de Zoologie* . . . [Paris] vol 50: 319–329 + 3 pl.

Glasgow Herald, [1907] Index to the *Glasgow Herald* for the year 1906. Glasgow, G. Outram. & Ibid 1907 [1908] -1968 [1969].

Glasgow Herald, (1937) 2 Sept: 9c; 3 Sept: 7c; 6 Sept: 11g; 9 Sept: 9a; 20 Sept: 11e & 12; 21 Sept: 7c; 25 Sept: 10a; 27 Sept: 11; 2 Dec: 11g; 11 Dec: 9b; & (1938) 26 July: 7; & (1939) 24 May: 7; 7 June: 9c; 11 Aug: 5; & (1945) 2 Jun: 5g; 3 Sept: 3e; 5 Sept: 3c; 6 Sept: 3e; & (1955) 5 Mar: 3.

Goodlad, C.A., (1971) Shetland Fishing Saga. [Lerwick], Shetland Times.

Graham, M. (ed), (1956) Sea Fisheries: Their Investigation in the United Kingdom. London, E. Arnold.

Grange, J., (1992) Maws. *BBC Wildlife*, Nov 1992: 56–61.

Gray, M., (1978) The Fishing Industries of Scotland, 1790–1914: a Study in Regional Adaptation. Oxford, Oxford University Press.

Greener, W.W., (1910) The Gun and Its Development. [Birmingham?] 9th ed. (1st edition 1881) (Reprinted. London, Arms & Armour, 1986)

Grieve, J., (1966) Plankton Study at Kaikoura: Answer Sought to Pelagic Fish Movements. *Commercial Fishing* [New Zealand] Sept 1966: 18.

Gudger, E.W., (1953) Maxillary Breathing Valves in the Sharks *Chlamydoselachus* and *Cetorhinus*. . ., *Journal of Morphology*, vol. 57, no 1: 91–104.

Gunnerus, J.E., (1765) Brugden (*Squalus maximus*). *Det Trondhiemske Selskabs Skrifter*, vol 3: 33–49 + pl 2.

Gunnerus, J.E. (1770) Nogle smaa rare og mestendelen nye Norske Sodyr Beskrevene. *Skrifter som udi det Kiobenhavnske Selskab af Laerdoms og Videnskabers Elskere*, 1765–1769, vol 10: 175.

Hallacher, L.E., (1977) On the Feeding Behaviour of the Basking Shark, *Cetorhinus maximus*. *Environmental Biology of Fish*, vol 2, no 3: 297–298.

Hancox, J., (1994) Harpoon Hunter Sails Back into a Storm: Outcry Fails to Stop Slaughter of Sharks. *Sunday Telegraph*, 18 Sept 1994: 10.

Harrison, R., (1987) Leonard Harrison Matthews 12 June 1901–27 November 1986: Elected FRS 1954. In *Biographical Memoirs of the Royal Society,* vol 33: 413–442.

Harvie-Brown, J.A. & Buckley, T.E., (1888) A Vertebrate Fauna of the Outer Hebrides. Edinburgh, D. Douglas.

Headrick, J., (1807) View of the Mineralogy, Agriculture, Manufactures and Fisheries of the Island of Arran. . . Edinburgh, G. Constable.

Henderson, D.S., (1972) Fishing for the Whale: a Guide-catalogue to the Collection of Whaling Relics in the Dundee Museum. Dundee, Dundee Museum & Art Gallery.

Herman, J.S., McGowan, R.Y. & Swinney, G.N. (1990) Catalogue of the Type Specimens of Recent Vertebrates in the National Museums of Scotland. Edinburgh, National Museums of Scotland.

Hett, G.V. (1937) Basking Sharks [letter]. *The Times,* 20 Sept 1937:13e.

Heuvelmans, B., (1968) In the Wake of the Sea-serpents. London, R. Hart-Davis.

Hilditch, T.P., (1956) The Chemical Composition of Natural Fats. London, Chapman & Hall.(3rd Ed)

Hillaby J., (1946) Shark Hunting. *Picture Post,* vol 32, no 12, 21 Sept 1946: 7–10.

Hillaby, J., (1947) Operation Adventure. London, Peter Lunn.

Holdsworth, R., & Lavery, B., (1991) The Ropery: Visitor Handbook. Norwich, Jarrold Publishing.

Home, E., (1809a) On the Nature of the Intervertebral Substance in Fish and Quadrupeds. *Philosophical Transactions of the Royal Society of London,* pt 1: 177–187.

Home, E., (1809b) An Anatomical Account of the *Squalus maximus* (of Linnaeus) Which in the Structure of Its Stomach Forms an Intermediate Link in the Gradation of Animals Between the Whale Tribe and Cartilaginous Fishes. *Philosophical Transactions of the Royal Society of London,* pt 2: 206–220.

Home, E., (1813) Additions to an Account of the Anatomy of the *Squalus maximus,* Contained in a Former Paper; with Observations on the Structure of the Branchial Artery. *Philosophical Transactions of the Royal Society of London,* pt 2: 227–241.

Hutchinson, R., (1998) Tex Geddes [Obituary]. *The Herald* 14 Apr. 1998: 7.

Izawa, K. & Shibata, T., (1993): A Young Basking Shark, *Cetorhinus maximus,* from Japan. *Japanese Journal of Ichthyology,* vol 40, no 2: 237–245.

Jackson, G., (1978) The British Whaling Trade. London, A. & C. Black.

Jonstonus, J., [1649] Historiae Naturalis: De Piscibus et Cetis. Libri V . . . Frankfurt am Main, Meriani.

Joung, S-J., Chen, C-S., Clark, E., Uchida, S. & Huang, W.Y.P. (1996) The Whale Shark, *Rhincodon typus,* is a Live-bearer: 300 Embryos Found in One 'Megamamma' Supreme. *Environmental Biology of Fishes,* vol 46: 219–223.

Karnovsky, M.L., Rapson, W.S., Schwartz, H.M., Black, M., & van Rensburg, N.J. (1948) South African Fish Products. pt 27.The Composition of the Liver Oils of the

Basking Shark (*Cetorhinus maximus,*Gunner) and the Spiny Shark (*Echinorhinus spinosus*, Gmelin). *Journal of the Society of Chemical Industry*, vol 67: 104–107.

Kibby, L., (1996) Sharks in Deep Trouble. [Scottish] *Daily Express*, 4 Sept 1996: 26.

Knox, J., (1787) A Tour Through the Highlands of Scotland and the Hebride Isles in 1786. Edinburgh, Mercat Press. (1975 edition.)

Kristjansson, L., (1983) Islenzkir Sjarrhaetir, vol 3. Reykjavik, Bokautgafa Menningarsjods

Kuban, G. J., (1997) Sea-monster or Shark? An Analysis of a Supposed Plesiosaur Carcass Netted in 1977. *Reports of the National Center for Science Education.* vol 17, no 3: 16–28.

Kunzlik, P.A., (1988) The Basking Shark. (Scottish Fisheries Information Pamphlet no 14.). Edinburgh, Department of Agriculture and Fisheries for Scotland.

Landsborough, D., (1875) Arran: its Topography, Natural History, and Antiquities. Ardrossan, Arthur Guthrie. (3rd edition, David Landsborough Jnr, editor).

Largs & Millport Weekly News & North Ayrshire Advertiser, 9 Sept 1994: 1 & 6.

Leach, W.E., (1818) Some Observations on the Genus *Squalus* of Linne, with Descriptions and Outline Figures of two British Species. *Memoirs of the Wernerian Natural History Society,* vol 2: 61–66.

Lee, A. & Langer, R., (1983) Shark Cartilage Contains Inhibitors of Tumor Angiogenesis. *Science*, vol 221, no 4616: 1185–1187.

Lien, J. & Fawcett, L., (1986) Distribution of Basking Sharks, *Cetorhinus maximus*, Incidentally Caught in Inshore Fishing Gear in Newfoundland. *Canadian Field Naturalist*, vol 100, no 2: 246–252.

Linnaeus, C., (1766) Systema Naturae: Editio 12, Tomus 1 Regnum Animale (1766): Caroli Linne . . . London, Natural History Museum 1991. (Microfiche)

Long, D.J. & Jones, R.E. (1996) White Shark Predation and Scavenging on Cetaceans in the Eastern North Pacific Ocean. In Klimley, A.P. & Ainley, D.G. (eds) Great White Sharks: the Biology of *Cacharodon carcharias.* London, Academic Press: 293–307.

Low, G., (1813) Fauna Orcadensis . . . Edinburgh, Constable.

Lucas C.E., (1956) Plankton and Fisheries Biology. In Graham, M. (ed) Sea Fisheries: Their Investigation in the United Kingdom. London, E. Arnold: 116–138.

Lum, M., (1996) Every Mouthful of Shark's Fin in High Demand. *Straits Times* (*Sunday Times*) 19 May 1996: Sunday Plus 9.

Lytle, T.G., (1984) Harpoons and other Whalecraft. New Bedford, Old Dartmouth Historical Society.

MacCaig, N., (1969): A Man in My Position. London, Chatto & Windus.

McCulloch, J., (1824) The Highlands and Western Isles of Scotland . . . London, Longmans, Hurst *et al.* 4 vols.

MacDonald, F., (1992) Island Voices. Irvine, Carrick Media.

McKay, M.M. (ed), (1980) The Rev. Dr. John Walker's *Report on the Hebrides* of 1764 and 1771. Edinburgh, John Donald.

McLean, G.R.D., (1961) Poems of the Western Highlanders. London, SPCK.

McLean, J., (1992) Hunter Stares at Jaws of Defeat. *Scotsman (Scotland on Sunday)* 12 July 1992:[?].

McNally, K., (1976) The Sunfish Hunt. Belfast, Blackstaff Press.

Marine Conservation Society, (1994) Basking Sharks (Factsheet SP/08/94). Ross on Wye, Marine Conservation Society.

Marshall, S. M. & Orr, A. P. (1955) The Biology of a Marine Copepod *Calanus finmarchicus* (Gunnerus). Edinburgh, Oliver & Boyd.

Martin, A., (1981) The Ring-net Fishermen. Edinburgh, John Donald.

Martin, A., (1995) Fishing and Whaling. Edinburgh, National Museums of Scotland.

Martin, M., (1703) A Description of the Western Islands of Scotland. Stirling, E. Mackay (1934 edition).

Matthews, L.H., (1950) Reproduction in the Basking Shark, *Cetorhinus maximus* (Gunner). *Philosophical Transactions of the Royal Society,* vol 234B: 247–316.

Matthews, L.H., (1962) The Shark that Hibernates. *New Scientist,* no 280, 29 Mar 1962: 756–759.

Matthews, L.H. & Parker, H.W., (1950) Notes on the Anatomy and Biology of the Basking Shark (*Cetorhinus maximus* (Gunner)). *Proceedings of the Zoological Society of London,* vol 120: 535–576.

Matthews, L.H. & Parker, H.W., (1951) Basking Sharks Leaping. *Proceedings of the Zoological Society of London,* vol 121: 461–462.

Matthews L.H. & Parker, H.W. (1952) The Basking Shark. In Maxwell, G. Harpoon at a Venture. London, R. Hart-Davis: 255–264.

Maxwell, G., (1952) Harpoon at a Venture. London, R. Hart-Davis.

Memoirs of the Wernerian Natural History Society, vol 2, 1818: 638–640

Molaug, S., (1985) Var gamle kystkultur, vol 1. Oslo, Dreyer.

Myklevoll, S., (1968) Norway: Basking Shark Fishery. *Commercial Fisheries Review,* July 1968: 59–63.

N. [Neill, P.] (1809) Monthly Memoranda in Natural History. *The Scots Magazine and Edinburgh Miscellany,* vol 71, Sept 1809: 645–646.

Neill, P. (1811) A List of Fishes Found in the Firth of Forth, and Rivers and Lakes Near Edinburgh, with Remarks. *Memoirs of the Wernerian Natural History Society,* vol 1: 526–555.

Nicolson, J.R. (1992) The Summer of the Brigdies. *Shetland Life,* Nov 1992: 5–8.

NSA (1845) New Statistical Account of Scotland . . . vols 5, 7, 13, 14 & 15. Edinburgh, Blackwood.

Nordgard, O., (1931) Gunnerus, Johan Ernst, 1718–73. In *Norske Biografisk Leksicon* vol 5: 98–103.

Nuttall, N (1996) Oriental Appetite for Fins Threatens the Basking Shark. *The Times,* 22 Oct 1996: 10.

O'Brien G., (1918) The Economic History of Ireland in the Eighteenth Century. Dublin, Maunsel.

O'Connor, P.S. (1953) Shark-O! London, Secker & Warburg.

O'Dea, W.T., (1958) The Social History of Lighting. London, Routledge & Kegan Paul.

Olsen's (1940) Olsen's Fisherman's Nautical Almanack . . . 1940. Scarborough, Dennis & Sons. & 1948, 1950 & 1994 editions.

'Orcadensis', (1809) On the Great Sea Snake Found in Orkney. *The Scots Magazine and Edinburgh Miscellany,* vol 71, Jul 1809: 507–509.

OSA (see Sinclair, J. (1799))

Paisley Daily Express, 2 Sept 1937: 4.

Parker, H.W. & Boesman, M., (1954) The Basking Shark, *Cetorhinus maximus,* in Winter. *Proceedings of the Zoological Society of London,* vol 124: 185–194.

Parker, H.W. & Stott, F.C., (1965): Age, Size and Vertebral Calcification in the Basking Shark, *Cetorhinus maximus* (Gunnerus). *Zoologische Mededelingen . . . Leiden,* vol 40, no 34:305–319.

Parnell, R., (1838) Prize Essay on the Natural and Economical History of the Fishes ofthe Firth of Forth. *Memoirs of the Wernerian Natural History Society,* vol 77: 161–460.

Pavesi, P., (1874) Contribuzione alla Storia Naturale del Genere Selache. *Annali del Museo Civico di Storia Naturale di Genova,* vol 6: 5–72 + 3pl.

Pavesi, P., (1878) Seconda Contribuzione alla Morphologia e Sistemica dei Selachii. *Annali del Museo Civico di Storia Naturale di Genova,* vol 12: 348–418 + 2 pl.

Pelster, B., (1997) Buoyancy at Depth. In Randall, D.J. & Farrell, A.P. (eds) Deep-sea Fishes. London, Academic Press: 195–230.

Pennant, T., (1769) British Zoology: Class III Reptiles: IV Fish. vol 3. Chester, E. Adams.

Pennant, T., (1774) A Tour in Scotland 1769 and Voyage to the Hebrides 1772. Warrington, W. Eyres (vols 1 & 2); Chester, J. Monk (vol 3).

Pennant, T.,(1776a) British Zoology: Class III Reptiles: IV Fish. vol 3. London, B. White.

Pennant, T., (1776b) Ibid. [Pennant's annotated copy in the Zoology Library of the Natural History Museum, London.]

Pennant, T., (1777) [Caledonian Zoology] In Lightfoot, J., Flora Scotica: the Native Plants of Scotland and the Hebrides. London, B. White : 1–66.

Pennant, T., (1793) The Literary Life of the Late Thomas Pennant, Esq: By Himself. London, B. & J. White.

'Piscator' (1792) Account of a Voyage to the Hebrides, by a Committee of the

British Fisheries Society, in the Year 1787. *The Bee or Weekly Intelligencer* (Edinburgh, J. Anderson) vol 8, 21 Mar 1792: 66–83 & 4 April 1792: 173–178; vol 9, 23 May 1792: 89–95.

Pollard, S. (1997) Basking with Sharks – Biology and Conservation of the Basking Shark *Cetorhinus maximus* in U.K. Waters. In *Proceedings of the Third European Shark and Ray Workshop* (in press).

Pontoppidan, E., (1755) The Natural History of Norway . . . London, A. Linde. [Translation of Det Forske Forsog Norges Naturlige Historie 1752–1754]

Pottle, F.A. & Bennett, C.H. (eds.), (1963) Boswell's Journal of a Tour to the Hebrides with Samuel Johnson . . . Melbourne, Heineman.

Priede, I.G., (1978) Satellite Tracking of Basking Sharks (*Cetorhinus maximus*): Report on Work Carried Out During the 1978 Season. (Unpublished Report). Aberdeen, University of Aberdeen.

Priede, I.G., (1984) A Basking Shark (*Cetorhinus maximus*) Tracked by Satellite together with Simultaneous Remote Sensing. *Fisheries Research* no 2: 201–206.

Rae, B.B., (1956) The Basking Shark Fishery on the West of Scotland. *Scottish Fisheries Bulletin* no 5, June 1956: 13–14.

Ralston, T., (1995) My Captains: Memoirs of a Scottish West Coast Fisherman. Aberdeen, Scottish Cultural Press.

Reipma, S.F., (1970) The Story of Margarine. Washington, Public Affairs Press.

Riedman, S.R. & Gustafson, E.T., (1969) Focus on Sharks. New York, Abelard Schuman.

Rose, D. A., (1996) An Overview of World Trade in Sharks and Other Cartilaginous Fishes. Cambridge, TRAFFIC International.

Sandison, C., (1968) Unst: My Island Home and Its Story. Lerwick, Shetland Times.

de Saussure, L.A.N., (1822) A Voyage to the Hebrides, or Western Isles of Scotland. London, R. Phillips.

Scotland – Fishery Board, (1900) *Selache maxima* (Gunner) The Basking Shark. *Eighteenth Annual Report of the Fishery Board for Scotland: Being for the Year 1899.* Glasgow, HMSO, pt 3: 291 & *41*[st] *Annual Report 1922* (1923): 18.

Scott, W.B., & Scott, M.G., (1988) Atlantic Fishes of Canada. Toronto, University of Toronto.

Seccombe, T., (1893) Low, George (1747–1795), Naturalist. In *Dictionary of National Biography*, vol 34: 182–183.

Senna, A., (1925) Contributo alla Conscenza del Cranio della Selache (*Cetorhinus maximus* Gunn.) *Archivio Italiano di Anatomia e di Embriologia*, vol 22: 84–122 + 2 pl.

Shark News (Newsletter of the IUCN Shark Specialist Group), no 5, Oct 1995; no 9, June 1997.

Shark Trust (1997) Save Our Sharks! Newbury, The Shark Trust. [Pamphlet]

Shaw, F.J., (1980) The Northern and Western Isles of Scotland: Their Economy and Society in the Seventeenth Century. Edinburgh, John Donald.

Sims, D.W., Fox, A.M. & Merrett, D.A., (1997) Basking Shark Occurrence off Southwest England in Relation to Zooplankton Abundance. *Journal of Fish Biology*, vol 51, pt 2 : 436–440.

Sims, D. W. & Quayle, V. A., (1998) Selective Foraging Behaviour of Basking Sharks on Zooplankton in a Small-Scale Front. *Nature*, vol 393: 460–464.

Sinclair, J. (ed), (1799) The Statistical Account of Scotland 1791–1799 *OSA*. (Withrington, D.J. & Grant, I.R. (eds), Wakefield, EP Publishing,1982. A reissue in 20 volumes.)

Sinclair, J., (1825) Analysis of the Statistical Account of Scotland. Edinburgh, Constable.

Singer, C. *et al* (eds), (1957) A History of Technology, vol 3. The Renaissance to the Industrial Revolution. Oxford, Clarendon Press.

Singer, C. *et al* (eds.), (1958) A History of Technology. vol 4. The Industrial Revolution. Oxford, Clarendon Press.

Smith, A.M., (1982) Jacobite Estates of the Forty-five. Edinburgh, John Donald.

Smith, H.D., (1984) Shetland Life and Trade 1550–1914. Edinburgh, John Donald.

Smith, J.B.L., (1967) Pugnacity of the Whale Shark, *Rhincodon*. *Copeia*, no 1: 237.

Smith, W.A., (1883) Curing and Preserving Fish at Home and Abroad. In Herbert, D. (ed.), Fish and Fisheries . . . International Fisheries Exhibition, Edinburgh, 1882. Edinburgh, Blackwood & Sons: 93–105.

Springer, S. & Gilbert, P.W., (1976) The Basking Shark, *Cetorhinus maximus*, from Florida and California, with Comments on Its Biology and Systematics. *Copeia*, no 1: 47–54.

Squire, J.L., (1990) Distribution and Apparent Abundance of the Basking Shark, *Cetorhinus maximus*, off the Central and Southern California Coast, 1962–1985. *Marine Fisheries Review*, vol 52, no 2: 8–11.

Steel, R., (1992) Sharks of the World. London, Blandford.

Stevens, J., (1996): Archival Tagging of Sharks in Australia. *Shark News* (Newsletter of the IUCN Shark Specialist Group), no 7, June 1996: 10.

Stevens, J.D., (1987) Sharks. London, Merehurst.

Stott, F.C. (1967) The Basking Shark in Western European Waters. *Fishing News*, 10 Nov 1967: 10.

Stott, F.C., (1974) Why ignore the basking shark? *Fishing News*, 24 May 1974: 8–9.

Stott, F.C., (1980) A Note on the Spaciousness of the Cavity around the Brain of the Basking Shark, *Cetorhinus maximus* (Gunner). *Journal of Fish Biology*, vol. 16: 665–667.

Stott, F.C., (1982) A Note on Catches of Basking Sharks, *Cetorhinus maximus* (Gunnerus), off Norway and Their Possible Migration Paths. *Journal of Fish Biology*, vol 21: 227–230.

Stott, F.C. (1984) The Growth of *Cetorhinus maximus* (Gunnerus) – a Reply to Criticism. (Unpublished Paper – CM 1984/H:2). [Copenhagen], International Council for the Exploration of the Sea.

Sund, O., (1943) Et Brugebarsel. *Naturen*, vol 67, pt 9: 285–286.

Swinney, G., (1983) The Stronsay Monster: a Case of Mistaken Identity. *Current/The Journal of Marine Education*, Winter 1983: 15–17.

Taylor, L.R., Compagno, L.J.V. & Struhsaker, P.J. (1983) Megamouth – a New Species, Genus and Family of Lamnoid Shark (*Megachasma pelagios*, Family Megachasmidae) from the Hawaiian Islands. *Proceedings of the California Academy of Sciences* vol 43, no 8, July 1983: 87–110.

Taylor, W.,(1900) Sharks in the Moray Firth. *Annals of Scottish Natural History*, no 33, Jan 1900: 52 & [later title] *The Scottish Naturalist*, no 172, Jul/Aug, 1928: 123; no 174, Nov/Dec 1928: 187; no 190, Jul/Aug 1931: 112; no 197, Sept/Oct 1932: 167; no 215, Sept/Oct 1935: 170; no 222, Nov/Dec 1936: 163; no 228, Nov/Dec 1937: 173.

Tennyson, A., (1992) Basking Sharks: New Zealand's Largest Fish. *Forest & Bird*, no 265, August 1992: 38–42.

Thomson, K.S. & Simanek, D.E.(1977) Body Form and Locomotion in Sharks. *American Zoologist*, vol 17, no 2: 343–354.

The Times (1937) 2 Sept: 12e; 6 Sept: 17d; 20 Sept: 12e; 21 Sept: 16c; 27 Sept: 9f. & (1956) [Maxwell v. O'Connor] 27 Nov: 5f; 13 Dec: 2f. & (1969) [G. Maxwell obit.] 8 Sept: 10f & (1996): 10 June: 8; 3 Sept: 15.

Traill, [T.S.] (1854) On the Supposed Sea Snake Cast on Shore in the Orkneys in 1808, and the Animal Seen from HMS Daedalus in 1848. *Proceedings of the Royal Society of Edinburgh*, vol 3: 208–215.

Tressler, D.K. & Lemon, J.McW., (1957) Marine Products of Commerce . . . New York, Reinhold. (2nd edition.)

Tucker, D.W. (1956) A Cornish Ichthyologist in Fact and Fiction: 'Q' (Sir Arthur Quiller-Couch) on His Grand-father, Jonathan Couch. *Journal of the Society for the Bibliography of Natural History*, vol 3, pt 3, 1956: 137–151 & Postscript. *Ibid* vol 3, pt 4, Jan 1957: 195.

Turner, [?] (1879) The Structure of the Comb-like Branchial Appendages and of the Teeth of the Basking Shark (*Selache maxima*). *Journal of Anatomy and Physiology: Normal and Pathological*, vol 14, pt 3: 273–286 + 1 pl.

Tyler, P., (1992) Big Mouth: Is the Basking Shark being Fished Out? *Scottish Wildlife* (Magazine of the Scottish Wildlife Trust), no 15, winter 1991/92: 16–17.

Wagner, E.G., (1995) Gentle Giant of the Sea. *The Times*, 16 Sept 1995: Weekend 8.

Walton, J.K., (1992) Fish and Chips and the British Working Class, 1870–1940. Leicester, Leicester University Press.

Waterer, J.W., (1946) Leather in Life, Art and Industry . . . London, Faber.

Watkins, A.T., (1937) Basking Sharks: a Hunt and a 'Rescue'. *The Times*, 25 Sept 1937: 11f & 12a.

Watkins, A., (1958) The Sea My Hunting Ground. London, Heinemann.

Webster, D., (1817) A Topographical Dictionary of Scotland Containing a General Description of the Kingdom . . . Edinburgh, the Author.

Went, A.E.J. & O'Suilleabhain, S., (1967) Fishing for the Sun-fish or Basking Shark in Irish Waters. *Proceedings of the Royal Irish Academy*, vol 65C: 91–115.

Wheeler, A. & Jones, K.G., (1989) Fishes. (Cambridge Manuals in Archaeology) Cambridge, Cambridge University Press.

White, E.G., (1937) Interrelationships of the Elasmobranchs with a Key to the Order Galea. *Bulletin of the American Museum of Natural History*, vol 74, pt 2: 25–138.

Wilson, D., (1996) Giants of the Deep . . . *Natural World* (The National Magazine of the Wildlife Trusts), no 48, winter 1996: 18.

Workman, W.H., (1906) Loch Broom Sea Monster. *The Zoologist*, vol 10, no 783, Sept 1906: 355–357 & [other correspondents] no 784, Oct 1906: 396–398.

Wroth, W., (1895) Pennant, Thomas 1726–1798, Traveller and Naturalist . . . In *Dictionary of National Biography*, vol 44: 320–323.

Index